D0706751

For Renie Kulz –

with much gratitude

and appreciation –

J. White

LIVING SPEECH

LIVING SPEECH

RESISTING THE EMPIRE OF FORCE

James Boyd White

PRINCETON UNIVERSITY PRESS · PRINCETON AND OXFORD

Copyright © 2006 by Princeton University Press
Requests for permission to reproduce material from this work should
be sent to Permissions, Princeton University Press
Published by Princeton University Press, 41 William Street,
Princeton, New Jersey 08540
In the United Kingdom: Princeton University Press,
3 Market Place, Woodstock, Oxfordshire OX20 1SY

All Rights Reserved

Library of Congress Cataloging-in-Publication Data
White, James Boyd, 1938
Living speech : resisting the empire of force / by James Boyd White.
p.   cm.
Includes index.
ISBN-13 : 978-0-691-12580-0 (hardcover : alk. paper)
ISBN-10 : 0-691-12580-5 (hardcover : alk. paper)
1. Law—Language.   2. Judgments—United States—Language.
3. Violence in literature.   4. Violence.   I. Title.

K213 .W495 2006
306. 44—dc22
2005032670

British Library Cataloging-in-Publication Data is available

This book has been composed in Sabon

Printed on acid-free paper. ∞

pup.princeton.edu

Printed in the United States of America

1 3 5 7 9 10 8 6 4 2

To My Students

No one can love and be just
who does not understand the empire of force
and know how not to respect it.
—Simone Weil

Table of Contents

☙❧

Preface

꙳

THIS BOOK DERIVES from a long-standing interest in what is at stake—intellectually, ethically, politically—when the human mind meets and tries to use the languages that surround it, in the law and elsewhere: languages that are made by others, that are full of commitments to particular ways of imagining the world—describing it, judging it—and that carry deep within them the habits of mind, the values, of the world in which they are made.

What I think is at stake at such moments of expression is practically everything, including both the integrity of the individual person and the quality of our larger culture and polity. In our struggles with our languages we define and reveal the nature of our own processes of thought and imagination; we establish characters for ourselves and relations with others; we act upon the materials of meaning that define our culture, sometimes replicating them, sometimes transforming them, for good or ill. The activity of expression is the heart of intellectual and ethical life. It has an inherent public and political dimension too, for there is always the question whether we shall find ways to insist upon our own freedom and responsibility in a world of constraint, to respect the humanity and reality of other people and their experience, and to contribute to the formation of a culture and a polity that will enhance human dignity—or whether we shall instead lead lives imprisoned in dead modes of thought and expression that deny the value of ourselves and other people, and the activities of life we share.

In the introduction I try to show how it is that whenever we speak or write, in any context whatever, we reveal, in the terms suggested by the epigraph from Simone Weil, that we understand (or do not understand) and respect (or do not respect) what she calls "the empire of force." Succeeding chapters will deal with various aspects of what happens, in the law and ordinary life alike, when we work to free our minds from the control of the dead or sentimental forms of speech through which that empire works and try to achieve possibilities for living speech that will resist the empire of force, in the various guises in which it is at work in our minds and hearts.

ACKNOWLEDGMENTS

My thanks go to many friends for their helpful comments and ideas, especially Milner Ball, A. L. Becker, Patrick Brennan, Alison Cornish, Thomas Eisele, Anis Memon, Herbert Morris, Matthew Morris, Robert Post, Jefferson Powell, Eric Stein, Joseph Vining, Genevieve Vose, Peter Westen, Emma White, Mary White, and the members of the Monday Night Group. I also want to thank Sharon Rice and Laura Harlow for their important help in preparing the manuscript.

In the process of composing this book over several years, I have given talks or lectures on each of its chapters, in early and somewhat shorter versions, as follows: chapter 1 was delivered as the inaugural Mellinkoff Lecture at UCLA Law School and published as "Free Speech and Valuable Speech," *UCLA Law Review* 51 (2004): 799; part of chapter 2 was given at a conference at Amherst College on law and the liberal arts and published as "Meaning What you Say," in *Law and the Liberal Arts,* ed. A. Sarat (Ithaca, N.Y.: Cornell University Press, 2004); part of chapter 3 was delivered as the Margaret Howard Lecture on Law and Literature under the auspices of University College, London, and published as "The Desire for Meaning in Literature and Law," *Current Legal Problems* 53 (2000): 131; part of chapter 4 was given at a conference on law and literature held at University College London and published as "Writing and Reading in Philosophy, Law, and Poetry," *Current Legal Issues* 2 (1999): 1; and part of chapter 5 was delivered as a lecture to the Supreme Court Historical Society and published, in an earlier form, as "Human Dignity and the Claim of Meaning," *Journal of Supreme Court History* 27 (2002): 45. I am most grateful to the publishers named for their permission to use these talks and lectures as the basis for the chapters of this book.

My quotations from Dante are taken from Dante Alighieri, *The Divine Comedy*, ed. and trans. Charles Singleton (Princeton, N.J.: Princeton University Press, 1970 [*Inferno*], 1970 [*Purgatorio*], 1975 [*Paradiso*]).

In reproducing passages from judicial opinions I have regularly omitted citations without indication.

LIVING SPEECH

INTRODUCTION

❦

The Empire of Force
and the World of Words

IN AN IMPORTANT sense this entire book is an extended essay on the single sentence that stands as its epigraph, taken from Simone Weil's wonderful essay on the *Iliad* : "No one can love and be just who does not understand the empire of force and know how not to respect it."[1] For the purposes of this book it is a crucial fact that our knowledge of the empire and our capacity not to respect it—and the opposite of these things—all show up constantly in our uses of language, in what we confirm and what we resist, in what we reveal and what we hide, as we speak and write.

---

[1] Simone Weil, "L'Iliade, ou le poème de la force," first published in *Cahiers du Sud* (December 1940–January 1941). In French the sentence reads: *Il n'est possible d'aimer et d'être juste que si l'on connaît l'empire de la force et si l'on sait ne pas le respecter.* The translation given above is my own, made after discussions with Alton Becker, David Curtis, Anis Memon, Piotr Michalowski, and Joseph Vining. A more literal translation would be: "It is impossible to love and be just unless one understands the empire of force and knows how not to respect it." The essay has been reprinted in *The Simone Weil Reader*, ed. George A. Panichas (Mt. Kisco, N.Y.: Moyer Bell, 1977), 153, with the quotation appearing at page 181 and rendered into English as follows: "Only he who knows the empire of might and how not to respect it is capable of love and justice."

Each of the translations has its own merit. What I mainly like about the one I use is that it maintains the order of the French, which assumes the reader's interest in "loving and being just" as obvious goals of any human life worthy of the name and emphasizes by its placement at the end the psychological, literary, and social act of "not respecting"; that it avoids the formality and abstractness of the more literal translation, which tends to sound lifeless in English, though not in French; and that it distinguishes between the two kinds of knowledge expressed in the French verbs *connaître* and *savoir*: "understanding by experience," which is the knowledge one must have of the empire, and "knowing how to do," which is the knowledge one must have if one is to be effective in not respecting the empire. In the terms to be developed in this book, one kind of knowledge is a reader's knowledge—understanding a situation and its meaning; the other is a writer's knowledge—knowing how to use language to create meaning of an appropriate and valuable kind.

THE EMPIRE OF FORCE AS WAR

Weil wrote her essay on the *Iliad* during the period of fascism in Europe, just at the beginning of World War II, and saw the ancient poem as speaking directly to the horrible moment in which Europe and the world found themselves. The *Iliad* is of course about a stage in the Trojan war, which it describes in great and bloody detail. For Weil, this poem at once presents and criticizes the practice of dehumanization that is an inseparable part not only of a war between peoples but also, as we have since discovered, of that other kind of war that a government may wage against its own people. In this poem Homer sees, and brings the reader to see, the equal value and humanity of Greek and Trojan, of the human beings on both sides of this war. That is in fact the poem's central achievement: to identify and to criticize, indeed to undermine, what Weil calls the empire of force—the ideology, the way of imagining the world and oneself and others within it—that is always present in war and required by it, but present also in our lives whenever people deny the humanity of others whom they destroy, manipulate, or exploit.

What Weil says about war is undeniably the case. If one is not a psychopath, one can engage in war only by denying the full humanity of those one is trying to kill. This is true even for a person fighting out of deeply felt idealism, on the side of democracy and decency, say, against tyranny and genocide. Think, for example, of the mentality that would make it possible to participate in the firebombing of Dresden or Tokyo in World War II. The people one is trying to incinerate—children, old people, tram conductors, electricians, musicians, laborers, factory workers, clerks, secretaries, mothers—are themselves of course no threat to our nation or its safety, and one knows this perfectly well. The thought is that if we destroy enough of them, in a hideous enough way, those in charge of the military that does present such a threat will lose their will to fight. We are killing civilians by fire to persuade generals and politicians to surrender.

In purely military engagements the situation is not so very different: the people you are trying to kill, who are also trying to kill you, would in other circumstances be recognized as people—in our own country as tourists perhaps, or as the locals if we were traveling abroad, or even as neighbors and friends if one of us came to live in the other's country. It is through the operation of the military draft, or the work of war fever and propaganda, or by some deep political failure on one side or the other, or on both—by some horrible mistake—that you find yourselves fighting each other to the death. You naturally experience triumph when you succeed, as does the soldier you oppose. Yet whenever anyone dies, on whichever side, a world of possibility dies with him or her, a web of relationships of caring and concern. A part of the fabric of humanity and human community has been torn to bits.

In a sense we know all this, of course. But we cannot allow this knowledge to be present and active when we are engaged in war, whether as a soldier or as a civilian cheering on the troops. It would not be endurable. And the dehumanization of which I speak is present as well in the psychological and political process that leads to war. It is a way of justifying war: you begin to paint "them" as monstrous, superstitious, barbarian, ignorant, savage, inhuman, and then you can go to war against them.[2] Think of the Serbians who were married to Croatians in what was once Yugoslavia, or of the Hutu and Tutsi living at peace in Rwanda, all of whom suddenly discovered that there were lines of murderous enmity where before there were none.[3]

In her essay Weil shows that for Homer, and for us, the dehumanization of others is an inherent psychological cost of war, a denial of truth that corrodes the mind and will. Perhaps it is necessary, if the war is necessary, but it is always present, as an ineluctable cost of the activity. To take an event that occurred during the writing of this book, recall the American effort to kill Iraq's Saddam Hussein by bombing a restaurant in which he was thought to be dining. In the reports I read of this event, the only topic considered was the question whether we had succeeded in killing him. I saw no reflection of the fact that we had surely killed other people who were having dinner at the restaurant that evening, workers

[2] Compare what Stuart Hood says in his memoir of World War II in Italy (speaking here of a local partisan leader): "Franco, for his part, remembered his father dosed with castor-oil and tied in a sack [by the Fascists], like a calf ready for the market, to lie in his own filth and weakness. He knew that Fascism degrades and by degrading its victim finds justification for murder." Stuart Hood, *Pebbles from My Skull* (London: Hutchinson, 1963), 51.

[3] For a brief account of the Hutu and Tutsi, see Alex de Waal, "The Genocidal State," *Times Literary Supplement*, July 1, 1994, 3 (review of *Ethnicity and Conflict in the Horn of Africa*, edited by Katsuyoshi Fukui and John Markakis [Columbus: Ohio University Press, 1994]; *The Cohesion of Oppression: Clientship and Ethnicity in Rwanda, 1860–1960*, by Catharine Newbury [New York: Columbia University Press, 1988]; and *Human Rights and Governance in Africa*, edited by Ronald Cohen, Goran Hyden, and Winston P. Nagan [Gainesville: University Press of Florida, 1993]).

in the kitchen, waiters, passersby, and so on. Their deaths were, in the jargon of our day, collateral damage, like the shattering of plates and glasses. Yet each of these persons was a center of meaning and life; presumably all had friends and relations, children or parents, whose lives were injured, perhaps destroyed, by this violent killing. It is Homer's achievement in the *Iliad* to bring to our attention where we cannot deny it the recognition of the common humanity of people on both sides of a war, a recognition that the very activity of war requires us all to suppress.

Of course, as Homer also makes clear, it is true that on these dreadful conditions human beings can be capable of extraordinary virtue and achievement—courage and loyalty and mercy. Homer loves and admires the people of his world, trapped as they are in a system of war. But that system is his ultimate subject. It is overcome only occasionally in the lives of his characters, at rare moments of understanding and feeling; but it is overcome constantly in his text, which recognizes and never forgets what no one in the poem can wholly see or act upon, the common humanity of Greek and Trojan.

All this is not necessarily to say that war is always wrong—though that is what some people may conclude—or that a good person cannot make a career with real nobility in the military, for that is surely possible, but rather that a necessary cost even of what we denominate a just war is that in it we erase the reality of other human beings and of what we do to them. This is a serious evil; maybe a justified evil, but an evil nonetheless.

THE EMPIRE OF FORCE AS A HABIT OF MIND

What interests me in this book is not so much the phenomenon of war itself as what lies behind war, and behind not only war but all the forms of power that enable or require us to reduce other people to objects, to deny their equal claims to a life of meaning and fulfillment. These are the systems of thought and imagination at work in our heads and hearts that make up an empire of force with which it is a duty, a necessity, to come to terms if we ourselves are to realize our own best capacities of mind and feeling. My question is not whether this or that particular war is justified, given the attitudes and arrangements of power that led to it and to the situation in which it breaks out, but what is to be done about those attitudes and arrangements and situations in the first place—about, that is, the empire of force with which we always live, even in peacetime, and which is in a sense always preparing for the war in which it will attain its fullest expression. That is the subject of Weil's essay and of this book.

One form this empire takes is the familiar one of which I have been speaking: that of armed men systematically destroying other people, armed and unarmed, and almost of necessity taking pleasure and satisfaction in so doing. Each person who is the object of destruction becomes, as Weil says, a thing in the mind of the other, not a person. But as I have suggested, the empire of force is at work not only in those who are engaged in the actual practices of war, but in others as well. Behind the men and women at the front are other people, all of us, committing ourselves to this activity, and necessarily engaging in our own ways of constructing those on the other side as things or animals or monsters, not people. Beyond even that, both for Weil and for the purposes of this book, the empire exists in other forms, in ordinary life and politics, throughout our lives in fact—whenever we find ourselves denying each other's full humanity in the way we speak and think.

For the "force" of the empire of which Weil speaks is not simply military or physical in nature, but also psychological, emotional, and ideological. Though power may come from the barrel of a gun, as Chairman Mao once said, it is a real power only by virtue of the understandings among people that make the guns and bombs and spears usable and effective. All power rests on agreement among those exercising it. You can only order the secret police to sweep a neighborhood, to spy on citizens, to kill or torture opponents, if they are willing to accept orders and, in a democracy, only if the people become willing to accept the existence of a secret police who will do such things. And the members of the secret police themselves will obey orders only because they accept a vision of the world that supports this role and because this vision is confirmed by others.

What looks like external and physical force thus always depends upon—is really a manifestation of—forces at work within the mind and imagination. These forces are as real, and in their own way can be ultimately as destructive, as physical power. This means that the empire of force has presence and power in the minds of each of its agents and servants and supporters—in each of us who does not oppose it, who does not understand it and know how not to respect it. This is in fact where it really lives, in the mind; without that life it would have no force at all.

This dimension of empire can be deliberately created by a master manipulator, like Joseph Goebbels, or it can be something that looks quite different, simply the culture working itself out in our imaginations and our hearts. Each of us grows up surrounded by languages, codes, manners, expectations—ways of imagining the world and oneself and others within it—that tell us what to say and how to say it, what to do and how to do it. Mastery of these systems of meaning is essential to social competence: you have to know how to talk to your schoolmates, to your teacher, to your employer or employee, to the vendor at the newsstand, and so on, or you will be unable to achieve any of your objectives in life, indeed be unable to formulate objectives in the first place. But mastery of a culture's resources for social interaction, for claiming meaning for experience, is also a kind of submission to them.

This submission may be to something deeply evil. Think of the "Aryan" child raised as a good German by his loving parents in the 1930s, for example, or a "white" child in a slave-owning family in our own country before the Civil War, each learning patterns of thought and feeling, even as very young children, that supported such horrors as mass murder and hereditary racial enslavement. The American language of race, from which none of us in this country can escape, is its own version of the empire of force, ruling each of us from inside our minds and hearts.

But the empire extends beyond such obvious evils to reach whatever modes of thought and imagination we unthinkingly or unconsciously adopt that deny our common humanity: our failure to see that the child born into poverty in an inner-city public hospital is as fully a human being, with the same value and rights and claims, as our own more privileged children; our collective acceptance of the values of a consumer economy, which systematically reduces life to the stimulation and gratification of desires without any attention to their larger meaning for the individual or the community; our repeated insistence on an inherent difference between "us" and those "others" who are different, across a wide range of familiar contexts; and, to take an issue of special interest to me and to this book, our ways of thinking of our political leaders, not as people whom we can expect to speak to us in a genuine way about our nation's life and the problems that confront it, but as figures defined by a set of images and gestures, slogans and sound bites, just like those used to advertise commercial products on television. These systems of thought and imagination—in which all of us participate—tend to erase the reality and humanity of other people, and in doing so to make us agents of an empire of force. This Weil saw clearly; it means that for her the *Iliad* is a profound criticism not only of the heroic culture of war presented in that poem, but of forces at work every culture, every human society, every human life. The empire of force lives within us, each of us.

KNOWING AND NOT RESPECTING THE EMPIRE OF FORCE AS A PROBLEM OF WRITING

How are we to respond to the reality of our own participation in the systems of dehumanizing thought that make up so much of our own world, our own thinking, our own characters? Simone Weil's own life was a constant struggle to find an answer to that question, leading her to work in factories under soul-destroying conditions and ultimately to affirm her connection with the victims of war by refusing to eat more than she would have had in a concentration camp, a practice that led to her early death. That was the course she set for herself.

In the sentence I have quoted she suggests one place we might begin in shaping our own lives, telling us that the essential thing is to "understand" the empire of force and "know how not to respect" it. Yet how are we possibly to do this? How can we recognize the empires of force already at work in each of us, in the form of humanity-erasing languages— ways of imagining and thinking and speaking and acting—that exist in our minds, that shape our sense of the world? How can we learn not to respect these things, which are so much part of us? What *are* we to respect? What would it really look like to "recognize the humanity" of another person? Such are the questions that animate this book.

It is crucial for Weil, and for my purposes here, that the "understanding" and "not respecting" of which she speaks are internal activities of the individual mind. There is no adequate solution to the problem she identifies to be found in national policy, international law, programs or principles adopted by the National Council of Churches, philosophical systems, codes of conduct, or any other collective statement or action. These can of course all be good things or bad; but for us as individual people the only real remedy, and it is necessarily imperfect, lies in our own struggle to come to terms with the systems of meaning, with the languages, that shape our world: our effort to learn to understand the empire of force and how not to respect it.[4] To fail in this endeavor, she tells us, is to fail to be capable of love and justice, the central ends and fulfillment of human existence. It is a task for a whole life.

Her sentence is not a call to quietism or removal from the world. Once we begin to see what happens when people successfully claim power over the lives of others, when an empire of force is created in language and in life, we should of course try to find ways to resist it in our conduct: in our voting, our political and social action, our contributions of money and time and energy. But—and this is crucial to the power and meaning of her sentence—the problem she identifies does not go away when we act on the side of the poor and the oppressed, when we are reformers of the system, good as those things are. For when we explain and justify what we think, and what we do, we shall still be working with language, language will still be working with us, and our own formulations can quickly become the language of another empire, full of slogans, sentimentalities, falsities, and denials, of trivializations and dehumanizations. What we think and say can in a deep way replicate just what we should be most trying to resist.

As you may have noticed, for example, I have talked about "dehumanizing" others and its opposite, "recognizing their full humanity," without giving either phrase much content. These are still what might be called thin or shallow expressions, in danger of being used as clichés or slogans. To think of Homer's achievement as the recognition of the humanity of both Greek and Trojan is a fine start, but if we were to continue to work with that text we would need to capture and express, so far as we could, exactly how he does that and with what precise effect. That would be the central critical task.[5] In this book I shall not proceed

---

[4] Compare what the Dalai Lama has said about peace: "Although attempting to bring about world peace through the internal transformation of individuals is difficult, it is the only way." Foreword to Thich Nhat Hanh, *Peace Is Every Step* (New York: Bantam, 1991), vii.

[5] For an extended reading of the *Iliad* with such an object in mind, much influenced by Weil's essay, see James Boyd White, "Poetry and the World of Two: Cultural Criticism and the Ideal of Friendship in the *Iliad*," in *When Words Lose Their Meaning* (Chicago: University of Chicago Press, 1984), chapter 2. For an earlier articulation of a similar basic insight about Homer's humanity, see Gilbert Murray, *The Literature of Ancient Greece* (1897; reprint, Chicago: University of Chicago Press, 1956), 43: "It is the true pathos of war; the thing seen on both sides; the unfathomable suffering for which no one in particular

with Homer but shall turn instead with such questions in mind to other texts that manifest the problem I am trying to define, from the writing of children to Supreme Court opinions to Dante's *Divine Comedy*.

All of this work can be seen as a way of trying to give deeper content to the terms—"dehumanization," "full humanity," "empire of force"—that I am using to frame the investigation. Or, to put it another way, my object is to give the sentence from Weil the kind of attention that will resist the impulse we have to reduce language to slogan and cliché and instead keep this sentence alive as the complex challenge to the mind and soul that it is. Whether I succeed is another question; what I want to stress here is that the internal aspect of the problem, what might be called the literary aspect, is permanently with us, present in my own use of language and yours, all the time—including in this book, this paragraph—and requires our constant and unrelenting attention. Learning to understand the empire of force, and how not to respect it, is a task and responsibility for each of us. It is this task that is the subject of this book. Even when I talk about judicial opinions, then, I shall accordingly deal very little with arguments about legal doctrine, policy, or rule, for those arguments, and the choices they imply, can be made well and responsibly only if we find ways to acquire the understanding and knowledge of which Weil speaks, and to demonstrate those things in our thought and writing. Language is always dying in our minds, and it is our responsibility to give it life.

THE EMPIRE OF FORCE AND THE LAW

Weil's sentence invites us to attend constantly to our own minds and language as they interact to form one another—to what we do when we read and listen, speak and write. The threat of the empire is constantly present in our lives, whenever we use language to think or talk, even in our most private moments. But our speech can have direct public consequences as well, perhaps nowhere more obviously than in the law, where public power is given shape and reality in language.

At first the law may seem to be by nature a primary agent of the empire of force, a crucial instrument through which that empire works in

---

is to blame. . . . [Is] it not a marvel of the sympathetic imagination which makes us feel with the flying Hector, the cruel Achilles, the adulterous Helen, without for an instant losing sight of the ideals of courage, mercifulness, and chastity?"

the world to organize brute power—guns, and police, and bailiffs, and sheriffs—to dominate the weak, to erase distinction and difference, to obliterate the force of the individual mind and of individual life. But is that right? It can obviously be these things, but is the law *inherently* an instrument of the empire of force? Or can it be not the servant of the empire but something of a counterforce to it, a way—a structured and learnable way—of not respecting it? Can it in fact be an organized way of respecting the humanity of others? If not, can it at least be a place where these positive possibilities can be defined, and the forces that oppose them be contested? If so, what would that contest look like?

As a way of elaborating the line of thought suggested by these questions, I examine in what follows certain ways in which people have found it possible to speak in the law, good and bad. I look especially at some Supreme Court opinions that interpret the First Amendment to the U.S. Constitution, for here the Court must simultaneously address and exemplify the activity of speech itself.[6]

In this book, then, I weave together three lines of thought that would usually be regarded as distinct but are in my view deeply connected. The first is suggested by the body of this introduction and could be put as a question: How, as individual minds and persons, might we come to understand the ways that the empire of force is always present in our thought and speech, and learn how to resist its power by refusing to respect it? The goal, as Weil suggests, would be to render ourselves more nearly capable of love and justice.

The second line of thought concerns the law made under the First Amendment, largely by the Supreme Court, and concerns in particular the way the Court defines and thinks about the kind of speech the amendment protects. Should the constitutional phrase "freedom of speech" include all acts of verbal expression? That construction seems to almost everyone plainly impossible, since there are well-established crimes that can be committed by words alone, such as conspiracy, aiding and abetting, and incitement, and many forms of speech are traditionally the ground of civil action, such as defamation, copyright violation, and the like. It is almost impossible to think that the First Amendment should invalidate these well-established bodies of law.

---

[6] The amendment reads in part: "Congress shall make no law . . . abridging the freedom of speech."

But if the phrase "freedom of speech" does not include all speech, and if it also does include, as virtually everyone agrees it should, some forms of nonverbal expression (such as flag waving and marching and dancing), how are these words to be given meaning? In this book I do not propose a comprehensive answer to that question, which would require a book of its own, but I do make this suggestion: that we should start our thinking by assuming that the amendment singles out speech from other forms of conduct for a reason, and that the reason has to do with the extraordinary value of some acts of speech—what I here call living speech—to the individual speaker and hearer and to the larger world as well. Forms of speech that are manipulative at their core and in no way expressive of any person's thoughts or feelings, such as commercial advertising, should be placed at the margin of protectability, while speech that is deeply meant and alive—speech above all that understands the empire of force and knows how not to respect it—should be placed at the center of the amendment's protections.

The third line of thought relates to the writing, reading, and criticism of judicial opinions. Briefly stated, the idea is that the justices of the Supreme Court, and other judges too, are under even greater temptation and pressure than the rest of us to speak in dead, mechanical, or bureaucratic ways, and that they should resist these forces strenuously, seeking to attain in their own compositions the kind of life, the presence of mind and imagination, that can alone prevent the law from becoming a central actor in the empire of force.

This book is thus built on three ideas, all related to what I call living speech: an idea about the living speech by which alone each of us can resist the work of the empire of force in our lives; an idea about the First Amendment, namely that it should be read to protect living speech above all; and an idea about the work and writing of judges, and lawyers too, namely that in their effort to do justice it is crucial that they learn, as some indeed have done, to engage in living speech in their own performances. To say this is of course to present the question how the phrase "living speech" is to be defined and given meaning. It cannot I think be done by a stipulative or purely conceptional definition—by the elaboration or substitution of terms—but only by the experience of particular examples and reflection upon them, which is what I intend the rest of this book to offer.

My examples are drawn from law and from various other sources, ranging from the Bible to children's writings to poems by Robert Frost and William Carlos Williams. In each chapter I turn as well to passages from Dante's *Divine Comedy*, a poem that perhaps surprisingly seems to have a concern with the empire of force close to its center. I should also say that because each chapter addresses living speech in each of the contexts mentioned above, and in doing so calls on both legal and non-legal materials, the chapters are somewhat lengthier (though fewer in number) than is usual in a book of this kind.

This book is not centrally about war, then, or the brutality of the empire in its most florid and fully realized forms, but about the origins and sources of that kind of empire in our own thought and speech. Its real subject is writing and speaking, regarded as an activity of ethical and political significance. All of human life involves this activity. To do it well we must understand the languages, the habits of thought and expression, that surround us, that have their life within us; we must think critically about these forces and resources of meaning, which means thinking critically about our own uses of them; and we must learn the art by which we can begin to control these languages, turning them to our purposes, rather than becoming their agents and slaves—which means learning to have confident purposes of our own in the first place. In all of this we need to ask what kinds of relations we establish with others, those we talk to and those we talk about. This is what it would mean to "understand the empire of force and know how not to respect it."

It is to explore these themes and questions, all of them prompted by Weil's sentence, that this book is written. Chapter 1 is in a sense a continuation of this introduction, elaborating more fully the questions the rest of the book addresses. Each of the other chapters focuses on a different aspect of the problem, in what I intend to be a sensible and progressive order; but certain motifs and themes necessarily recur, some in every chapter, others more sporadically, giving the book as a whole a structure that is more spiral than linear in nature. We come back again and again, from different starting points, to the same central questions, in the process transforming our sense of what they mean.

CHAPTER ONE

W

Speech in the Empire

Silence; valuable speech; Dante's Divine Comedy; our world of public speech; advertising and propaganda; the "marketplace of ideas"; Robert Frost's "The Road Not Taken"; Frankfurter and Jackson in the flag salute case; Abraham Lincoln's letter to General Hooker.

ONE DAY WHEN I was a teenager I read about the monastic order of the Trappists and its rule of continual silence. As a highly voluble young person this seemed horrible to me, unimaginable really, and I said so to a friend and teacher, who suggested: "Perhaps a life of silence would teach us how pointless and empty almost everything we say actually is." This struck me powerfully at the time and lives in my mind still. Later in life I happened to spend several years as an active participant in the life of the Society of Friends, or Quakers, whose meetings for worship are almost entirely silent. The idea is that this shared silence is profoundly valuable, to be interrupted only when someone feels that they simply must speak. When someone does speak, what they say is to be given deep attention, of a kind made possible by the silence.

The practices of the Trappists depend upon and make real a sense of the deep value of silence itself, of a life without spoken words; those of the Quakers stress both the value of silence and the value of a certain kind of speech—speech taking place against silence, speech made possible by silence. In both cases the silence is communal: people are together yet not speaking; they are sharing silence.

Though the practices of the Trappists and Quakers are in a sense at the edges of our social world, they invite us to think about silence and speech—about the activity of speech and the silence against which it works—in ways that may help us understand both the dangers and the opportunities that confront us whenever we speak or write.

SILENCE AND SPEECH

To begin with silence: in one sense silence is necessary to all meaningful expression. Think of the silence that precedes the concert in an orchestra hall, or the lesser silences, called rests, that make up an essential part of the music. In drama, too, silent pauses are part of the material of art, often full of significance that is expressible in no other way. Or recall how a poem looks, printed on the page, surrounded by an expanse of white—a sort of visual silence that makes the poem itself stand out where it can be seen and responded to. Much the same kind of spatial silence can be observed on museum walls where pictures are displayed, and we all know that some museums are simply too crowded to permit any picture to be seen, to be heard as it were. Silence is in fact necessary to any kind of speech, for without silence the words and phrases and syllables could not be distinguished from each other or from the noise that surrounds them; and silence is especially necessary to significant speech—speech that makes a real claim upon one's attention and promises to reward it—for it is silence that makes attention possible and gives space for reflection.

Silence is a crucial element of speech in another way, for at least some utterances carry with them the shadows of other things: things that are not said but assumed, and which we must reconstruct or intuit or figure out from what is before us; and things that might have been said instead, other versions of what we hear, which we half-consciously construct as we proceed. Think of the way a lawyer listens to a good legal argument, for example: wondering about what is unstated but assumed as a premise, asking herself why the speaker did not make it explicit and whether he leaves himself open to attack at such a point; and at the same time contrasting what he does say, as his argument proceeds, with what she thinks that she or someone else might have said in his place.

In this kind of reading, or listening, we attend to what is before us partly by imagining what is not there, filling the spaces around the speech with our own thoughts and bringing them to bear upon it. This is an inherent part of the process by which we attend to what we read or hear. As we read we think we know what is coming next, though we are not sure; when it does come, it either confirms our judgment or surprises us by being different. And we look backwards as well as forwards, repeatedly going over in our minds what we have read or heard, tentatively putting it in retrospective order, an order that may change as new material is added to it. When we get to the end we find that in both directions what *was* said derives much of its meaning from what was *not* said.

In such ways the meaning of any expression worth real attention comes in part from silences, external and internal, silences that reflect both what is not said and what is not sayable at all. We cannot really imagine it, except as surrounded by silence; and if it invites and rewards the kind of attention I describe, it will seem to come not from the familiar part of the mind that is full of tags of remembered speech and gesture, rote pieces of speech that we assemble without thinking, but from some deep place within the self—silent, below the words, a place where language can be the subject of conscious attention and where it can be remade.

An essential feature of this kind of speech or writing is that its use of language is not automatic, but shaped or chosen. The speaker or writer tries to be aware of his language and its limits, and invites his audience to be so too; this requires of both of them an inner as well as outer silence. And this silence is not simply empty space or time, an absence of words; it is a state or condition that must be attained, by work and art and discipline, and it must be used, and used well. It is a crucial part of what we mean by the engagement of the whole mind.

Much of what we say and hear is of course not like this—not shaped by inner and outer silences—but is simply a stitching together of locutions in predictable and uninteresting ways, locutions that are not in any significant way made our own. On these occasions we speak or write as if our words and phrases were simply stored in an antechamber to the mind, ready for immediate use upon demand. Lawyers are all too familiar with this sort of speaking and writing, of which a certain kind of brief can be taken as an example: one that pieces together rules and quotations, makes distinctions, argues to conclusions, but without ever making it the work of the individual mind—as though the writer were trying to approximate a Platonic ideal of the brief that should be written in the particular case, an ideal that has its origins outside of his mind, which it is not his place to judge or shape but simply to approximate. His effort is not actually to think through the legal problem and express his thought in legal language—to say what he means in the language of the law—but to sound like someone doing those things: to sound like a lawyer, not to be one. The reader of such a brief is offered not the work of a mind with which he or she can engage, but something very different, a stitching together of phrases and formulas, none of which is truly meant.

These habits of mind and expression can of course be found outside the law as well, wherever one can find clichés and received ideas and formulas and slogans presented as though they could carry the work of thought and writing, wherever we see a system of thought applied without regard to what else can be said. As writers we fall into these habits often without knowing it. As readers we often simply acquiesce in them. Yet at some level we know that we simply cannot attend to such utterances, nor do we want to, certainly not in the same way in which we attend to expressions more deeply shaped by the internal processes I describe, of which silence is an essential element.

What I am saying then—and it is in one sense perfectly obvious—is that not all of our speech is of the same quality or nature, indeed not of the same value. What I mean by "value" here is not some instrumental effect on the world, but the real value of the speech as such, for the speaker and his or her audience: the value of speech that invites and deserves and rewards real attention, that makes possible the engagement of one mind with another. At one extreme we have the reiteration of clichés, formulas, slogans—dead language really; at the other, speech that is deeply meant and alive, coming from a place of inner silence, directed to a similar place in its audience. I assume that we all in a rough way recognize the difference between these two kinds of speech, and the kinds of thought and life they each reflect and invite, at least in their extreme forms; but how to put that recognition to work in our lives and judgments is another matter entirely, and a central subject of this book. Can we be confident that we perceive this difference accurately, as readers and hearers, when we are faced with the expressions that make up our world of speech and language? Can we protect ourselves against the appeal of the first kind of speech and resist our own desires to use and submit to it? Can we ourselves attain speech of the second kind—speech that comes from the center of the person, and is addressed to the center of its audience; speech worthy of real attention; speech upon which both individual and shared life can be built? These are our questions, and much is at stake. For it is only this kind of speech, which I call living speech, that can express the workings of the individual mind and imagination. It is what makes possible the real—if always imperfect—communication of mind with mind, person with person. Indeed it is what enables any of us to be a person in the first place.

SILENCE AND MEANING IN DANTE

Here and from time to time throughout this book I shall turn to Dante's *Divine Comedy* as a work that addresses, often with astonishing success, certain central questions about language and power. At its heart it is a text that shows us both how to understand, and how not to respect, the empire of force. This may be at first a surprising claim: after all, Dante's plainly stated political position is in favor of a vigorous and powerful empire; and in the course of the poem he elaborates a complex theological vision, drawn to a large degree from the *Summa Theologica* of Saint Thomas Aquinas, which it would be easy to regard also as a kind of empire—and one in which the element of "force" is beyond doubt, for Dante's theological emperor, the Deity, is omnipotent and has used his power, especially in creating the Inferno, to define and maintain the moral coherence of the universe as he has imagined it into existence. Nonetheless—indeed partly by virtue of these commitments both to the temporal empire and the eternal rule of the Deity—this poem has much to teach us about the kind of speech and writing that understands the empire of force and how not to respect it.

In thinking about Dante's poem, I shall pursue my themes of quality and silence, asking in particular how silence of various kinds is at work in it; how these silences shape our experience in reading it; and how that experience puts into question the various empires of force that Dante may seem on the surface to accept and promote.

Here is the famous opening of Dante's *Inferno*:

> *Nel mezzo del cammin di nostra vita*
> *mi ritrovai per una selva oscura,*
> *che la diritta via era smarrita.*   (I, 1–3)

Or, much more flatly: "In the middle of the road of our life I found myself in a dark wood, because the straight way was lost."

For most of us the most salient feature of this passage will necessarily be that it is written not in English but Italian; it must entirely depend upon the resources of that language for its effects, and we may not even understand it at all. This is an instance of the general truth that in every act of expression the speaker must choose one language or another, and whatever language he chooses to speak will silence other possibilities. To write in Italian is to be silent in every other language, and the consequences are real.

This poem is written, for example, in a verse form Dante invented for the purpose, the terza rima, which works well in Italian but not in English. This form consists of interlocking three-line stanzas, in which the first and third lines rhyme; the second line, unrhyming in one stanza, provides the rhyme for lines one and three of the next, and so on, indefinitely. In Italian this can work well, for that language has an enormous number of words that rhyme, but, as every translator discovers, terza rima does not work well in English, which does not have these resources.[1] This means that the most basic element of the verse cannot easily be carried over into English.

This is not a small matter: the hope of the poem to create an ordered and coherent poetic universe, mirroring God's creation and running in imagination from the beginning of time to the day of judgment, is in a sense enacted or performed in the very structure of the verse, which runs through the whole thing. If this pattern of the verse were continued without interruption, it would connect every part of the poem and its imagined world in a seamless woven tapestry of language from beginning to end. But each Canto begins a new sequence, breaking the pattern established by its predecessor, a fact that works as a poetic admission either that the structure of the universe may not be totally coherent after all or, at least, that it cannot be represented as wholly comprehensible in human language. It would not I think be possible to use English rhymes to create such a sense of immense coherence threatened by incoherence.

The richness of Italian rhymes has more local consequences too, as these three lines reveal: its rhyme of *vita* and *smarrita*—echoed in *diritta via*—unites these terms to tell us that life, like the straight way, is lost, lost in confusion. The sound connects these words to establish the psychological and spiritual starting point of the entire poem. As we read a bit further we see the poem connect *oscura* (dark) with *dura* (hard) and *paura* (fear) to forge these words into a single set of associations.

Dante is aware of the resources of his written Italian—a language he is in fact doing much to create—and he deploys them to make meanings

---

[1] The best effort at terza rima in an English translation of Dante is probably that of Henry Wadsworth Longfellow. See *The Divine Comedy of Alighieri*, trans. Henry Wadsworth Longfellow (Boston: Ticknor and Fields, 1867).

that could not be replicated in another language. For us, the language of comparison is naturally English; for him, it was Latin, and his choice of the vernacular has enormous significance not only in the technical ways I am describing but in a much larger theater of culture and politics. In writing in the speech of Tuscany he helped to create what we know as modern Europe. His ambition is to do for Italian what his guide and model, Virgil, did for Latin, namely to demonstrate its full capacities for meaning.[2] His self-consciousness about his language—his understanding of its potentialities and limitations—is thus crucial to both the aesthetic and the political aspects of his achievement. For our purposes it is important that this awareness depends upon a kind of silence, an inner distance from his language that makes it possible for Dante to use it for his own purposes—to have purposes of his own in the first place—and not simply to replicate its forms. Silence is part of what gives life to this text, and to us as we read it.

Let us now look at these three lines as a story. What does the narrator of the poem *not* tell us? He does not tell us who he is; how the right path was lost; what the dark woods consist of; whether this is a dream or an allegory or an invention, or something else; he does not tell us why he is telling us this story, or who he imagines us to be, himself to be. He just gives us this sketch: I was lost, in the woods, at middle age.

Everything in the poem will come from this moment: the narrator's frustrated attempt to make his own way out of the woods; the sudden and mysterious appearance of Virgil, who will lead him, as it were, not out of his problem but through it—through the Inferno and almost all of Purgatory as well, where he will be handed over to Beatrice, his guide to Paradise. Much of the effect of these lines would be ruined if Dante rendered himself more particular, like a character in a novel, say—telling us about his prior history and education, his social location, his qualities of mind and aspiration, the special sense in which he is lost—for at the moment he is speaking for us as well as for himself. To overspecify would prevent us from reading our own way into the story, as people who can

---

[2] As Sordello says of Virgil in Canto VII of the *Purgatorio*:

> "O gloria di Latin," disse, "per cui
> mostrò ciò che potea la lingua nostra."   (16–17)

"Oh glory of the Latins, through whom our language showed what it can do."

also imagine ourselves in the middle of life to have lost our way, surrounded by dark woods.

This kind of silence is also a way of posing questions, questions that will keep us engaged with this poem, one of which is surely: Who actually is this "Dante," the character in the story, and what relation has he with that other "Dante" who composed this poem? It will turn out that this Dante, our fellow traveler, is among other things himself a questioner, asking of Virgil, and those damned in the Inferno, and later of Beatrice, and those saved in Paradise, the most frank and embarrassing questions. He asks Piccarda, for instance, in the lowest level of the heavens, whether she is disappointed not to have been placed higher; he asks Virgil, who is obviously Dante's ideal figure as artist and as mind, why he is condemned to Limbo with the other great figures of the classical world instead of being placed in heaven; he asks whether the suffering of the damned will be greater or less after they are restored to their bodies on the day of judgment; he asks how it is that the gluttonous in Purgatory can suffer the pangs of hunger when they have no need for food. Later he asks Adam what language he spoke in Eden, and how long he enjoyed the bliss of the garden before his expulsion. (Answers: he spoke a language that was extinct before Nimrod built the Tower of Babel, and six hours!) He is a kind of Candide before his time, irrepressibly asking just the questions you can imagine yourself wanting to ask but being afraid to do so.

The largest of these, repeated in one form or another over and over, has to do with the justice of the Deity. How can it be right that Virgil and Homer and Plato are consigned to the dark world of Limbo, where they huddle by the fire? Or that Paolo and Francesca should suffer forever, for what is after all human love? Or that the great Ulysses, the impassioned embodiment of the desire to know and understand, should be consigned to the Inferno? As readers we necessarily feel that the persistent questioning of Dante the traveler must present him (and us) with real dangers in a universe that is so evidently governed by a single omnipotent authority—its God—who punishes with such severity. Yet as this Dante exhibits his gift for insistent questioning, the other Dante, the writer, holds it out to the reader as a quality to admire. More than that: his questions are real for us as well as for him—he asks what we would like to ask—and they thus at once stimulate and confirm our own capacities for questioning. And the deepest question of all is this: What are we to think of this universe and its Governor?

Consider the famous case of Paolo and Francesca, a man and woman who fell in love reading a book of romance and now find themselves in the Inferno. Dante does not explicitly tell us this, but in the historical case upon which this episode is based, the lovers were apparently adulterers, killed by Francesca's husband upon discovery. This is significant because Dante's original audience was raised on the romantic conventions of courtly love, of which at least the fantasy of adultery was an essential ingredient. How can it be right that for this understandable, indeed culturally validated act, these two souls should drift emptily in the dark, for ever and ever? To think that this is right or just is nearly impossible for the reader of the poem, and the same is true of the disposition of many of the souls in each of the realms. Let me stress that this is the poet's doing. We tend to forget it, but it is Dante who presents Paolo and Francesca so sympathetically. He does not just find them in the Inferno, he places them there, and does so in such a way as to make us question the justice of God himself.

I think that it is in fact an essential part of the design of this poem that the reader be dissatisfied, over and over again, both with the eternal disposition of many of the souls and with the explanations offered in justification. It is not against the intention of the poem but in accordance with it that you as a reader experience the resistance I describe. To put it another way: one central function of the poem, a central part of its meaning, is to constitute its reader as the kind of person who can learn to ask the questions Dante the traveler asks—questions that the text in a real way makes inevitable—and learn to live with what this questioning habit means.

Suppose this were not the case and that as you read you found that the disposition of every soul, in each of the three realms, made perfect sense to you. You would have no objections, for the judgments would accord perfectly with your own. How long could you read such a poem, and what would it mean to you while you did so? There would be none of the tension essential to art, just a predictable elaboration of premises; there would be no life in the text, or in the reader. And, for our purposes crucial, this would be not an aesthetic failure only but a political one: in such a case you would be submitting to an ideology working out its iron logic without hitches or gaps or cracks, a system of thought and imagination in which there was no place for you, except as a subordinate—no place for the independence of thought and judgment that Dante exhibits and stimulates. It would be perfectly authoritarian.

In the poem as composed, Dante finds a way to present this highly judgmental order—eternal judgments by the Judge of the Universe!—yet at the same time to leave room for the reader; more than leave room, to stimulate and confirm in the reader the capacity to question, to insist;

and thus to call into life a capacity in the individual mind that is essential to real thought, real action.

Not that our first instinct is always to be taken as right: as fallen creatures, our first response is often wrong, as we shall see those of Dante the character to be too. Like him, we are in need of education, an education the poem itself will offer us, and a crucial part of it is that we can never be totally sure of our own judgments. As I argue in later chapters, we are forced upon our own resources, then challenged, then forced upon our own resources again, all in a definition of responsibility as ultimately ours. The reader of this poem is thus not simply put in a position in which he must exercise independence of judgment, finally on his own; the reader is compelled at the same time to establish a responsible relationship with an intellectual and juristic structure that is represented as having real authority. He is not pushed off, that is, to make his own way in a world of radical existential uncertainty, but, far more maturely and significantly, he is presented with the inescapable problem of reading, understanding, learning from, disagreeing with, and reimagining the reigning modes of thought of the time—of Dante's time—as they are represented in the theological world of the poem. It is not right answers that Dante offers us in the end, then, but a special kind of silence, the silence that follows posed but unanswered questions. He uses this silence to engage us in a process of imagination and thought and feeling in which we are constantly forming and reforming our own judgments, and to leave us with the responsibilities he has defined.

Are the tensions concerning the justice of God ever resolved? If so, how? These are questions I shall pursue throughout this book. Here suffice it to say that at a formal level Dante the traveler receives from certain authorized speakers—Virgil, Beatrice, Bernard—answers to his questions and doubts, and these are, at least on the surface, offered and accepted as conclusive. But at an imaginative level the tension remains, for these resolutions are often unsatisfactory to the very part of us that the poem has been calling into existence. To this extent the poem seems to resist its own teachings.

Yet the poem goes further, for when we bring our dissatisfactions back to the text we sometimes find material for explanation and response, never articulated as such, that will carry us to a somewhat more satisfactory position than any explicitly stated there. For example, on reflection we discover that no one consigned to the Inferno seems to see that what he or she did was wrong and to repent it. In the implied theological narrative the soul is being punished for what it did, and who it was, before its human death, and it is now assumed to be totally incapable of repentance or any other change; but in a psychological or poetic sense the damnation seems to us continuously chosen, even at the present moment. Of course the sinner does not like the pain he or she is subjected to, but will not say, "I now see how wrong I was": rather, the sinner confirms the sin, insists on it, even while being punished. Francesca herself speaks of her eternity with her lover as a good, without any capacity to see it otherwise.[3] She is in a sense a captive of the language of courtly love, and cannot see beyond or beneath its formulas to deeper possibilities of human definition and connection.

Likewise Ulysses, seemingly representing in purest form the impulse of human knowledge, is the prisoner of his own beautiful language. He says to the men he is leading to their doom:

> "*Considerate la vostra semenza:*
> *fatti non foste a viver come bruti,*
> *ma per seguir virtute e canoscenza.*"   (XXVI, 118–20)

"Consider your origin. You were not made to live like beasts, but to pursue virtue and knowledge."[4]

Yet in saying these inspiring words he is in fact calling his men to certain destruction, urging them to sail west across the unknown sea, and without any expressed awareness of the meaning of what he is doing to them. He is conscious and overtly proud of the power of his rhetoric, his capacity to bend his men to his own will:

> "*Li miei compagni fec' io sì aguti,*
> *con questa orazion picciola, al cammino,*
> *che a pena poscia li avrei ritenuti.*"   (XXVI, 121–23)

---

[3] At one point Francesca says that the pleasure in Paolo that love gave her has never abandoned her (V.105) and, at another, that she will never be divided from him (V.135). The latter remark may be felt by the reader as grim indeed, and, on reflection, the first may come to seem a statement of what has in fact condemned Francesca to the Inferno, a misplaced love that she cannot give up. I think we are to read her as being unaware of these significances. For more on Francesca, see chapter 2.

[4] My translation fails to capture the crucial tension created by the fact that in Dante's Italian, *virtù* and *virtute* mean not only "virtue," as with us, but something like "force" or "power" as well.

"I made my companions so keen for the journey, with this little oration, that after it I would hardly have been able to restrain them."

On rereading, that is, we can come to question both our admiration for Francesca and Ulysses and our own susceptibility to their appeal. This works as one kind of resolution to the tension I spoke of, between the poet's apparent commitment to the justice of God and the contrary judgments and feelings we find emerging within us as we read.

A different kind of resolution occurs, at once imaginative and imperfect, in the closing Cantos of the *Paradiso*, where Dante and the reader are so caught up in the splendor, the light, the magnificence, the love, that everything else, in the *Inferno* and *Purgatorio* alike, is simply forgotten. The concerns of justice disappear in the light of truth and love. Perhaps that is after all the best answer possible; or, to put it another way, perhaps the closest the poem comes to a theological answer is no answer at all, again a kind of silence, the invocation of mystery. In this the poem would be in a grand tradition from Job to the present day. After all, no human being has ever been able adequately to reconcile the presumed power and goodness of the Deity with the sufferings and injustices of human life.

The souls that Dante the traveler meets in each of the three realms of the afterlife will often sum up in a few lines the essence of their whole lives. This is in the end a matter of moral and spiritual quality. Everyone has sinned, of course; the question is what attitude one has towards the damage one has done to others and oneself, what effort one makes to correct and improve, what kind and degree of trust one can attain, and so forth. This means for the reader—however remote he or she may be from Dante's specific religious commitments and understandings—that an essential part of the experience of this text is a certain anxiety and doubt it generates: Where in this imagined world would I be placed? What would I have to say for myself, about the moral and spiritual center of my life and being, and what would my statement look like in this context? What kind of meaning, in short, does *my* life have—the life that I have made?

Perhaps worse: When I turn from Dante's poem to my own experience, what way of imagining the world, and myself and others within it, does my culture offer or have I myself made? What do I have, that is, that takes the place of Dante's medieval Christian theology? Does my way of imagining, whatever it is, imply standards by which I can judge myself or another person, standards that will enable me to claim significance for my own experience? (If not—?) Finally, we are led to ask analogous questions about other people, and about organizations and nations and cultures too: tested by the highest standard of human excellence and possibility I can imagine, how does this person—or institution or culture—measure up?

That the poem does this is a great gift to us, even if in the end our standards are different from Dante's, for it is a way of calling upon us to recognize our own deepest values and best selves, and thus requires us to face the questions what those values are, how they can be expressed, and what our own sense of a "best self" is. The threat is that we shall find that we have no adequate way to imagine the world and ourselves, no way to claim meaning for our experience or that of others, no sense of a character made over time by its conduct, no sense of the deep value of our own lives.

In the chapters that follow I return frequently to Dante's poem and to the questions I have raised about it. At the moment my main point is a comparatively simple one: that this poem works by creating a crucial realm of silence defined by the unanswered questions, the unanswered questionings, that it stimulates in its reader. This is how it can present what looks like a complete and universal structure—an empire—and at the same time create the possibility that it will not be an ideological apologist for it. In the terms of my quotation from Simone Weil, Dante tries to keep the highly juridical world that he imagines into existence in this poem from becoming an empire of force in part by creating silences that confirm—that make necessary—the presence and place and judgment of the reader.

The center of this poem lies in what it calls upon each of us as a reader to do and to be as we read it: a questioner, as I have said, and in this sense a resister; one who must be satisfied in his or her own mind, and not simply rest on a set of authoritative declarations. It calls upon us to be present at the deepest place in our own imaginations, as one person and mind engaged with another, facing the great question of the meaning of this or that human life, of human life itself. That there is no systematic structure of thought that can automatically meet the responsibilities it defines, that the authoritarian is not to be respected, is one of the great teachings of this poem.

TRIVIALIZING AND DEMEANING NOISE

I want to turn now from the silent worlds of the Trappists and the Quakers, and from the empire-resisting poem Dante has built partly out of silences and questions, to look at the world we ourselves inhabit, and ask some very general questions: What is our own public speech-world like? What is its value? In what respects does it constitute an empire of force?

Propaganda and Advertising

It seems obvious that our world of public speech is very different indeed from the silences of the Trappists in their monastery, of the Quakers at their Meeting, or of Dante's great poem. While we each enjoy personal islands of peace and privacy—moments of silence—we are for the most part immersed in a world of speech of many kinds, in many formats and means, from newspapers to radio to the telephone to television and the internet, much of it insistent and demanding, some of it blaring, and very little of it calling for or rewarding real attention. We live in a very noisy world, and we contribute to that noise. And, if I may say so, it is plain to me at least, as my friend implied in his comment on the Trappists, that a great deal of what we hear and say is junk.

It is a little embarrassing to talk in this way about the character of our verbal world, for it makes me sound like a sourpuss, a repressive spoilsport, maybe a snob. But I do think we are out of balance. If you are inclined to resist, let me suggest that you pretend that you are told that you must spend an hour, or a day, thinking about the world in the terms established by television or newspaper ads, billboards, newspaper editorials and op-ed pieces, or, dare I say it, by presidential debates and speeches. You could not bear it because no self-respecting person could. I think it is fair to say that this world consists largely of one cliché or slogan after another; that much of it is misleading or dishonest; and that its tendency is to suppress, not stimulate, independence of thought and judgment. This speech does not come from inner silence, and it depends for its effect upon the fact that it does not take place in outer silence either, for it could not bear the attention that such silence would invite. And it is not neutral in its effects—not mere noise or chatter—but trivializing, dehumanizing, and demeaning. To consider the most important case: When is the last time you felt that you were addressed by a candidate for public office, or someone who holds such an office, in a way that made you feel that he was speaking directly and honestly about a difficulty he thought was real and hard, and speaking to you as a person of independent mind and judgment?

In my view far too much of our world of public speech consists of forms of expression that are designed simply to promote the sale of commodities or to advance a political position, and to do so with very little respect for the audience or regard for the truth. Speech of this character works not by appealing to the thought and experience of the person it addresses, imagined as a whole being and mind, but through the manipulation of instincts, instincts that it in fact does a lot to form. To put it briefly, I think our public world is too much dominated by the evils of advertising and propaganda; that these constitute in their own way an empire of force; and that what to think or say or do about this fact is a serious problem for us both in our individual lives and in the law.

We ought not simply to disregard this kind of speech, for it can have real effects, including on our own minds, which it does not improve. If we believe, as we sometimes no doubt do, that advertising and propaganda cannot reach us, for we are too intelligent, too aware of what they are doing, we are fooling ourselves. Surely those who spend billions of dollars on advertising are under the impression that they are not wasting their money; equally surely, the cumulative effect of advertising, virtually all of which promotes the same trivialized view of human life and the human person, must be more effective than any one advertising campaign. Much the same can be said about political propaganda, in which, as in advertising, bad speech always tends to drive out the good, partly by simply swamping it but more tellingly by destroying the sense of self and the world upon which all meaningful speech ultimately depends. I think that such trivializing and degrading forms of speech in their own way present as great a danger to the real value of speech as censorship does and need to be resisted for many of the same reasons.

This is not just a matter of aesthetics or taste. Advertising is largely built upon a diminished and diminishing image of the human being as merely a cluster of wants and desires, and upon a conception of speech as the manipulation of those desires. The view that the good life is a life of the gratification of desire, without critical attention to the nature of the desire in question or to the nature of the proposed gratification—a life of consumption or "entertainment"—is simply not an adequate conception of human felicity or an adequate image of the meaning of human experience. Our habituation to the forces in our culture that promote this view, in the economic and political arenas alike, makes it difficult for us to defend our most important institutions and values, those that imply and require a richer conception of human action, thought, and flourishing. I think here of our deep and admirable cultural commitments to human equality, to caring for others, to independence of judgment, to public education, to the practice of self-government—all of which presuppose a very different image of human life from that of the consuming economy or the politics of self-interested voting.

There is, then, a kind of speech, of which I use advertising and propaganda as key examples, of which one can say not only that it is itself not valuable as speech, but that it does much to destroy the possibility of valuable speech by what it does to us and to the world, for it corrodes the conditions that are necessary to that kind of speech—the silence without, the silence within, the possibility of openness and depth, the very sense of the human being as one engaged in a search for meaning in one's life and expressions. Propaganda and advertising and related forms of expression are not simply noise we must put up with, but deeply affect the character of the culture and our minds. They constitute a kind of speech that destroys real speech.

I need not go on. No one could sensibly argue or believe that the purpose of human life is acquisition or emulation of the kind stimulated by our advertising culture, or that this kind of life or talk is worthy of us in the political realm either. Imagine that we suddenly found ourselves to be collectively a character in Dante's poem: How would we talk to Dante the traveler? How would we explain our collective life and history? What kind of life would we represent ourselves as having, and what meaning would we claim for it? For Dante, what matters most is what he would call the state of the soul; we do not usually use that kind of language outside of religious discourse, but we do say something similar, that what matters most is who we are, who we are becoming, who we help each other become. This is the deepest question of life, and not only for us as individuals, but for us as a nation, and for an institution like the Supreme Court too: Not what we do, what we have, but who we are. And who we are, in the domain of public speech, is not so good.

Our Talk about Speech in the Law: The "Marketplace of Ideas"

For a person interested in the quality of speech, in freedom of speech, and the First Amendment, as I am, the disturbing point to which I have been building can be put this way: that our beloved freedom of speech has been in some ways the enemy of valuable speech—especially of the most valuable speech—both by creating the conditions on which it can be swamped or driven out or perverted and by undermining its assumptions about the possibilities of human life. We normally think of free speech as perhaps the most precious resource we have in resisting the empires of force at work in our world, and this is in a sense true enough; but it is also true that sometimes—in our world of public speech very often indeed—what we call "free speech" does not resist the empire of force but serves it, reinforces it, in some ways makes it possible. Our right to speak meaningfully and well—and in this sense freely—requires protection not only from the state but from the culture, from each other, and from ourselves.

How do we think about this problem? How should we do so? What place should silence have in the way we think? In the larger world?

1.

These are questions of particular importance in the law, which ought to be the place above all others where the value of speech is recognized and protected. Yet as I suggest in what follows, the law too often falls victim to the kind of trivializing and demeaning language upon which the empire depends for its life and effects.

Let me start by asking you first to reflect on your own response to what I have just said about certain strains of speech in our culture of which I have said I disapprove, especially my use of the word "junk." If you are like me, a side of you will have reacted very strongly, saying something like this: "Who are you to refer to any speech as junk? As Americans we are committed to our liberties, to our liberty of speech above all. The explosion of speech in our public spaces is an inherently good thing, not a bad one, even if you don't like it. What kind of elitist are you anyway?"

Some such response—in you and me and all of us—is deeply built into our minds and our culture. It is an instinctive reaction, so well established among us as to be a kind of second nature. At the faintest signs of what looks like censorship or even disapproval of any form of speech, we are likely to find ourselves resisting strongly. We boldly say that we are cheerfully willing to pay the price of too much speech—and of trivial or even dangerous speech—and that we do this for what seem to us to be several very good reasons: in order to avoid the evil of government censorship; in order to make truly democratic politics possible; and in order to respect the right of the individual to form her mind, and her relations with others, in such manner as seems to her best. Free speech is an aspect of autonomy, of the sovereignty of the individual over herself. We believe that if speakers are, within very generous limits, simply allowed to say whatever they want, this will be productive of great public and private good. As Voltaire is supposed to have said, we may detest what you say but we will fight to the death to preserve your right to say it. This is a key part of what it means to be an American.

Notice that in its dominant formulation this view is based upon deep skepticism: skepticism about anyone's claim to be able to judge in any enduring way the value of another's speech—to call it junk, for example. Yet, with happy inconsistency, we often join this skepticism with an affirmation of the deep faith that, over time, the best speech will prevail in the process we label, in the metaphor made famous by Justice Oliver Wendell Holmes, the "marketplace of ideas."[5]

I have stated in the briefest possible terms what I take to be a standard view of free speech in our country, not only among lawyers but in the culture more generally. It is simply a part of our minds. It is what I myself think and say, most of the time at least. There are of course many competing theories and visions of the First Amendment, but when I think of the responses of my colleagues, students, and indeed of myself, none of them begins to have the force and staying power of the image of the "marketplace of ideas." This is the position we instinctively resort to when someone challenges the idea that speech should be free.

2.

What interests me at the moment is the peculiar fact that we—I include myself—tend to hold on to this position even though we know, as every First Amendment class teaches, that there are serious difficulties with

---

[5] Holmes did not in fact use that phrase in the famous opinion in which he spoke to the question, but in our culture it has come to stand for his position. What he did say was this: "[M]en may come to believe . . . that the ultimate good desired is better reached by free trade in ideas—that the best test of truth is the power of the thought to get itself accepted in the competition of the market." *Abrams v. United States*, 250 U.S. 616, 630 (1919). For further comment see note 10 below.

it—difficulties so serious that in its usual formulations at least, it is really not tenable.

Consider this, for example. When we really do believe that speech can advance truth, or when we value what it can do for other reasons, we normally do not free it from constraint but instead do the opposite: we regulate it, sometimes with extreme severity, and we do so in ways that directly reflect a collective judgment of usefulness or quality or value. Take the courtroom, for example: this is an institution that works almost entirely by words, but in it there is very little of what one would call freedom of speech. The law of procedure and evidence is actually a way of declaring who can say what, on what occasion, and to whom, and one is not free to deviate from what it declares. No trial judge would be receptive to the argument that your freedom of speech entitled you to disregard his or her courtroom rulings. Likewise the classroom—a bastion of freedom for the professor—is a place of radically controlled speech. Normally a student may speak only when called on and only to the issue. Scientific journals strictly regulate what can be published and under what conditions. One can readily think of other instances.

In fact all institutions regulate speech, from museums and theaters to businesses and churches to sports teams. In a sense, that is what an institution is: a complex set of expectations about the use of language, all of which are ways of repressing and excluding speech as well as enabling it. At a play, for example, the audience must be silent so the actors may be heard. This kind of regulation is not hostile to speech and what it can achieve but the opposite: its aim is to foster speech of a high quality, for it is upon such speech that the success of the institution depends. The goal is not to suppress truth, or some other social value, but to make its discovery or expression possible. To return to my first theme, notice that in each of these cases regulation works to a large degree through compelled silence: silence is the sculptor's chisel that shapes the speech, that creates the context that makes sustained attention to it possible and in this way enables one to build upon it. It is almost as though, despite our claims for the importance of freedom of speech, we allow speech to be relatively unconstrained only when we think it does not much matter.

Here is a second point. Despite what we say about the "marketplace of ideas," we also know, if we allow ourselves to reflect on it, that we simply cannot trust any such process as a metaphorical market to winnow out the bad and promote the good. We know that dreadful speech can survive and flourish, like a poisonous plant: think of *The Protocols of the Elders of Zion*, a venomous anti-Semitic text that has been wholly discredited for more than a century but, as a quick web search will show, is still in robust circulation. Or think of American racism, which—formed and maintained by speech—infects the mind of every person who lives in our country, including yours and mine. Each of us is partly made by the world we inhabit; this means that our most private and personal and apparently independent choices, the roots of our imagination, may be corrupted by something wrong, or evil, or demeaning, or trivializing in our world, which we have internalized. This in turn means that our choices in the world of speech, and those of others, ought not be granted perfect and unquestioned authority, either on the grounds that speech is harmless or that more speech is always all to the good. Think once more of the "white" child growing up in a system of black racial slavery, or of the "black" child doing so; the minds of both, their ways of imagining the world and themselves and others, will be perverted by the cultural system of which they are a part, and their speech will tend to confirm and promote this perversion. We owe it to ourselves and our world not to abandon our powers of collective judgment about good and bad speech, good and bad cultural forces, as the marketplace metaphor invites us to do, but to train and develop them, with the constant awareness that what now seems to us natural and right in us or in our world may in time come to seem false and wrong. Not to do this would be to abandon an essential human responsibility. What we say, and what others say, matters enormously to all of us. It is a form of action.

A third difficulty with the "marketplace" image is this. The standard ideology of free speech assumes as its model an independent-minded individual who is speaking unwelcome truths to the world, resisting power, and competing with others in an open market that will test both fact and value. It is with such speakers that we easily identify; it is they whose right to say what we detest we would die to defend. But very little of the speech that makes up our shared world takes this form. Rather, the bulk of our public speech is commercially and politically driven and as such is naturally dominated by a cluster of institutions, businesses, interests, and political organizations of great power. The "market" for public speech, if one is to use such a metaphor, is not individual and not a truly open one. This means that important threats to speech of the very kind we imagine ourselves as valuing most—freedom of speech in the individual person—may emanate from these immensely powerful private speakers as well as from the government. Like the government, the non-governmental world is a world of power, including power over speech: it shapes and suppresses speech—it drives out speech—both by the speech it fosters in others and by the speech it disseminates.[6] Think for example of the fact that a few television networks dominate the ways in which we conceive of and imagine what is happening in the world. We tend to assume that if the government just leaves the world alone, a garden of speech will spring into existence, but in some ways what we have made with our freedom is closer to a desert.

Finally, and perhaps most deeply, the very image of the "marketplace of ideas" is unclear at the center. After all, what is to be imagined here: a bazaar with tables and booths where people offer "ideas" for sale? But in most speech there is no ownership, and no buying and selling. The person who hears a good "idea," and adopts it, makes it his or her own and pays nothing for it; the promulgator gets nothing for it. The realm of copyright, a seeming exception where speech is indeed commodified, explicitly excludes ideas from its coverage, reaching only the form of an expression, not its content. What is more, the historical implications of the image of the "marketplace" do not suggest a zone that is to be free from regulation but one that is regulated to serve the public interest in all sorts of ways, from weights and measures to labels to pricing.[7] Finally, the image implies that the value of speech lies in things called "ideas,"

---

[6] This speech silences living and valuable speech in several ways: by drowning it out; by establishing the expectation that this sort of speech is the norm, and in this way making it harder to achieve, or to hear, speech of a deeper and more important kind; and by gathering into the hands of a few the effective power to speak in what is supposed to be a public arena. Such silencing perpetrates a unique kind of injustice, not often spoken of in the discourse of our day, which tends to focus on disparities of income, or wealth, or access to services. For another effect of our system of poverty and deprivation is the annihilation of the person's sense of his or her own real value, of his or her right to talk and be heard, inflicting an injury at the center of the soul that cannot be healed by the provision of material wealth or services.

[7] Perhaps, indeed, the seductive appeal of the image of the "marketplace of ideas," for some people at least, is the reverse of what one might at first think, namely that the idea of a market for *speech*, which is by our tradition and Constitution free, suggests that more traditional markets for *goods*, normally regulated, should be similarly free from state control. Ronald Coase in particular has made the argument that the reasons for freedom in the market for speech apply with at least equal force to the market for goods. See Ronald H. Coase, "The Market for Goods and the Market for Ideas," *American Economic Review* (papers and proceedings) 64 (1974): 384.

thus erasing from the field of attention all the other valuable aspects of expression, from emotive force to political and ethical significance. How often is it an "idea" that makes speech valuable, for the speaker or the listener? Does *Hamlet*, for example, express an idea?[8]

One could sum it up by saying that the phrase, the "marketplace of ideas," functions as a cliché or slogan in something of a paradigmatic way. It assumes its own adequacy, and seems to resist any effort to complicate or challenge it or to locate it in a larger complex of thought and discourse. It neither comes from silence in one who uses it nor speaks to silence in one who hears it. Indeed it is normally used in a way that offers no place to its hearer except as one who will in turn repeat it.[9]

3.

Here, then, is the problem: in our very talk about speech, and freedom of speech—as evidenced by the force of the image of the "marketplace of ideas"—we can be seen to collapse into slogans and clichés of our own, signally failing to manifest the qualities of mind and expression for which speech itself at its best is properly valued. Why is this so? If the image of the "marketplace of ideas" has the rather obvious defects I describe, why does it have such force and power in our minds? Why can we in fact hardly remember its defects, when in some sense we know them perfectly well?

---

[8] Compare the institution at Harvard and perhaps elsewhere of a department of the history of ideas—as though there were a plane above the field of expression where "ideas" could be seen and described unproblematically and where they could in fact live out stories of their own. For good statements of the view that intellectual history can better be thought of as the history of language, in a generous sense of the term, see Quentin Skinner, *The Foundations of Modern Political Thought* (Cambridge: Cambridge University Press, 1978); and J. G. A. Pocock, *The Ancient Constitution and the Feudal Law* (Cambridge: Cambridge University Press, 1987).

[9] I should make clear that I am speaking of the cliché that the "marketplace of ideas" has since become, not of Holmes's original use of similar language in *Abrams*. His opinion might indeed be taken as an example of living speech in the law, not a reduction of law to a slogan. In fact, the main image of his opinion is not the market but the process that most deeply marks his mind, that of evolution by survival of the fittest. His opinion is marked by tensions—between skepticism and faith, brute power and idealization, tolerance and judgment, dominance and truth—that characterize his work as a whole, calling upon the reader to exercise independent and complex judgment of his or her own and in this way giving life to the text and to the law. For further analysis of this opinion along these lines, see James Boyd White, "Legal Knowledge," *Harvard Law Review* 115 (2002): 1396, 1416–24.

This feature of our experience, this puzzling fact of our own psychology, is important not only for its own sake but for a more general reason: this is a point at which we can actually catch ourselves succumbing to the temptation to fall into slogan or cliché. Paradoxically, we do this at exactly the moment at which we think of ourselves as most powerfully taking a stand for freedom of speech, as resisting the authoritarian, as protecting the individual mind, and so on.

I do not claim to understand all the reasons for the force of this language, but part of it I think is that the metaphor of the "marketplace of ideas" replicates in the field of speech a cultural system or mentality that is so widely prevalent in our world, in the law and elsewhere, that it is hard to resist in any context. What I refer to, as I suggested earlier, is the habit of imagining human life simply as the satisfaction, or not, of human wants or desires, which is the principle upon which our advertising culture, and much political propaganda, rests. If I want it I should presumably have it. This is a premise not only of advertising but of most economic thought as well, which takes human wishes for granted and conceives of itself as the science of their satisfaction; it is also sometimes said, erroneously in my view, to be a premise of democracy as well. When we are thinking in this mode, we imagine a world of competent adult people, each making choices that will serve what they believe to be their interests; and we believe that so long as they do not interfere unduly with the rights of others, each person should be free to act and speak with maximum liberty. In that way the desires and wants and values, or what are sometimes called tastes or preferences, of each—and all—will be achieved to the maximum possible extent. Our image of speech as a market thus acquires much of its force and staying power from our larger ideological commitment to that kind of thinking—our imagining democracy as a market, life itself as a market. Consumer choice and electoral choice are alike: you will try to get what you want, I will try to get what I want; the function of government is to protect this process in a value-neutral way.

As a general matter, and not only with respect to speech, all this seems not only to constitute a depreciated view of the possibilities of human life but, even on its own terms, to rest upon a highly exaggerated faith. Just as our experience tells us that the cultural processes we call the "marketplace of ideas" will not always lead to truth or justice or fairness, so it tells us that the basic assumption that a series of "rationally self-interested choices" will lead to the best possible outcome is not true.[10] Aside from the dubious "rationality" of many of our choices in the first place, it is perfectly possible for a series of individual choices, each in some sense "rational" on the conditions presented, to produce a result that no one could sensibly want. Our patterns of land use demonstrate this as well as anything: no one would want a highway leading into a beautiful and historic resort town to look like the standard American strip, with gigantic signs, bright lights, ugly buildings. But this is all too often what we have, and it is the result of individual "rational" decisions. The person who owns a piece of land on the highway and wants to use it for business purposes is compelled to compete for attention by contributing to the visual blare, even if he or she thinks it hideous. Or think of the new-style American suburb, which owes its origins to similar processes. Under current conditions it is "rational" for developers to create housing subdivisions that are wasteful of scarce resources and "rational" for people to buy such houses, given the alternatives available, even if all the actors agreed that it is not good to live without the shops, restaurants, sidewalks, and neighborhood life that denser communities make possible.

Much the same is true in the field of speech, with similar results. Who would for a minute think that what our television networks produce is worthy of a great people? Only those who could see no farther than their ideology of private choice would let them. The market cannot be an automatic test of value, as that ideology insists, for to use my earlier term, it so often produces junk. The ideology of the market refuses on the surface to make "value choices," supposedly leaving them to be worked out by consumers, but in fact it is deeply resonant of value, especially in its way of imagining what a human being is, its sense of what motives drive us, its limited conception of human reason, and its image of what would constitute a fulfilled human existence.

4.

The image of the market seems even more obviously wrong as a way of thinking about democratic government. I do not think that the central idea of democracy is that it provides a framework in which the maximum number of things can be done or said, shaped only by human will and

---

[10] One way to attempt to solve this difficulty is to define all decisions as equally "rational" as a matter of first principle—on the grounds that no person can really judge the quality of another's decision—but this obviously strips the term "rationality" of any content at all.

preference.[11] At least one point of democracy is to give a nation the special character that arises from the fact that all people have an equal right to participate in the activities not only of voting but of government itself; this is to subject the government, and the nation, to a special discipline, one that will make it capable of moral and ethical action on behalf of its citizens in a new way; and this should in turn give the nation the possibility of a meaningful past, a meaningful future, of a new kind. Democracy is built upon the hope that our lives and experience can have meaning, meaning of a kind that the language of the market cannot express or imagine.

Democracy is a method by which the people choose their collective values, shape their collective conduct, and assume their collective responsibilities as a nation. Or, to put it slightly differently, it is a way in which people commit to a shared identity and history while they struggle over these things. It is not about the pursuit of self-interest. Quite the reverse: for democracy to be real it requires what it makes possible, an identification of the individual with his government—his sense of pride or shame at the moral history of his nation, at what is said and done in his name. It is built upon, and requires, a sense of public responsibility leading to collective self-education. In a sense, one test of any nation is the willingness of people to die on its behalf, and no one could willingly die for enhanced economic welfare. For that sacrifice, without which one cannot have a nation, one needs such a thing as justice, or truth, or community.

As for the economic model, it is of course not life but a way of looking at life. One could look at life in other ways. One might begin by noticing, for example, that no person is independent of all others, as the economic model assumes; we all live in relations of dependency, or caring, from birth until death. We are a bit like parents and children to one another, working out relations in which one person cares for another: sibling, friend, teacher, doctor, lawyer. Most of our life actually takes place in networks of such relations, in which we find ourselves constantly alternating roles. The arm's length "deal," except in the life of a trader, and then only a piece of it, is a small part of life, surely not a model of human experience as a whole. On this view the fundamental questions about human life and relations could be put this way: When are we good and bad par-

---

[11] Consider here: "Democracy functions as a religion, because it expresses in politics the secular faith that satisfying desires is the point of being alive." Kenneth Minogue, review of *On Democracy*, by Robert A. Dahl, *Times Literary Supplement*, June 18, 1999, 8.

ents, and children, and friends, in these relations? When do we take good care of each other, when not? What kinds of structures and relations promote care for each other? What kind of community does so?[12]

Our Desire to Submit

The Trappist—or Dante—might see more clearly than we can that the part of our culture that works through advertising and propaganda, and that imagines the world of speech as just another market, represents a fundamental emptiness. He might also see more readily than we can do that it creates a force in our minds that makes it very difficult to think about the question I have been elaborating from the beginning of this chapter, namely the tension between free speech and valuable speech. And this is what interests me: the pressure that the image of the "marketplace of ideas" exerts in our minds, so strong as to make us forget its obvious defects and limits.

I think this image has the power it does not only because its assumptions are deeply mirrored in other aspects of the culture, as I have been suggesting, but for an additional and deeper reason: because there is something in us that leads us to want to reiterate it, to resort to it, even when we know how inadequate it is, in a way *because* it is inadequate. It is a kind of slogan, the function of which is to suppress independent thought and judgment; its power comes in the end from our very desire to submit to that kind of language, that kind of thought, because this is easier than facing the responsibilities of a full human life. Its power comes from our own desire to submit to the empire of force.

In thinking about this kind of speech, and our susceptibility to it, I am often reminded of Robert Frost's most famous poem, "The Road Not Taken," which closes by celebrating the choice of the road "less traveled by." I am sure it is read at high school graduations all over the country as a way of urging young people to follow their own path, even if unpopular; to listen to the drummer only they can hear. But, as you may recall, in the poem itself we are explicitly told, when the choice of path is de-

---

[12] Compare Robin West, *Caring for Justice* (New York: New York University Press, 1997), which works out a vision of the world somewhat similar to the one I sketch here. Also see Alasdair MacIntyre, *Dependent Rational Animals* (Chicago: Open Court, 1999).

scribed, that the two roads were in fact not different but virtually the same:

> Two roads diverged in a yellow wood,
> And sorry I could not travel both
> And be one traveler, long I stood
> And looked down one as far as I could
> To where it bent in the undergrowth;
>
> Then took the other, as just as fair,
> And having perhaps the better claim,
> Because it was grassy and wanted wear;
> *Though as for that the passing there*
> *Had worn them really about the same,*
>
> *And both that morning equally lay*
> *In leaves no step had trodden black.*
> Oh, I kept the first for another day!
> Yet knowing how way leads on to way,
> I doubted if I should ever come back.
>
> I shall be telling this with a sigh
> Somewhere ages and ages hence:
> Two roads diverged in a wood, and I—
> I took the one less traveled by,
> And that has made all the difference. (Emphasis added)

We are explicitly told that there was no real difference between the paths; yet when we get to the end we find that we have utterly forgotten that fact of our experience. Despite our prior knowledge, we accept and even celebrate the false and sentimental phrase with which the poem concludes.

We forget what we know. Our desire for an image of sentimental meaning—for an apt phrase to slide over the true difficulties of describing and judging experience, and thus to give us an illusion of significance and control—is just too deep. This is the real subject of the poem—not the nature of human choices, but the way in which a phrase or slogan can take over the imagination, colonizing it, making the mind no longer fully one's own. The true aim of the poem is not to say something vapid about human life-choices, but to resist the very impulse toward cliché that it stimulates in us and captures, and freezes in amber, and holds up for our examination.

It does this in a most complex and artful way. The rhythms of the poem, for example, include an anapest in almost every line,[13] giving it an almost soporific quality, drawing our attention away from what is said to the sound of the chant. This effect is reinforced by the paratactic structure of the sentences—"and . . . and . . ."—a structure that consists of sequence alone, rejecting hierarchy and consequence, once more having the effect of lulling our critical capacities to sleep. The poem is not only about our preexisting susceptibilities, then, but also about the way in which language can carry a charm or magic that will work on us, against our own minds, against our critical judgment, against our knowledge of the facts. In this sense, it is itself like a piece of what I have called "advertising," but one that presents itself for criticism and rejection. What the poem teaches is the necessity of being on guard when the Siren sings.

HOW CAN WE RESPOND?

If I am right that in our world we have too much speech, and speech of the wrong kind—speech that does not come from silence within, is not deeply meant, and destroys the silence without; speech that trivializes human experience, including human expression itself; speech that confirms an image of life as the gratification of want or desire—this is not an unimportant issue, but crucial to all of us, especially those of us in the law. At stake is the quality and character of our culture and therefore of our own experience and identity, collectively and as individuals. We cannot properly wash our hands of it. Nor will it do to inhabit our private islands of silence, closing our ears to the sea of trivializing and demeaning noise that surrounds these protected spaces, any more than it would do to inhabit our peaceful houses and concert halls and museums and close our eyes to the ugliness of the world we have built between these places. Nor can our ideology of free speech excuse us, as individuals or as a community, from reflecting critically upon, and judging, the speech we hear, the speech we create.

To think about this well requires us to have an image of speech itself, an understanding of what is good and not so good, an image that cannot be collapsed into a process or metaphor—like the market—but one that reflects a fuller way of imagining human life and the world in which it

[13] An anapest is a metrical unit, called a "foot," consisting of two unstressed syllables followed by a stressed one. It tends to have a sing-song quality, as in : " 'Twas the night before Christmas and all through the house, / Not a creature was stirring, not even a mouse."

takes place. The dominant mode of our culture, economic in nature, seems obviously inadequate as a model of life or speech. I have held up the Trappists and the Quakers and Dante as representing different possibilities, based on different principles. The question is what these principles might be—and not so much for them as for you and me. How are we to think of these things? As people and as lawyers, how are we to define the speech that is most valuable and explain why it is so? How are we to achieve, nourish, protect it?

To begin with, I think we are right to value speech, or some speech, very highly indeed, but for a reason quite different from a commitment to the ideology of the market: rather, out of a deep intuition that speech is essential to our humanity, to what it means to be human, and in particular, that our full dignity as individual people and as a culture depends upon our being able to claim meaning for our lives and experience. We are meaning-making creatures. This is what distinguishes us from other animals. This capacity is the deepest nerve of our life, and our instinct to protect it and its freedom at almost any cost is a right one. This is not a view of speech as a market or even as an evolutionary process; the kind of speech we hope for with this part of ourselves is not advertising and propaganda, not commodity or entertainment, but speech that is deeply meant, that expresses and offers engagement of the mind, that invites and rewards attention—speech that comes from inner silence and takes place in outer silence.

With respect to the law, this raises the question: Is it imaginable that the law could be a place for the kind of speech I describe? This question actually has two distinct forms. The first is this: Can those of us in the law find a way to imagine the speech of others—the speech that is the subject of the First Amendment, say—as exhibiting the possibilities, positive and negative, that I have been trying to describe? The second asks: Can those of us in the law ourselves speak, as lawyers and as judges, in ways that achieve the quality of speech we most admire? Both questions require us to recognize that our speech falls on a spectrum, from speech that has extraordinary value, for us as individuals and for the world, to speech that is destructive of that very value.

We cannot ask of the Supreme Court, for obvious reasons, that it create a world in which only living speech exists, and in which advertising and propaganda, and other forms of trivializing and dehumanizing speech, have no place, but we can ask of our courts, as of ourselves, that they seek to imagine speech in a worthy way—to distinguish what has real value as speech from that which is destructive of the value of speech, and to demonstrate the distinction in their own expression.

Imagining Speech

To start with the first task identified above: if not as a "marketplace of ideas," how should the law imagine the human activity of speech? The First Amendment, our central text and authority, is part of the puzzle here, for it is on both sides of the tension between freedom and quality. It is obviously committed to freedom of expression, yet its commitment presumably rests on the belief that the speech that will emerge under its protection will have real value, and this suggests a scale of better and worse. Yet the amendment can still provide real help, if we ask, as we did of Dante's *Commedia*, how it imagines the world it seeks to create. The answer—so obvious as to be hard to see—is that it imagines the world not as a market, not as a world of people trading, but as a world of people speaking to each other. Primacy is given to the act of speech itself, not to what is achieved by it. Perhaps this is in fact its greatest single achievement: to suggest that there is something about speech itself, about the activity of using language, that sets it apart from other forms of human activity.

To imagine people as speaking is to imagine them in some deep sense as equals, for it is to recognize that each person has her own place in the world, her own mind and her own experience, her own right to express the meanings she finds in existence, from her own perspective. It is to create a polity based upon communication across difference, committing us to the acknowledgment of the reality of the experience of others. The consequences are large, reaching even straightforward social and economic policy, for once you hear the voice of the person who is poor, or oppressed, or poisoned by industrial effluents, it is much harder to dismiss her claims than if you imagine her simply as a player in a complex game in which she happens to be a loser, not a winner.

This means that the First Amendment should be read as calling for an enhanced or elevated image of speech, not a reduced or reductive one—as a marketplace, for example, or as a system for the transmission of information or a mode of entertainment. Perhaps a preliminary sketch of such an enhanced image might run something like this.

As human beings, as users of language—as citizens of this new country based on new principles—we are not simply animals that have learned to communicate our wants and desires to each other, to make deals in which we swap or exchange our freedoms. As Dante shows, we are creatures with minds and imaginations, who can use language in a characteristically human way to claim identities for ourselves and others, to claim meaning for our experience—past, present, and future. We are actors in the world who are capable of significant action because we have ways of imagining ourselves and our conduct, and that of others, that can claim meaning and invite judgment. To do this we need ways of conceiving of the natural and social world, ways of defining our values, ways of thinking about our own thinking; and ways of limiting, by silences, the languages that we use. It is in these capacities of mind and spirit as much as anything else that human dignity resides.

Our speech has real value for us and for the world—value of the kind the First Amendment presumably contemplates—insofar as it is deep, original, self-testing, revealing awareness of the limits and resources of its language; insofar as it is truly composed, organized to call upon the reader or hearer to respond in a deep, not superficial, way; insofar as it has genuineness of voice, and character, and relation; and insofar as it has a life and shape of its own that work against the various reductive and dehumanizing forces in the world that I have been calling the empire of force.

Not, I hasten to add, that I think the Supreme Court should interpret the Constitution as permitting the government to prohibit all speech that has low value on this or any other scale. But the Court should reflect in the way it imagines the world and talks about it a view of speech that reflects the importance and value of this activity.[14]

---

[14] In particular terms, whenever the Court, for what seem to it to be good First Amendment reasons, decides to tolerate speech that it believes to be base, empty, manipulative, dead, or disgusting, it should recognize, express, and explain what it is doing. Even if it wanted to—and no matter how hard it tried—the Court could not entirely avoid the question of quality of speech, whether by using the formula or ideology of free speech I outlined earlier or in some other way. One reason is that—as every teacher of the First Amendment knows—it is not at all clear what ought to count as the "speech" to which that amendment affords its special protections. "Speech" does not include everything done with words, for this would include conspiracies to kill, agreements in restraint of trade, treasonous revelation of secrets, perjury, and so on. And "speech" almost certainly should include expressive activities that do not consist entirely, or not mainly, of words—for example, protest marches, musical performances, picketing, and so forth. How is the scope of the term, and the amendment, to be determined? Built into the very structure of this field is a question of judgment about the character of the activity at issue, and this question is necessarily connected with judgments of worth and value. For an analysis of the cultural process by which some acts of communication come to be thought of as presenting First Amendment issues, others not, see Frederick Schauer, "The Boundaries of the First Amendment: A Preliminary Exploration of Constitutional Salience," *Harvard Law Review* 117 (2004): 1765.

Speech in the Law

This brings me to the second dimension of my question: how we ourselves engage in speech not in the world but in the law, and especially in the judicial opinion. For it is in the opinion, if anywhere, that a more adequate way of imagining language will receive its clearest and most important definition. This will not happen through routine or formal protestations, but only if the Court itself can exemplify the qualities of mind and speech we ought to value most. Exactly what these qualities are and how to think about them are important subjects of this book as a whole, to be addressed by positive and negative examples, by comparison with other forms of literature, and by examining the way we ourselves think and write. But this can already be said: that we can properly ask of an opinion whether in it we see the presence of a distinctive mind speaking out of inner silence to a similar place in the reader; whether we see a composition that is not the reiteration of dead and routine forms, but has a figure and life of its own that resist the appeal of ideology, slogan, and cliché; whether we see a text that defines its reader as an independent mind and offers him or her an opportunity to make a judgment on the merits, a judgment that the opinion will inform but not dictate.

The hope would be that those of us in the law could create a community of minds engaged in a conversation that proceeded from and to the deepest place in the human mind, the point at which it imagines itself and the world anew. If we could do this, we would advance in a most important and immediate way the fundamental value upon which democracy rests, namely the essential dignity of human experience and identity. If we fail, we fail in this, perhaps the most important of our collective endeavors.

The law is perhaps surprisingly a place where the kind of valuable speech I have been trying to identify can already be heard, more often than in many other segments of our culture. There are good reasons for this. The oppositional nature of legal thought tends to put in question both the assumptions we bring to an argument and the language in which we express them. Legal thought and argument are inherently individual, not in the sense that they are not cooperative but in the sense that there is—or should be—always an individual mind behind whatever is said and responsible for it.[15] And law works, or should work, under the persistent pressure of silences: silences that shape the argument, recog-

[15] The practice under which opinions, especially in the Supreme Court, are no longer written by the justices but by teams of clerks is I think a perversion of the fundamental

nizing what cannot be said, or should not be said; silences that recognize the limits of our understanding; silences that create the possibility of real attention to what is said. Our hope for a law that can talk about speech in a deeper and truer way than we now do, and itself exemplify or embody speech at its best—not trivializing human experience but conferring dignity upon it—will ultimately rest on our capacity to speak out of silent places within ourselves, to places of silence in others. So long as the law does not collapse into the language of theory—the authoritarian impulse to claim to know all, to explain all—or, even worse, into political cant and slogan, it may remain a discourse in which new truths can be discovered and expressed.

Barnette

As a brief example of what the Supreme Court can sometimes do, let me call upon the opinions in *West Virginia State Board of Education v. Barnette*,[16] the famous flag salute case. The question was the constitutionality of a West Virginia statute requiring all children in public school to salute the flag, and pledge allegiance to it. The two main opinions are by Justices Robert Jackson and Felix Frankfurter, the first writing for the Court in striking down the salute and pledge requirement, the second, in dissent, arguing that it should not be held unconstitutional.

For Jackson the requirement of the salute and pledge is a form of forced expression, of which he speaks in these terms: "If there is any fixed star in our constitutional constellation, it is that no official, high or petty, can prescribe what shall be orthodox in politics, nationalism, religion, or other matters of opinion, or force citizens to confess by word or act their faith therein."[17] As Jackson puts it, the issue is whether the "slow and easily neglected route" to national loyalty, which consists of education in

---

premise of law that one is entitled to be spoken to by the person acting as one's judge. Among other things, opinions written by clerks understandably tend to be far too long, to consider arguments that have no real force, and to speak in a voice to which no one can seriously attend. The clerks are, after all, not explaining why they decided the case one way or the other but producing a text for someone else's signature. The most serious difficulty with this practice is that it erases our expectation that the justice will speak to us as a person responsible for making the judgment he or she has reached and for explaining it to us. See the discussion of *Ashcroft v. Free Speech Coalition*, 535 U.S. 234 (2002), in chapter 4.

[16] 319 U.S. 624 (1943).

[17] *Id.* at 642.

the history and structure of our government, can be "short-cut by substituting a compulsory salute and slogan."[18] He thus imagines the world of speech as important and complex, crucial to the life of the individual person and to the development of his or her capacities of judgment, and here he protects it against an imposition of untoward simplicity. Yet at the same time he recognizes that any of us might find ourselves sharing the impulse lying behind such an imposition: "Struggles to coerce uniformity of sentiment in support of some end thought essential to their time and country have been waged by many good as well as by evil men."[19] It is from our own temptations and proclivities to tyranny, then, not just those of other people, that the Constitution, and this opinion, seek to protect us. And Jackson sees that what is at stake in enforced conformity of speech reaches more than speech: "Those who begin coercive elimination of dissent soon find themselves exterminating dissenters."[20]

For Justice Frankfurter much of this makes sense. "One who belongs to the most vilified and persecuted minority in history is not likely to be insensible to the freedoms guaranteed by our Constitution."[21] His own inclination is strongly against the wisdom of the salute requirement. But here the Court is faced with a judgment reached by the West Virginia legislature, and it must hesitate to substitute its own view, especially where the Court's only mode of action is so severe, the permanent invalidation of a statute. The core of Frankfurter's argument is that the Court should systematically exercise self-restraint in striking down laws that are the product of the democratic process, both in the field of economic regulation, as several of his New Deal colleagues readily agreed, and with respect to civil rights and liberties, as they did not. For him, self-restraint is essential both to the integrity of the Court's thought and to its continued authority. Frankfurter says this about the requirement that children participate in this symbolic gesture: "[I]t is not for this Court to make psychological judgments as to the effectiveness of a particular symbol in inculcating concededly indispensable feelings, particularly if the state happens to see fit to utilize the symbol that represents our heritage and our hopes."[22]

[18] *Id.* at 631.
[19] *Id.* at 640.
[20] *Id.* at 641.
[21] *Id.* at 646.
[22] *Id.* at 662.

Both justices speak out of evident conviction; both find something external to themselves to respect—Jackson, the speaker's freedom; Frankfurter, the legislature's judgment. Neither reduces his position to a cliché or slogan; each of them, in his own way, resists that kind of thought. Both opinions are shaped by respect for silence, not only in the usual way in which an opinion is set apart from other texts but in their structure: Frankfurter's deepest claim is that the Court should be silent on the matter of the salute and pledge, and Jackson's is that one must permit the children to be silent. Especially as they work together, the opinions do indeed define a place of independent judgment for the reader of these opinions. This is not simply a matter of choosing the opinion you prefer, because each is so markedly the actual work of a distinctive mind that you could not adopt it as your own. Rather, they invite you to work through to your own judgment, expressed in your own terms. In doing this, both writers resist the forces of dehumanization and do so on behalf of the life and value of the individual mind, both yours and theirs. For both of these men respect and value the workings of their own minds, and evidently believe that it matters a great deal what they say and how they say it; this works for both of them as an affirmation of the importance of what others think too, and how they speak. In their prose, in somewhat different ways, these two justices thus perform and make real the possibility and importance of valuable speech.

In the law—as Dante shows us with respect to the Christian discourse of his time—the effort should be to resist the empires of force that seek to dominate our minds by manipulative or empty speech, and to do so by insisting on the presence of the individual mind and person, both as speaker and as hearer. Much more important than the outcome of any particular case or the adoption or rejection of a particular rule, it is only through such insistence, repeated over and over again, as actors in the law and as critics of it, that we can hope to create the life—the intellectual and moral life—upon which democracy depends.

Lincoln

I close this chapter with a small example of the kind of achievement I have in mind, not by a judge or lawyer, not by a poet like Dante or Frost, but by an American public man and political actor. Below I reproduce Abraham Lincoln's letter of appointment to General Joseph Hooker, which in a rather surprising way turns out to involve the issue of freedom of speech. Lincoln leaves neither us nor Hooker in any doubt as to his judgment on Hooker's acts of speech, but he tolerates them nonetheless. This is one mind speaking the truth to another, insisting on it in fact, and doing so in such a way as to invite the other to act out of his best self, not his worst. It can stand as a model of what I would call responsible and living speech, the opposite of advertising and propaganda, of slogan and cliché. For our purposes it is important that it is shaped in no small part by its significant silences. Notice, too, that Lincoln is here resisting, in a direct and effective way, the impulse towards what he calls dictatorship, and that this resistance is achieved both in his definition of himself as a person responsible for what he says and does and in the demand he makes upon his reader for independence of mind and judgment.

Executive Mansion,
Washington, January 26, 1863

Major-General Hooker:

General.

I have placed you at the head of the Army of the Potomac. Of course I have done this upon what appear to me to be sufficient reasons. And yet I think it best for you to know that there are some things in regard to which, I am not quite satisfied with you. I believe you to be a brave and skilful soldier, which, of course, I like. I also believe you do not mix politics with your profession, in which you are right. You have confidence in yourself, which is a valuable, if not an indispensable quality. You are ambitious, which, within reasonable bounds, does good rather than harm. But I think that during Gen. Burnside's command of the Army, you have taken counsel of your ambition, and thwarted him as much as you could, in which you did a great wrong to the country, and to a most meritorious and honorable brother officer. I have heard, in such a way as to believe it, of your recently saying that both the Army and the Government needed a Dictator. Of course it was not *for* this, but in spite of it, that I have given you the command. Only those generals who gain successes, can set up dictators. What I now ask of you is military success, and I will risk the dictatorship. The government will support you to the utmost of its ability, which is neither more nor less than it has done and will do for all commanders. I much fear that the spirit which you have aided to infuse into the Army, of criticizing their Commander, and withholding confidence from him, will now turn upon you. I shall assist you as far as I can, to put it down. Neither you, nor Napoleon, if he were alive again, could get any good out of an army while such a spirit prevails in it.

And now, beware of rashness. Beware of rashness, but with energy, and sleepless vigilance, go forward, and give us victories.

Yours very truly
A. Lincoln.[23]

See how Lincoln begins: by cataloging the moral and practical qualities he sees in Hooker that led him to appoint him head of the Army of the Potomac; then by specifying what he regards as grievous faults— Hooker's insubordinate ambition, leading him to undermine Burnside, and his pronouncement that both the army and the nation need a dictator. In saying this Lincoln tells Hooker that he is known for what he is and that Lincoln is not afraid of him. The effect may of course not be to abash him (as it should), but it will surely be to put him on notice that Lincoln has perceived and understood his course of improper speech. "Of course it was not *for* this, but in spite of it, that I have given you the command." Hooker's task is to bring victory, in which enterprise Lincoln will do all he can to help, including helping him resist the spirit of insubordination that Hooker himself has done so much to introduce. Lincoln will bear Hooker's destructive speech by facing it, calling it by its proper name, and demonstrating that it has no power over him or his mind. He does not retaliate in kind but insists upon speaking in the opposite way from Hooker himself in a text that can comprehend complexity and contradiction, make appropriate judgments of character and conduct, respect institutional roles, and perceive the importance and reality of what it calls "spirit." In this way Lincoln calls Hooker's best side into being, trusting him with the truth. In all of this Lincoln does much to show us how to understand, and how not to respect, the empire of force, especially in the form—dictatorship—to which Hooker has shown his susceptibility.

[23] Abraham Lincoln, *Collected Works of Abraham Lincoln*, ed. Roy P. Basler (New Brunswick, N.J.: Rutgers University Press, 1953), 6:78.

CHAPTER TWO

⚜

Living Speech and the Mind behind It

"Nature in her full glory"; the writing of children; Polonius' speech to Laertes; Francesca's story of her life in Dante's Commedia; John Ashcroft on military tribunals; the teaching of writing in college; Abraham's argument with the Deity about the fate of Sodom; Blackmun's opinion in Virginia Pharmacy Board; Jackson's opinion in Thomas v. Collins.

WE KNOW THAT sometimes what we say is unmeant and unmeanable, just the replication of empty phrases and formulas, while sometimes it is the opposite of these things: deeply meant, alive, manifesting the presence of a mind and person. In our culture—perhaps something like this is true in any culture—a great deal of the language we learn from others, from our teachers and friends and books and TV shows and newspapers, consists of what could be called stereotyped utterances or responses: phrases and formulas and gestures that come to us with the authority of our world, which seems to ask simply that we reiterate them. We often comply, without thought, without asking what it is we really want to say or do, or what the truth is as we see it—without, that is, making demands of our own on our language, our minds, or the minds of others. We find ourselves replicating shallow, unmeant, and unthought gestures—clichés and slogans—as though we were not responsible for what we are saying. In chapter 1 we saw this tendency exemplified in the image of the "marketplace of ideas," which is current in all of our minds when we think about freedom of speech, and also in our demonstrated susceptibility to the sentimental phrase, the way "less traveled by," in Frost's poem; and we saw it resisted, in Frost's poem itself, in Dante, in the opinions by Jackson and Frankfurter, and in Lincoln's great letter. In all of these texts one can see the presence of a person and the force of a mind at work, meaning something of its own.

How can we learn to understand our own tendency towards formulaic and sentimental speech and how to resist it? How can we learn, that is, to understand the languages that inhabit our mind; to establish sufficient distance from them so that we can make them, and our use of them, the object of our critical attention; to write not out of the languages themselves, simply replicating their forms and phrases, but out of the silent center of our minds, where we can work upon the ways of talking we have inherited, trying to make them serve our purposes; how, in short, can we learn to be present in our writing, as minds and persons saying what we mean? These are serious and complicated questions, to say the least. At every stage we are trying to see what is going on within our own minds, which is difficult at best, and always at stake, as the quotation from Weil makes plain, is whether we shall ourselves be capable of love and justice.

DEATH AND LIFE IN WRITING

Since the roots of our habits of speech and writing lie in our early years, and to no small degree in the way in which we were taught, I begin by turning to some passages written by the very young. The idea is that it may be illuminating to go to the root of the problem in early education, and see it in its most basic form.

Children's Writing

The passages reproduced below are all composed by boys of about twelve years in age, collected in England by David Holbrook in the 1960s.[1] One question for each of us in reading them is to what degree we can see ourselves in this writing, or in the teaching that produced it. Another is how we would hope to respond to such a passage as this, and to the boy who wrote it, if we happened to be his teacher.

---

[1] The first two passages are from David Holbrook, *Children's Writing* (Cambridge: Cambridge University Press, 1967), 83, the second two from David Holbrook, *English for Maturity* (Cambridge: Cambridge University Press, 1961), 148–49.

We started out on a beautiful morning with a bright sky above us and a cooling south wind. Nature was in her full glory, the air smelt sweet, birds were singing loudly, squirrels scampered up trees at our approach and rabbits' tails disappeared down burrows at our presence. Lambs jumped around friskily tormenting their mothers for nourishment. Cows lay lazily chewing their cud among the buttercups. A little foal galloped alongside her mother on its spindly legs. In another field a ploughman plodded along behind his horses furrowing the field. Butterflies fluttered from flower to flower.

And so our journey went on in the presence of Nature's glory. Oh what a wonderful thing to be alive!

At Langham we refuelled ourselves and continued our journey.

A teacher would almost have to regard this as unexceptionable writing, indeed as very good: it is grammatical, clear, and full of specific detail. It has a beginning, middle, and end. It has the elegance of alliteration and manifests a certain undeniable energy. What more could you want, especially from a twelve-year-old child?

But look again. There is a sense in which this paragraph is simply a series of unelaborated clichés: beautiful morning, bright sky, cooling wind, nature in her full glory. These are phrases the writer has heard over and over, here replicated in their baldest form. He does nothing to make them his own. As for the details that we are so eager to praise, in fact they are not organized into anything, but consist rather of a list, a list of creatures—birds, squirrels, rabbits, lambs, cows—each doing what is expected of it—singing, scampering, disappearing, jumping, chewing. What relation is established among these actors and activities in this paragraph? What was the relation among them in the real world?

There is no shape or sequence here, no sense of how these things actually happened, or in what order: there is no *composition*. When you try to imagine the scene it has some of the quality of a Disney cartoon—in what other genre would innumerable rabbits' tails be constantly disappearing down burrows as the boy walked along? How many rabbits do you think the boy actually saw, how many of them went down a burrow, and how did he know that is what they were doing? Likewise the lambs: how many did he see, how many of them were "jumping friskily," and how many were "tormenting their mothers"? Did he actually see the buttercups in which the cows were lying? Exactly where were the flowers between which the butterflies were fluttering? In fact: how confident are you that this boy actually took the walk he described? Maybe he just stayed home that afternoon and wrote out the paragraph before dinner.

Obviously I don't mean to pick on this twelve-year-old boy. If there is something troubling here it is not with him but with the expectations he has been trained to meet, the ways he has been rewarded, what he has been taught—something wrong, that is, in the world that is shaping him. But in his writing there is a quality simultaneously deeply false and deeply familiar, a quality that shows up in college essays, law school briefs and memos, official publications of all kinds, from university catalogs to Environmental Protection Agency releases to judicial opinions, and it presents a danger to and for us all.

Look at the next to last paragraph, where the boy says that it is a wonderful thing to be alive. Of course it is; but this very language invites us to ask what kind of life he reflects here: what kind of life as a walker in the woods, what kind of life as a writer? How wonderful is that? And what are we to make of the shift in tone in the very last sentence, from the self-consciously poetic to the utterly matter-of-fact—what does that imply? Has he brought his highly imitative, and in a sense deeply insincere, performance to a close just a sentence too early?

Compare the following, also from a twelve-year-old boy:

Turning the last bend we came to a halt by the river. The village at this time of the year is so unfrequented. Even so, a number of small boys were dipping jam pots into the river to catch minnows. One had caught a crayfish. We propped our bicycles by the buttress at one end of the bridge, and turned round to look at the memorial cross cut in the hill. Then riding on up the opposite side of the valley, we noticed a flock of house-martins wheeling in clusters above a farmhouse. They could not have been in England long, even though most summer visitors arrived early this year. Underneath the overhang of the farmhouse roof a row of mud nests could be seen. Some hung down limp and useless; others were inhabited by sparrows; but a few remained in a fit state for the martins. The slope from then on grew steep—so much so that we stopped for a moment at one bend and rested our bikes on the bank. We were now high above the village, and even the conspicuous white rumps of the martins could hardly be seen. Where the hill was too steep for farmland, Scots pines were growing. On the move again we emerged from among them into the sunlight at the top of the hill.

It may help us think about the difference between these two pieces of writing, and why it matters, if we try to look through the writing in each paragraph to the mind of the boy producing it.

Suppose the first writer were your own son: What would you think he was doing when he wrote this? Would you be bothered by its clichéd and empty quality? Perhaps not; he is after all succeeding in school, meeting the expectations others have of him and doing so with great skill and apparent ease. The ability to whip off a paper that gets an A is one that, with certain transformations, will enable him to do well in college or law school, and beyond that in life. He is a successfully socialized person.

Do you worry that his mind is being marked by the clichés he so cheerfully uses, that it is learning to run in utterly predictable channels? This is a real question, but I think the answer is probably not, or not yet: he has learned how to write stuff he does not mean, could not mean, but at least as I imagine him he knows that perfectly well. This paper has nothing to do with what are to him the important things of life, nothing indeed to do with what happened on that afternoon, whether he took the walk or not. He may write in clichés, but that does not mean he experiences life in that way: the walk, if he took it, may have been full of interest and importance to him, the occasion for observation and reflection and questioning—as may have been whatever he did instead of taking the walk, if he in fact skipped it. The energy of the boy shines through in the exuberance with which he dishes up what his teacher will like, and he is probably in fine mental and intellectual health. The response to his situation that he achieves in this writing, false as it is, may be both intelligent and sensible.

That is all true, yet there is something crucial missing here that is present in the second passage: the capacity to write in a real way about his experience, to put on paper, out in the world where others can see it, where *he* can see it, some of the processes of mind—of observation, of feeling, of understanding—in which he actually engaged. The second writer can do a lot of this. You really do know something about the nature of his experience, and about his capacity to think about it as he renders it into language. "Underneath the overhang of the farmhouse roof a row of mud nests could be seen. Some hung down limp and useless: others were inhabited by sparrows; but a few remained in a fit state for the martins." You know what happened, in what order, and the position from which he observed and judged what he saw. You know something about *him*, for he is present in his prose, and not merely as a student but as a person.

This is writing that he can mean. And the fact that he is doing it in school, under compulsion, does not keep him from creating a passage with qualities of immediacy, authenticity, and care—a passage that is of real significance to him and perhaps to others.

I have said that one cannot confidently infer from the first passage that the writer sees the world in clichés. This may be a way of talking he has learned in school, a language he must speak to succeed. Perhaps he can do it without much effort or sincerity, and hence without much consequence, beyond the important fact that he is not learning to do what the second writer can do.[2] But consider this passage:

> On my return from school on Wednesday afternoon, my father invited me to accompany him on a visit to the Zoological Gardens. I answered in the affirmative, and we at once boarded a tramcar bound for the city. Here we caught the omnibus, and soon arrived at our destination.
>
> We had heard such a lot of talk about the new polar bear pit, we decided to visit this modern structure first of all. After a good discussion on this piece of workmanship, we made our way to the Monkey Temple. Here we had a gay half-hour watching the peculiar antics of the monkeys, who seemed almost human in some respects. We then partook of a frugal tea, and continued our tour by a visit to the noisy parrot house. This was very interesting despite the deafening shrieks of the brightly coloured birds. Next came the most exciting time of our excursion—a call at the Ape House. Alfred, an ape, and Adam, a baby chimpanzee, were the chief entertainers. On looking at the clock we saw that it was twenty minutes past seven, so we concluded our journey by viewing the humming birds.
>
> We soon arrived back at our abode, and I retired to bed, feeling that I had gleaned much knowledge during the evening.

What would you think if this were the work of your nephew, say, or some other child in whose welfare you had an interest? I read it very differently from the first passage: here the boy is not simply manipulating empty forms to get his teacher off his back, but seems desperately anxious to manage forms of speech that are utterly dead. He is conforming to rigid and empty patterns, perhaps of his father, to which he has granted authority. He speaks in terms of conclusion—"good discussion," "gay half-hour," "frugal tea," "exciting time," "chief entertainers"—which he does not elaborate, does not define, by reference to his experience. We cannot know what these words mean. It is as though for him these

---

[2] It is also possible that the dullness and deadness of the last sentence may express his true condition of mind. This would be far less favorable than the possibility I have been suggesting in the text.

things *must* be so. If only I can speak this way, he seems to say, I will be safe. Here there is no sense of a cheerful cynicism or manipulation, but an intensely serious need to acquire rigid, dead, hopeless forms of thought and speech, and, as I imagine it, not only in this paper and in school, but in life more generally. I have difficulty imagining this boy rushing out into the schoolyard after class with a joyous shout, ready to engage in life after hours of imprisonment. He is building his own prison.

Just to complete a pattern, consider the following:

> When I leave school I am going to be a comosole traveler ["commercial traveler," British for traveling salesman], I would go to all sorts of shops and see what goods they want. I would go to the sweet shops espeshly. Why I would like to be a comosole traveler is because you get good money and on sunday you can keep the car and go out to the seaside free. I have a long time to go before I leave school yet because I am only ten. My mother wants me to be a comosole traveler as well. At first my mother wanted me to be a macanicle engineer. She said you can pay up for a car weekly the boss would take it out of your wages but I would rather get a car free. If I would get the sack which I most probably will I would like to be a coal miner and dig coal from the pit. Theres one thing I would not like to happen to me or eney miner in the mine is the coal to fall in. What my mother thinks of it is too dangerous but I like using my musles of caurse you have to have only a vest and trouses on. You get good mony on it because it is a dangrous job of course.

This writer is not in a prison of his own construction. He does as he will with his words. Neither spelling nor grammar is any restraint upon him. He expresses the run of his mind directly and authentically—this is not made up; he means it all—and it is very attractive and appealing. As I read it, I find myself liking him, caring what happens to him, more than any of the others.

Here we come to a fact of the world in which these boys are working, and one with which the first writer, for all the emptiness of the exercise, deals very well indeed. While the last writer is not in a prison of his own imagination, of internalized expectations, he is in a prison of another kind, a social prison: unless he manages to learn how to spell, and to compose grammatical sentences, and to put it all in an order that meets the cultural demands of the classroom, he will have very limited opportunities in the world, not only in school but in the life that school can lead to. He will indeed "get the sack," as he so cheerfully and touchingly foresees. This is one reason I find the passage so affecting: here is this boy, full of life and energy, full of appeal—where will he end up?

Now think of these passages from the point of view of the teacher of writing. You need to teach your students—in college and law school just as in elementary school—how to master the forms of speech and writing that are authorized by the culture into which you are introducing them. Yet in both cases it is common for this to be an experience for the student, and sometimes for the teacher, that alienates the student from his own mind and experience as he struggles to produce a simulacrum of expression—something that looks like something he ought to say or write rather than something he can actually mean. He learns to produce falsity and is rewarded for it.

It may indeed be a sign of a certain kind of psychological strength that a writer like the first succeeds in treating the demand to "write a paper" as a requirement that he will do his best to manipulate, reducing it all to an exercise, for in this he is distancing himself from the empty. But in its way his situation is as tragic as that of the last student discussed above if it is true that he never learns to use language in a formal context— the class, the courtroom, the political speech, the academic article—to say what he means. Or, to put it another way: if he never gives himself a mind sufficiently engaged with life to be capable of meaning something of his own—something grounded in his distinctive experience and imagination—in the first place. He may in a sense succeed in life as a manipulator of forms, but that is its own species of lifelessness and despair.

The worst outcome, well known in college and law school and beyond, is represented in the third writer, who is so taken over by the language he uses that he is incapable of meaning anything except his desire to be defined by it. The consequences for him are serious indeed: a kind of emptiness of life, deadness of mind, that deprives him of what should be his birthright as a human being, namely his capacity to describe his experience and claim meaning for it, to express his own way of imagining himself and his world, to form real relations with others. He is the prisoner of the expectations that surround him. He denies his own humanity—the reality and value of his own experience, his own mind—which is necessarily to deny the humanity and reality of others as well. This habit of mind is of real importance not only to him but to the world, for it is upon such deadness of mind and self, and the fear associated with it, that the propaganda of tyranny utterly depends for its force and power.

As teachers we struggle to help our students master their forms of expression so that they can turn them to their own purposes, transforming them when appropriate, placing them in constructive relation with other ways of talking, and so on, producing pieces of writing that are both formally correct and actually meant by the writer. We hope that in the process they will acquire a new sense of language and its relation to the mind, a new sense of what it is like to say something they can mean, indeed a new sense of self. I sometimes sum up what I am looking for in the teaching of writing by asking myself the question: "Knock! Knock! Anybody home?" If there is a person there, in the prose, we can readily deal with the problems of form and diction, the expectations of the audience, and so forth; if not, the struggle for the student is to try to change that, to find a way to be present as a mind and to write something he or she can mean.[3]

Polonius and Hamlet

How far beyond the world of twelve-year-old English boys do the problems suggested by these passages run? Very far, I believe. Think for a moment of Polonius in *Hamlet*, who gives his famous advice to his son, Laertes:

> There; my blessing with thee!
> And these few precepts in thy memory
> Look thou character. Give thy thoughts no tongue,
> Nor any unproportion'd thought his act.
> Be thou familiar, but by no means vulgar.
> The friends thou hast, and their adoption tried,
> Grapple them to thy soul with hoops of steel,
> But do not dull thy palm with entertainment
> Of each new-hatch'd, unfledged comrade. Beware
> Of entrance to a quarrel; but, being in,
> Bear't, that th' opposed may beware of thee.
> Give every man thine ear, but few thy voice;

---

[3] For a fine book on the teaching of writing as an activity of self-creation—as a way of giving yourself simultaneously something you can mean and the capacity to express it—see William E. Coles Jr., *Teaching Composing: A Guide to Writing as a Self-Creating Process* (Rochelle Park, N.J.: Hayden Book, 1974).

Take each man's censure, but reserve thy judgment.
Costly thy habit as thy purse can buy,
But not express'd in fancy; rich, not gaudy:
For the apparel oft proclaims the man;
And they in France of the best rank and station
Are most select and generous, chief in that.
Neither a borrower nor a lender be;
For loan oft loses both itself and friend,
And borrowing dulls the edge of husbandry.
This above all: to thine own self be true,
And it must follow, as the night the day,
Thou canst not then be false to any man.
Farewell: my blessing season this in thee! (*Hamlet*, I, iii, 57–81)

One of the main points of this speech is that Polonius does not mean it; in a sense no one could mean such a string of platitudes, all in a sense "true" but adding up to nothing. When Polonius says, "Give thy thoughts no tongue," he is advising Laertes never to say anything he can mean, as he himself cannot mean this series of phrases that might have come from sixteenth-century advice books. He speaks of "friends," but what kind of friendship could be expressed or maintained in such a language, either between Polonius and Laertes or between the person he is assuming Laertes to be and anyone else? This is a world of calculation and management, all expressed in terms that have a pretended, not an actual, meaning. The end of the passage gives it all away, making suddenly visible the secret of what he has been saying: "to thine own self be true" is an impossible phrase in this passage, for neither Polonius nor Laertes is in this speech imagined as having a self.

What is Polonius really saying about how to live life, his ostensible subject? For that, you have to turn to his conduct, including his use of Ophelia as bait to test Hamlet's madness—"I'll loose my daughter to him" (II, ii, 161)—and this shows him to be far worse than a purveyor of platitudes. Not the genial fool he is often thought to be, Polonius represents real evil, and evil of a highly particular form: he is utterly untrustworthy because utterly incapable of trust. In the quoted passage he offers his advice to Laertes as if he were a wise and kind old man, passing on the benefit of his wisdom, such as it is, to his son; this in turn implies a certain view of his son, as capable of understanding, of remembering, of following his advice—as a person who can and will respond to what he is saying; but this implication is a lie, as Polonius reveals in his conduct when he sends spies to follow Laertes and report upon him. The platitudes are foolish, but they mask, as platitudes often do, something much more serious, both morally and psychologically. Polonius cannot mean what he says for he is not capable of expressing coherent meaning. You could not listen to anything he said with the attention you accord someone you respect. There is in a real sense no one there in the words, and the person behind them is a monster.

Whether—and how—one can mean what one says is a large theme of the play as a whole, perhaps its largest theme. This is what Hamlet struggles constantly to do, and finds impossible. He can never quite find a way to imagine the world, and himself and others within it, in such a way as to make possible coherent speech or intelligible action. He compares himself to the actor who is able to express a powerful lament for Hecuba in the play he is rehearsing and asks: "What's Hecuba to him, or he to Hecuba, that he should weep for her?" (II, ii, 532–33). Think what this actor would be able to say, Hamlet goes on, if he had my real-world cause and ground for speech. But Hamlet can neither speak nor act effectively; it is not so much that there is no "objective correlative,"[4] in T. S. Eliot's famous phrase, to his internal life, as that his internal life itself has an incoherence that makes it impossible for him to ground action and speech upon it. Instead he becomes something of an increasingly despairing commentator on the events that thrust themselves upon him.

One of the major reasons for his failure is that he is surrounded by false speech: in Claudius, pretending to be a substitute father but eventually ordering Hamlet's murder; in Polonius, whom Hamlet understands and mocks with meaningless speech of his own; in Gertrude, who cannot face what she has done; and in his "friends" Rosencrantz and Guildenstern, who become the murderous agents of Claudius. He does to Ophelia what the world does to him, torturing her with inconsistent and unmeant claims, and drives her into despairing insanity. It is really only Horatio, who knows how to be silent, modest in his claims, who is solidly reliable—who can mean what he says—to whom Hamlet can speak. Our experience of this relation of trust in an untrustworthy world is the reason why Hamlet's famous closing words are so deeply touching:

> If thou didst ever hold me in thy heart,
> Absent thee from felicity awhile,

---

[4] T. S. Eliot, *Selected Essays 1917–1932* (New York: Harcourt, Brace, 1932), 124–25.

And in this harsh world draw thy breath in pain,
To tell my story. . . . (V, ii, 333–36)

Paolo and Francesca

Let us now turn from the speech of Polonius to something far more appealing, the famous self-description of Dante's Francesca, whom we met briefly in chapter 1.

The relevant passage appears in Dante's account of the second circle of the Inferno. Here the spirits of those who gave themselves to lust are ceaselessly battered by strong and blustery winds, whirled in the dark and cursing divine justice. Virgil, Dante's guide, identifies many of the lost souls. When Dante sees two with whom he would like to speak, Virgil tells him to invite them by the love that leads them, *per quello amor che i mena*, and they will come. They are of course Paolo and Francesca.

They come to Dante the traveler, as the poet says, like doves to their nest. Francesca makes a highly formal and gracious speech, enacting the elegant manners that are an essential attribute of the courtly lover and beloved. She says that if the King of the Universe were friendly to her she would pray to him that Dante should have peace, "since you have pity for our perverse evil," *poi c'hai pietà del nostro mal perverso*. This is an extraordinary gesture, at once touching and incoherent, for it affirms the value of peace and the value of "pity," *pietà*—Dante's own word for his response and a term that also means "piety"—while at the same time apparently accepting the characterization of her own conduct as perverse and evil. But if what she has done is truly *mal perverso*, how is pity—much less pious pity—the appropriate response? If we read the word *"mal"* to refer not to her conduct, but to her punishment—so that the phrase might be translated, "the perverse evil we are suffering"—the implication that his pity is pious is even odder. Her phrases are stuck together in a way that does not in the end make sense. Perhaps the opacity of this phrase is a sign that she is incapable of meaning anything she says.

She then tells her story. Love, she says, "which is quickly kindled in a gentle heart," *ch'al cor gentil ratto s'apprende*, seized this man, Paolo, because of her beautiful body, *bella persona*, which has since been taken from her. The statement that love "is quickly kindled in a gentle heart" is a kind of truism or cliché of the language of courtly love, here completely unexamined. It assumes that a "gentle heart," that is to say one belonging to a person of a certain social class who conforms in feeling to the social practices of courtly love, is the best kind of heart to have, and that it is a good thing for it to be quickly aroused to "love," even where, as here, the occasion of love is simply the sight of a *bella persona*. Francesca then invokes another rule of courtly love: "love, which pardons no beloved from loving in return," *amor, ch'a nullo amato amar perdona*, seized her with a delight in him so strong that it does not leave her even now, *ancor non m'abbandona*.

Dante the traveler is moved with sympathy for what he calls the "sweet thoughts and so great desire," *quanti dolci pensier, quanto disio*, that brought them to this disaster, and we naturally share those sentiments. But Dante the poet shows us that Francesca's expectations, her feelings, her way of imagining the world, had been formed and shaped by the language of courtly love, or a certain version of it, to such a degree that she could not—and still cannot—imagine thinking, or making judgments, in any other way. She has made herself the prisoner of her version of this language. There are many kinds of love, after all, and what kind of love is this? In fact, as Francesca tells the story, her love has no content at all except in its conformity to the conventions of courtly love.[5] One could imagine someone asking, for example, whether the fact that this love is "quickly kindled" is really a sign of a fine heart in Paolo, or a shallow heart, or whether one should respond to erotic attentions, as Francesca does, with an automatic, indeed obligatory, reciprocation, rather than with thoughtful self-examination of the heart. But Francesca is incapable of questioning her commitment to the language that brought her to this condition in the Inferno.

On more careful reading we discover that Francesca's fate is not so much a punishment for an act or course of wrongdoing as a vivid expression of the life she has made on earth, especially her incapacity to think about what she has done, or the way she has made herself the captive of her language. After all, there are plenty of former sinners in heaven: in Canto IX of the *Paradiso*, for example, we meet the adulterous and promiscuous Cunizza, the hedonist troubadour Folquet, and the harlot Rahab, all of whom engaged in much more systematic and serious

---

[5] She is still connected with Paolo, true, but who is he to her? What is the nature of the love that connects them? We never hear what he has to say on these matters, for he is eloquently silent. In the courtly love tradition, the lover and beloved are never joined in body but remain connected in their love. Here Paolo and Francesca, who were joined in body, not soul, have now lost their bodies yet keep company forever. No wonder Paolo has nothing to say.

acts of sexual sin, but who repented before they died. They came to see the emptiness of the way of life in which they had been engaged. In each of them there was present both the side of the self that was committed to the sin and another side or aspect of the self that resisted or regretted it. Not so with Francesca, who still affirms the language and motives that led to her disaster. She cannot see this, for she is still under their spell. She seems to have within her no other voice defining another possibility. Francesca has made herself completely subject to the way of thinking defined in her use of the language of courtly love. What Dante represents as her "damnation" is really another way of expressing the totality of her chosen subjection, first as a reader, then as a speaker.[6]

It may seem to us that it is the formulaic and ritualized language of courtly love itself that is at fault here. Francesca made a mistake in her choice of language, and everything else followed from that. But the *Commedia* as a whole offers us a picture of the universe that has love— Francesca's word, *amor*—at its center, and as the poem proceeds it becomes clear that the language of courtly love can be used and used well to talk about this love, real love. Consider the language used, for example, by Virgil in *Purgatorio* XXII when he meets the poet Statius. Virgil says that he had heard from others how Statius loved his verse, and he naturally loved him in return, for "love, kindled by virtue, always kindles other love, if only the flame be seen," *Amore,/acceso di virtù, sempre altro accese,/pur che la fiamma sua paresse fore.* This is a direct echo of the courtly love principles we just saw Francesca invoke, "Love, which is quickly kindled in a gentle heart" and "Love, which pardons no beloved from loving in return." But the changes worked in Francesca's formulas are significant: for Virgil, it is not any love that kindles love in return but only love "kindled by virtue," and the statement is made more realistic, less formulaic, by the additional limitation that the love must be visible to have this effect. Dante's point here is to show us how

---

[6] As I suggested in chapter 1, the relevant theology tells us that this is a choice she made in life that she is now powerless to change, for that is the condition of those in the Inferno. But if we think of her as a character in a narrative, which she relives in her mind and relates to Dante and to us, it is really not possible to imagine her in such a way. If she is an actor in a story she tells, she has to be able to choose, at least to choose her attitudes. For us as readers, then, whatever we may be told doctrinally, her condemnation is eternally chosen by her, not only in her life but now, in the Inferno. In some sense it is her punishment to be continually repeating the choice to subject herself to these empty formulations.

it is that the language used by Francesca can in fact be used well, when it is used of the right kind of love in the right way.

Indeed, there are many moments when the language used to speak of Beatrice herself, or which she herself uses, reflects the courtly love tradition. At the beginning of *Paradiso* V, for example, Beatrice says, "Do not wonder if I flame on you in the warmth of love beyond the mode that is seen on earth," *s'io ti fiammeggio nel caldo d'amore/di là dal modo che 'n terra si vede.* One movement of the *Commedia* as a whole is from the abuse of the possibilities of this language to their theretofore unimaginably full realization. It is not the language of courtly love, certainly not the language of love itself, that is responsible for Francesca's fate, but her desire to use it in a way that empties it of distinction, life, and meaning. She has no desire to act on the material she has inherited to convert it from dead to living speech, no desire to be present as a mind engaged authentically with the difficulties and opportunities her language presents, and thus no real desire to be connected with other people: no desire to love.

Likewise, it is not Francesca's sexual conduct that is responsible for her fate but what she makes that conduct mean. She merges completely with the modes of thought and expression that validate her mode of life, indeed in some sense constitute it; there is no self or mind capable of putting either language or conduct into question. What she faces is the meaning of her total submission to a language that is in her hands empty and inadequate. To us as readers this may well—and perhaps properly—be more frightening than the image of a righteous God punishing misconduct.

Dante himself strongly experiences the pull of Francesca's way of thinking and imagining the world—it was in a sense once his own—and in our own way so do we, perhaps much more than we experience the pull of Polonius' sententiousness. We are seduced by the appeal of this language, and her way of using it, much as Paolo and Dante himself may have been seduced by it. In this passage, then, our desire for the empty and sentimental is stimulated so that it may be corrected, much as happens in Frost's "The Road Not Taken." We are led to participate imaginatively in emptiness and death so that we can come to see them for what they are, as forces in our world and in ourselves. This suggests that we might read the rest of the *Inferno* as a series of seductive misleadings, or confidence tricks, played on us by the speakers, then exposed by the poet, an idea that I shall test out in later chapters.

John Ashcroft

With the passages just discussed I would like to compare, very briefly, just a few sentences and phrases used by former Attorney General John Ashcroft to justify the military tribunals that were established by presidential order for the trial of people suspected of having committed crimes of terrorism. Under that order the tribunals may proceed without giving the defendants certain rights that we normally think of as essential to due process: rights to counsel, to a public trial, to confront witnesses against them, to judicial appeal, indeed to trial by jury or a judge.[7] In a news conference Ashcroft sought to justify these tribunals by saying that they were established "for trying individuals who had committed or perpetrated war crimes, and these would be war crimes perpetrated by foreign nationals." At another point he added, making his assumptions clear, "foreign terrorists who commit war crimes against the United States, in my judgment, are not entitled to and do not deserve the protections of the American Constitution."[8] In his testimony before the Senate Judiciary Committee, he said: "[T]he order indicates that those to be tried under the order have to have committed war crimes," and "a correct construction of the order would indicate that only persons who had committed war crimes would be subject to the jurisdiction of the commission."[9]

In a way it is plain enough what Ashcroft is trying to say: these tribunals are established not for the trial of ordinary crimes but to deal with people from other countries who commit acts of terrorism, or war crimes, against our nation. These are acts of war, and we need to respond accordingly. At a certain level of generality, and as a matter of military strategy or politics, this makes a kind of sense.

But Ashcroft is speaking here as the attorney general, the nation's chief lawyer, and to anyone with legal training it is obvious that he is

[7] Military Order of November 13, 2001: Detention, Treatment, and Trial of Certain Non-Citizens in the War against Terrorism, 66 Federal Register No. 222 (Presidential Documents). For one analysis of the legal issues presented, see Jordan Paust, "Judicial Power to Determine the Status and Rights of Persons Detained without Trial," *Harvard International Law Journal* 44 (2003): 503.

[8] See *St. Louis Post Dispatch*, November 18, 2001, and Department of Justice press release, November 14, 2001, at http://www.usdoj.gov/ag/speeches/2001/agcrisisremarks 11_14.htm.

[9] *Federal News Service*, December 6, 2001.

committing a most fundamental legal error, namely equating the fact that people are charged with crimes with the conclusion that they are guilty of them. This assumption is often made in the general culture: the "suspect" arrested by the police is thought to be guilty, as in fact he often is. But it is a central task of the law and of lawyers to counter these assumptions, not to reinforce them, and to insist upon the fact that we do not know who is guilty until they have been tried in accordance with the fundamental protections of the law. This is the crucial premise of due process itself. The tribunals Ashcroft is talking about exist to determine the very fact he assumes, namely whether the defendants have indeed committed war crimes. His formulation is in its way as conclusory as the phrases used by the twelve-year-old boy to describe his visit to the zoo—"frugal tea," "gay half-hour" and so forth—but with vastly more serious consequences for the world.[10]

The real question of course is whether the process by which the tribunals will work—with no right to public trial, no right to trial by judge or jury, no right to the assistance of counsel of one's choice, no right to private communication with the counsel chosen by the government, no right to judicial review, no right even to have the fact or location of one's detention known—is a fair and decent one and, as a constitutional matter, whether it meets the requirements of due process. To speak as Ashcroft did is to assume the very question that is to be tried and thus to erase the whole process of the trial itself. This is the reasoning and expression of the empire of force. That it renders one who speaks that way, or who acquiesces in such speech, incapable of justice, to use Weil's language, needs no elaboration.

TEACHING WRITING

It is perhaps dispiriting to read the student papers about the walk in the woods ("nature in her full glory") and the trip to the zoo ("gay half-hour"), and the passages from Polonius, Francesca, and Ashcroft as well, for they all present the question whether we can possibly avoid such unsatisfactory forms of speech ourselves and learn to meet the dangers they represent. How are we to do this? It is not merely a matter of

[10] Ashcroft was speaking in response to questions at a press conference or a committee hearing, not making a prepared statement, and we all make mistakes under such circumstances. But the mistakes we make may be significant, and in any event we are responsible for them.

choice, after all, but education: we need to become more fully aware both of the materials of meaning that the world affords us and of our own desires to submit to formulas and clichés, and these things are difficult at best.

One way to approach this set of difficulties is to think of the matter from the point of view of a teacher of writing. How are we to teach our students these things? To do this would require us to find ways to help our students see the difference between dead and living language: between a language of clichés and slogans and conclusions, on the one hand, and expressions in which they were themselves present as persons and as minds, asserting the value and reality of their own experience and judgment, on the other. To speak in such a way they would need to have something to say, something of their own and not merely replicative of others—something they could mean—and at the same time to understand the languages they use and the art of using and transforming them. How might such an education proceed?

There can be no easy or schematic way of talking about this kind of teaching and learning—just as there cannot be about good judging, or good lawyering, or good writing, or any other valuable human activity. But it is clear that a lot of what we do, in law school and college alike, cuts the wrong way, in the direction of teaching our students how to manipulate forms, meet expectations, please their audiences, without much regard to whether they can possibly mean what they say. Of course it would not be good for the student, assuming she could do so, simply to dump out on the page everything that went through her mind, however empty or vague; an essential part of the task is learning to think oneself to the point where one actually has something valuable to say or do. But this is vastly more likely if from the beginning the student has some sense that it might be possible—should be possible—to say something that she means.

What would such teaching look like? How might one try to teach others, or to learn oneself, how to resist the clichés—the dogmas, doctrines, received ideas, unchallenged metaphors, standard phrases, hackneyed truths—that populate the mind, in their own way constituting an empire of force? How to reshape one's linguistic inheritance with the aim of achieving an individual expression or statement?

Here I give a brief account of one especially powerful effort to engage in this kind of teaching of which I myself had experience, namely the famous composition course designed by Theodore Baird and taught at Amherst

College in the middle years of the twentieth century.[11] Here follows the first assignment that greeted one group of freshmen, a couple of years after I graduated, that addresses the themes and questions of this book.

ASSIGNMENT 1:

You are now a member of a community, a social organization, or rather of a number of communities (Amherst College, the freshman class, a particular dormitory, etc.). This world is often described as artificial and secluded, an Ivory Tower. (The origin of this metaphor is obscure.) You may yourself believe, you may feel, that you have left behind the Real World. After all this is "only" a college, you are "only" a college student, this is "only" a course.

In the form of an essay deal with the following questions:
1. What is real about the Real World?
2. How do you know when you really are in the Real World?
3. If you have been in the Real World, why did you get out of it?
4. If you are outside the Real World, how do you get into it?

Finally, define "The Real World."

You can see how this works. The assignment makes the student's own language an unavoidable problem: "The 'real world'? What can *that* mean? I use that phrase all the time, but what on earth do I mean by it, does anybody mean by it? How can I use it now?" The student thus faces this part of his inheritance, which he has always used thoughtlessly, and sees it as a problem for analysis and reflection, thought of a kind he can barely imagine. At the same time, the assignment makes the student's actual experience of life a problem too: "Where actually am I when I am at Amherst College? In what community, or set of communities? And what *is* this place really—the buildings, the grounds, the people? A set of social and verbal practices? What are its boundaries? How can I possibly talk about it?" With respect to both the "real world" and his new set of communities, the "Ivory Tower," the student will find himself saying: "I thought I knew, but I don't. What can I possibly say?"

---

[11] The course was called simply English 1–2. The questions are reprinted with permission. For accounts of the context in which it was offered, see Richard Poirier, "Reading Pragmatically: The Example of Hum 6," in *Poetry and Pragmatism* (Cambridge, Mass.: Harvard University Press, 1992); William Pritchard, "Ear Training," in *Playing It by Ear* (Amherst: University of Massachusetts Press, 1994); and Pritchard "Foreshadowing," in *English Papers* (Minneapolis: Graywolf Press, 1995).

None of this will look like any assignment the student has ever seen before. There is nothing in it from which he can devise or figure out a set of expectations that these questions are designed to make him try to meet. There is no right answer. The student who wrote the first excerpt examined earlier ("nature in her full glory")—who can in fact stand for all of us—would have no way of dealing with such an assignment. For these questions do not call for a performance of the kind the student has been trained to make; rather, in their interest, originality, and difficulty, they suggest very different possibilities towards which he might direct his energies. They are amusing, full of confidence and intelligence; their function is to create a vacuum that it is the student's task to fill. He is asked to speak to his reader as though he too is a person and a mind, capable of being interested and bored—as though his writing, like these questions, will achieve its completion only when it is read by another intelligence. The task is to find a way to respond to the assignment with something like thought, something like an effort to mean what one says, and this is likely to seem very foreign indeed.

Here is the second assignment:

ASSIGNMENT 2:

This is a genuine student's paper submitted in a writing course at Harvard in 1893.

The Paradise of Books

Books, I often think, are the best thing life has to offer us. No where else do we get pleasure that is so great and so lasting, that can charm us still, whatever our condition of mind and body. There we meet friends and lovers such as reality cannot acquaint us with, and adventures which furnish excitement without toil, and arouse sympathy without suffering. All the higher emotions, so incongruous with matter-of-fact existence, may be serenely enjoyed in the realm of poetry, and all the speculative flights which transcend cold common-sense may soar undisturbed in the aether of philosophy. As long as a man has eyes to read and brain to understand, he may feel sure of one unfailing resource which can amply compensate the strokes of fortune.

❦

We call this single paragraph a Perfect Theme. (There is also the five paragraph theme, using the structure: Introduction, Body, and Conclusion.)

[One] reader's comment on this Perfect Theme, "Simple and direct," now seems all wrong. It is not simple: look at the sentence structure and vocabulary. It is not direct: who is it who could speak in this tone of voice and yet be considered direct? Can you imagine anyone speaking these sentences to anyone else under any circumstances? Is this opposition of books and literature to reality and matter of fact existence and cold common sense a simple one?

What comment do you make on this Perfect Theme? What adjectives do you apply to it?

Define on the evidence of this example the Perfect Theme.

What is the alternative to such writing? How do you proceed if you are going to write really simple and direct English? Where do you begin? What models, what authors, what books, for simple and direct writing do you have in mind? What books do you think of when you think of writing in the Real World?

This assignment makes the problem of formal writing explicit: the quoted passage is in a sense perfect English, flawlessly written with complete confidence, but it is in a more important sense perfectly empty. This is an antique version of the prose the student has been taught to admire, to emulate, but here it is held out as the object of scrutiny, a problem of some sort. "Can you imagine anyone speaking these sentences to anyone else under any circumstances?"

How is he supposed to speak in this paper, then? In a twentieth-century version of this perfect theme? What *is* expected of him?

In assignment three the student's attention is drawn to the nature of his own language, the way he has learned to speak.

ASSIGNMENT 3:

This opposition between the Ivory Tower and the Real World becomes complicated when we consider how we ordinarily speak of education and of our private experience. A college, we know, protects the student from the outside world while it prepares him for it. A student's fundamental beliefs are challenged, yet no belief ought to be offered as a substitute. Education is a purely academic endeavor, yet it also assumes a concern in those areas beyond the classroom. Student and professor join in the selfless pursuit of truth, while the aim of all our efforts is individual commitment. Education is learning how to use symbols, but the man who does not participate in the reality going on around him is uneducated. Both student and teacher pursue the ideal while they shape and are shaped by the real. And so on.

The paradoxes appear wherever we generalize. Amherst College should provide a controlled environment where inequality and competition and their inevitable disappointments do not exist, where at the same time the forces operating in the real world should have their full effect. Behavior taken for granted off the campus cannot be tolerated in our society, yet everyone has perfect freedom to follow the dictates of his own conscience. At the same time that societies are formed to make music and produce plays and take part in real politics and support particular religious organizations, everyone should be free to be himself. Team spirit is most important, yet the man we respect goes it alone.

Write an editorial, as if for the *Student*, in which you deal with this perplexing conflict. Do not be afraid of your own clichés and metaphors. The object here is to get at a vocabulary for talking about such matters. Everyone has at his command a large and useful stock of words. Give it an airing.

Here the student is asked to look simultaneously at his experience of the institution he has joined—not only Amherst College but the whole world of higher education—and at the clichés he is given by his culture as the language in which the life of that institution, this part of his own life, is to be imagined and talked about. How is this language to be understood, thought about, transformed, replaced?

This series of assignments asks the student to begin to come to terms with what I have been calling the empire of force in a form in which he has actually known it, namely the expectation that he will produce in his writing a simulacrum of something, a performance to be evaluated by how thoroughly it complies with rules of composition and grammar, of self-presentation, just as he might be judged by how appropriately he dressed or by his table manners. The collection of clichés articulated in assignment three is just a sample of what we all have running in our heads, and the challenge of the assignment is that you think about this material, and not merely deploy it as the Harvard student deployed the material of his world. The hope implied here, and reiterated in every assignment for a year, is that the student can discover that he has something to say that he can mean, something he can say in his own way; that he has, that he can give himself, experience worthy of the attention of another; that he can have interests and values and a style of his own—in short that he can be a grown-up individual person, responsible for what he says as well as for what he does, making himself worthy of his own respect and interest. To put it in the terms suggested by our reading of the passages with which we began, the student is invited—urged, pressed, leaned on—to discover something of his own humanity, his own capacity as a mind and person, and to find a way to make that capacity present in his writing. If he cannot do this he will not be able to recognize effectively the humanity of other people in his speech and writing, even in his thought.

The course asks students to write to such topics three times a week for a whole year. The bright student can find safe and empty things to say, time after time, but the pressure of the questions, asking you to think in ways you never thought possible, is relentless, especially when coupled with the pressure of class discussion, which focuses on the writing of the students—on *your* writing—making it a public question whether you have managed to say or be anything of value in what you have written. To stick with the safe and empty becomes increasingly difficult. If the course works well, you will begin to speak in something like your own voice. You do not do this alone of course but as part of a community of people, all engaged in talking to each other and trying to mean what they say. This experience calls upon you, and the others, to understand the dead, empty, and formulaic uses of language in which you have been trained, and to resist them by calling your own mind, and the minds of others, into the kind of life that will insist upon the transformation of what you write and say into living speech.

THE LAW

Imagine that you are a lawyer or a litigant facing a judge who turns out to be the first young writer discussed at the beginning of the chapter ("nature in her full glory"), now grown-up but still maintaining the same attitude towards speech and writing that he reveals in that passage. Or perhaps your judge is Polonius or Ashcroft. How could you speak to such a mind? With what kind of honesty or authenticity? What kind of judicial opinion would you expect that person to issue? It would be a deep violation of justice to have a judge who was not present in his prose, who did not mean what he said, or who was incapable of meaning anything—a judge who had not made the case in an important way his own, the object of integrated thought and attention. Such a judge would be unable

to hear what you said, to attend to it, to respond to it. Or imagine yourself as a client and ask what you want from your lawyer. Not an empty
and skillful manipulator, nor one who thinks in conclusions, but a person
with a mind of her own, one who can think about the case, in its parts
and as a whole, and reach judgments of her own about it; one who can
hear what you have to say and respond to it; one who can turn from that
conversation to the law and find ways to use legal language, transforming
it if necessary, to say what she has come to mean about your case.

What happens if you imagine that the judge you address is the third
student writer ("the Zoological Gardens"), now grown up? Or the second writer ("the house martins")? Exactly what are the differences between them: in the way you would address them, how you would expect
them to respond, the kind of justice of which each is capable? (The kind
of love?)

It is common for people to try to learn law, at the beginning of the
process, as if it were a set of rules to be applied more or less routinely to
the facts of cases as they arise. This is to think of the law as a simple system of commands. But as almost every law student learns, often to his or
her profound discomfort, this image of the law will not work, either in
law school or in practice. The lawyer and judge are constantly presented
with real difficulties of interpretation and harmonization of the law, in
relation to facts that are themselves uncertain, all presenting a set of
problems about which much can be said on each side and through which
they must think their way as independent minds.

Good legal thought and writing accordingly involve the articulation of
arguments that can be made both ways—for and against the characterization of the letter as an "offer," say, which can be "accepted" and thus
form a "contract"—and their arrangement in a structure that leads to a
conclusion that fairly reflects the force of opposing arguments. The good
judicial opinion thus takes the reader through the process of thought the
judge herself engages in, with a fair representation of doubts, uncertainties, and the force of countering arguments. It should end with a conclusion that is not predetermined or shaped by considerations external to
the opinion but reached by the process of thought enacted in her writing.

The good brief is both different and similar: different because it does
lead to a predetermined conclusion; but similar because it too leads the
reader through an idealized process of thought, one that also gives weight
to countering arguments, plausible claims the other way, and so forth, or
it will fail. The opposite of this kind of writing is what in the law we call

conclusory writing, cast in terms that bury argument and thought in one's premises, reducing it all to a set of unargued assertions.

The key element present in good legal writing, missing in bad legal writing, is a certain kind of life: the life of the mind, of thought and argument, that is generated by the recognition that we live in a world in which there are many valid things to say, from many points of view, with which it is the task of the legal mind to come to terms. In the law, as elsewhere, the task is to find a way to be present as a mind, a person, a voice, in a context that seems to invite the replication of standard forms. The lawyer who simply moves phrases around in his head and on the page, never really meaning anything he says—and there are plenty of lawyers like that—is never actually thinking about the case, or the law, and is certainly incapable of saying something fresh or transformative. He will be thinking only about his effort at manipulation, not the merits of the question before him. Once this is perceived, as it usually is by intelligent people, he will not be listened to by his audience. Why should he be? By contrast, there are lawyers who command respect and attention whenever they speak or write. One reason they have this power is that it is apparent that they are present in their speech and mean what they say.[12]

As for judges, the need to be present in one's speech and writing is even more crucial, for there are serious public consequences. The judge

[12] One might ask whether a lawyer *can* mean what he says when he speaks in the interest of a client and, if so, in what sense. It may well be that the argument he makes is not, so far as he is aware, one that he would base his judgment on if he were the judge in the case. But that does not mean that he is false or hypocritical, for the question he is implicitly answering is not how he would decide the case if he were a judge but something quite different, and of enormous help to those who do have the responsibility of decision: What is the best argument that can responsibly be made with the existing materials of law on behalf of his client in this case? His brief and argument constitute his answer to this question, and it should be an answer that he can mean. Compare the actor on stage: there is a sense in which he too must mean what he says or fail utterly, even though he is playing a total villain like Iago or a paranoid tyrant like Creon. I think that as a lawyer functioning well one does mean what one says, often in a more rigorous and intense and thought-out way than one does in other roles and contexts, and I imagine the same is true of the actor as well. To speak personally, my own experience of practicing law in fact helped me learn that it was possible to mean what I said, in a grown-up and whole-minded way; it was here that I learned that I could produce a text that could bear the weight of scrutiny and attention. For further consideration of the ways in which a lawyer can mean what he says, see James Boyd White, "Plato's *Gorgias* and the Modern Lawyer: A Dialogue on the Ethics of Argument," in *Heracles' Bow: Essays on the Rhetoric and Poetics of the Law* (Madison: University of Wisconsin Press, 1985), 215–37.

who simply articulates phrases, concepts, or ideas in an unmeaning way can likewise not be attended to, for he is not present as a mind or person. This means that his opinion cannot be read with the care and attention lawyers are trained to give authoritative texts in the law; it means, too, that he in a real way cannot be responsible for what he is doing. This kind of writing, to use the distinction made prominent by my colleague Joseph Vining, is authoritarian, not authoritative.[13] It is part of what Simone Weil would call the empire of force.

As an example of an argument—a kind of legal argument, in fact—that is simultaneously shaped to one's audience and actually meant, consider the following famous exchange between Abraham and the God of Israel, as recounted in Genesis (the King James Version). The Lord is contemplating the destruction of Sodom for its grievous sins and decides to reveal this plan to Abraham. ("Shall I hide from Abraham that thing which I do; seeing that Abraham shall surely become a great and mighty nation, and all the nations of the earth shall be blessed in him?" [Genesis 18:17–18])

And Abraham drew near, and said, "Wilt thou also destroy the righteous with the wicked? Peradventure there be fifty righteous within the city: wilt thou also destroy and not spare the place for the fifty righteous that are therein?

"That be far from thee to do after this manner, to slay the righteous with the wicked: and that the righteous should be as the wicked, that be far from thee: Shall not the Judge of all the earth do right?"

And the Lord said, "If I find in Sodom fifty righteous within the city, then I will spare all the place for their sakes."

And Abraham answered and said, "Behold now, I have taken upon me to speak unto the Lord, which am but dust and ashes: Peradventure there shall lack five of the fifty righteous: wilt thou destroy all the city for lack of five?" And he said, "If I find there forty and five, I will not destroy it."

And he spake unto him yet again, and said, "Peradventure there shall be forty found there." And he said, "I will not do it for forty's sake."

And he said unto him, "Oh let not the Lord be angry, and I will speak: Peradventure there shall thirty be found there." And he said, "I will not do it, if I find thirty there."

[13] See Joseph Vining, *The Authoritative and the Authoritarian* (Chicago: University of Chicago Press, 1986).

And he said, "Behold now, I have taken upon me to speak unto the Lord: Peradventure there shall be twenty found there." And he said, "I will not destroy it for twenty's sake."

And he said, "Oh let not the Lord be angry, and I will speak yet but this once: Peradventure ten shall be found there." And he said, "I will not destroy it for ten's sake."

And the Lord went his way, as soon as he had left communing with Abraham: and Abraham returned unto his place. (Genesis 18: 23–32)

This is a highly complex moment, for not only does Abraham find words to say what he means—in essence, "Do not destroy the righteous with the wicked"—he does so in the form of an argument, a cross-examination really, of a kind familiar to the law. He is trying to persuade the Deity to a course of action. To do that he must speak the language of the Deity, appeal to his nature and character; Abraham must offer him a way of speaking to the situation that would enable him to withhold his punishment and explain why. This is persuasive but not manipulative. Such is the effort of the modern lawyer too, at his best: to say what he means and to offer the person to whom he is speaking something she can mean as well.

One way to state what is so remarkable about this passage, and indeed about the whole relationship between the Deity and Abraham (and Moses too) is to say that it shows that Abraham can trust the Deity with the truth—the truth of his perceptions, thoughts, feelings—even though to do so is obviously risky in the extreme. Likewise, the Deity trusts Abraham with the truth of his intentions, almost as though he is asking for a response of approval or criticism. Each can say to the other what is displeasing. The one without power can speak to the one with all the power, and make claims upon him—can make in a sense the ultimate claim, based upon his character and nature: "Shall not the Judge of all the earth do right?" Through the pressure of questioning, Abraham forces the Deity to recognize something about the world and himself. Trust is the condition that makes it possible for both to speak with such frankness and honesty across the enormous gap between them, that enables them each to be present in their speech and to mean what they say to each other.

Would it be possible for a person to be present in his speech and mean what he says if both he and what he means are deeply evil? In some sense of course the answer is yes; just think of the speech of a Nazi politician or that of an American racist. But the assumption I make throughout this book is that we—the reader and I alike—regard the possibility of becoming capable of love and justice as the proper aim of a whole human life; it is this, as Weil says, that requires us to understand the empire of force and know how not to respect it. Our Nazi and racist fail to do these things, really as a matter of definition.

Is there then a class of persons who do fully understand the empire of force and what it means, yet affirmatively and deeply wish not only to respect but to support it? I am not competent to answer such a question, but my own instinct is to believe that every case of human evil is based upon distortion, damage, injury—upon other evil—and that at the center of every human being is the desire for justice and love, to which the empire of force is always opposed. On this view everyone, even the tyrant or Nazi guard or prison torturer, wishes at the deepest level to love and be just and therefore wishes, though he may not know it, to understand the empire of force and know how not to respect it.

THE JUDICIAL OPINION

Virginia Pharmacy Board

I now turn to an instance of modern legal writing, namely a passage from Justice Harry Blackmun's opinion for the Court in *Virginia State Pharmacy Board v. Citizens Consumer Council.*[14]

First, some background. The question this case addressed was the constitutionality, under the First Amendment, of a Virginia statute that prohibited pharmacists from advertising the price of prescription drugs. The asserted reason for this prohibition was to protect the real and perceived professionalism of pharmacists, on the theory that the price competition stimulated by advertising would lead pharmacists to work to a lower margin of profit, which would in turn lead them to take shortcuts both in the preparation of drugs and in the consultations they have with prescribing doctors and with the patients themselves. Further, it was thought that price advertising would damage the image of the profession, reducing the confidence the public has in it as a profession, not merely a business. As for any free speech interests involved, the pharmacists were free

[14] 425 U.S. 748 (1976).

to reveal their prices when asked, and consumer groups, such as the plaintiffs here, were free to publish their own price surveys. All that was prohibited was price advertising by the pharmacists themselves.

As a matter of economic theory the statute is of course not beyond challenge. Under its regime drugs were sold, as one would expect, at widely differing prices in different stores in the same city, which seems to be unfair in general and to disadvantage the less sophisticated customer in particular. On the other hand, the defenders of the statute might say, if price competition were allowed it would lead to the concentration of the profession in a small number of high-volume, cut-rate drugstores, which would in the nature of things be difficult and expensive for many people to reach. But that would not necessarily follow, the opponents of the statute would argue: perhaps small local drugstores would stay in business, charging more than the cut-rate places but being less expensive to reach. In this way those who wanted convenience would pay for that, those who preferred to travel for bargains would do that.

The arguments on the wisdom of the statute go back and forth, in what looks like a classic case of economic regulation. But if this is how the case is regarded, the statute should almost certainly be upheld, for courts normally defer to legislative judgments about the probable real-world effects of alternative economic regimes—judgments the courts are not authorized or well situated to make or to review, depending as they do on information not readily available to them. The Court concedes as much.

The crucial question for the Court, then, is the bearing, if any, of the First Amendment upon the case, on the grounds that the conduct regulated here takes the form of "speech." The obvious problem with this line of argument is that this speech is commercial in character, simply a way of doing business. While there are many proposed rationales for the First Amendment, most of them conceive of it as protecting political speech, or the discovery of socially valuable truth, or the autonomy and dignity of the speaker, not purely economic processes. Not surprisingly, when first presented with the question decades ago, the Court held that commercial speech was simply beyond the protection of the First Amendment.

Later cases complicate this picture, however, making clear that speech is not unprotected simply because money is spent to convey it, as in a political advertisement; or because it is sold for profit, as a book or newspaper is; or because it has a commercial subject—surely one would have a First Amendment right to complain that the anti-advertising rules in this very case were unjust, for example. Nor is it disqualified because the motives of the speaker are primarily economic, for the First Amendment protects certain forms of speech in labor disputes, not to mention forms of highly commodified speech of rather doubtful quality, from B-films to television shows to romance novels. But none of these cases present the question in its purest form, as *Virginia Pharmacy Board* does: here there is a simple proposal to engage in an economic transaction without any further artistic, ideational, political, literary, or other value. As the Court frankly says, "the 'idea' [the speaker] wishes to communicate is simply this: 'I will sell you the X prescription drug at the Y price.'"[15]

The Court nonetheless holds that the First Amendment should indeed reach this form of speech, saying that the interest of the particular consumer in "the free flow of commercial information" may be "as keen, if not keener by far, than his interest in the day's most urgent political debate."[16] It goes on to express the core of its position in these terms:

> Advertising, however tasteless and excessive it may sometimes seem, is nonetheless dissemination of information as to who is producing and selling what product, for what reason, and at what price. So long as we preserve a predominantly free enterprise economy, the allocation of our resources in large measure will be made through numerous private economic decisions. It is a matter of public interest that those decisions, in the aggregate, be intelligent and well informed. To this end, the free flow of commercial information is indispensable. . . . And if it is indispensable to the proper allocation of resources in a free enterprise system, it is also indispensable to the formation of intelligent opinions as to how that system ought to be regulated or altered. Therefore, even if the First Amendment were thought to be primarily an instrument to enlighten public decisionmaking in a democracy, we could not say that the free flow of information does not serve that goal.[17]

Notice that although this is a First Amendment case, Blackmun does not really talk in First Amendment terms. He does not discuss in any

[15] *Id.* at 761.
[16] *Id.* at 763.
[17] *Id.* at 765.

depth the aims of that amendment or the nature of the speech it is designed to protect, either as a theoretical matter or in connection with his reading of the cases.[18] What is wrong with this scheme of regulation, in his view, is not that it suppresses an independently valuable activity called speech, but that it interferes with the efficiencies of the market in prescription drugs. He might have struck the statute down on those grounds, but, as I suggest above, such a course would have been inconsistent with the law the Court had been making for decades concerning economic regulation. This looks like a case in which the Court disapproves of the regulation on economic grounds but, having no feasible

[18] In some respects the Court's opinion follows the established forms of legal thought rather well: explaining clearly the grounds upon which Virginia had adopted the statute, addressing the technical but important question of the plaintiffs' standing to bring this action, and fairly describing the relevant cases the Court had earlier decided on the subject of "commercial speech." But on closer reading this compliance with formal expectations turns out to be rather superficial—a bit like the similar compliance demonstrated by the first student writer discussed above. This is true especially in Blackmun's treatment of precedent, where he summarizes the outcomes of the earlier cases clearly and fairly enough, but does so simply in terms of rules they adopt, without seeing the judgments as motivated by competing visions and understandings of the purposes the First Amendment, of the nature and importance of speech, and so forth. This can be seen as a kind of legalistic, not legal, thought, the reduction of purpose and reason and vision to rule.

Likewise, Blackmun's basic articulation of the question before him skews his thinking: it is whether this communication is "wholly outside" the First Amendment or lacks "all First Amendment protection" (425 U.S. 748, at 761.) This is one way to put the issue of course; but even if you decide that the Court should not dismiss entirely any claim of protection for this kind of speech, you need to face the question whether price advertising should be protected exactly like other forms of speech, those that are plainly central to First Amendment concerns—like political debate, for example—or to a lesser degree, and why. The reasons and factors that had once led the Court to exclude this kind of commercial speech from protection might still have force after that position had been abandoned, and lead the Court to protect advertising significantly less than speech that is more central to the aims of the First Amendment. But, apart from a few observations at the end of the opinion, Blackmun regards his task as mainly done when he has argued to the conclusion that this kind of advertising should not be entirely without protection, when in fact his main work still lies before him, namely to explain how it should be protected, to what degree, and why. The Court will later address this question in *Central Hudson Gas v. Public Service Commission*, 447 U.S. 557 (1980).

Finally, Blackmun never really addresses the question of the relation between the Court and the legislature: he thinks price advertising desirable, the legislature thinks otherwise, both making their judgments on the basis of facts and expectations about human behavior. By what warrant does the Court substitute its judgment for that of the legislature here? There may be reasons, but Blackmun does not give them.

way to strike it down for such reasons, reaches for the First Amendment instead.[19] It is hard to regard Blackmun as actually meaning what he says about the First Amendment here.

In looking at Blackmun's use of economic language, we may be reminded of the young boy writing about "nature's glory" or of Polonius, each speaking as though his words were effective without regard to whether they were meant. The issue here is not the economic language Blackmun uses but the way in which he does so. One might imagine market language being used in a rather different way, metaphorically, with an awareness of its obvious difficulties—of what it leaves out—and as part of a larger vision of human life and our constitutional system. But that is not what we have here. Instead we have a dull replication of an ideology. Blackmun virtually constitutionalizes the "free enterprise system," for example, without any recognition of the fact that our economy is profoundly managed, by regulation, by taxation, and by government spending. The phrase as he uses it is really just a cliché, and much the same can be said of the rest of the formulaic language he employs. This is language that in a profound sense no one could mean.

Consider, for example, the passage already quoted, in which Blackmun says that the particular consumer's interest in "the free flow of commercial information" may be "as keen, if not keener by far, than his interest in the day's most urgent political debate." You can see where this sentence comes from: a person with crippling pharmaceutical bills and little political engagement is indeed likely to focus his or her attention on the former, not the latter. But aside from the fact that many "consumers" do not fit that example, there is a deep ambiguity in the word "interest": it can mean actual engagement of attention or even simple curiosity on the part of an individual; or it can be the equivalent of value or worth, as in the citizen's "interest" in free elections. While it may be factually true that some people care more about prices than politics, in the sense that they focus more time and energy on shopping and prices than they do on

---

[19] To strike it down on economic grounds would involve a revival of *Lochner v. New York*, 198 U.S. 45 (1905), which at the time of *Virginia Pharmacy Board* was thoroughly discredited. The last sentence in the passage quoted does hint at a First Amendment basis for the decision, namely that the advertising of prices will contribute to the quality of public decision-making. But it is hard to see how that could in any substantial way be true, and in any event the sentence does not reflect any judgment about the expressive value of the speech in question, which is obviously low. The decision does not really offer a way of reading the First Amendment but is based on quite other considerations.

political arguments, to say that they have a greater *interest* in "the free flow of commercial information" than in "the day's most urgent political debate" is to suggest either that the former is as a matter of plain truth of greater worth or value than the latter, or that this is what the people in question think. The former position seems directly contrary to the choice made in the Constitution itself, which declares the primary value of "freedom of speech," with no suggestion that this value has any economic dimension. As for the second claim, the Court may be right that, if asked, many consumers would say that the price of drugs is more important to them than a political debate. But under our constitutional system our "interests" are defined not only by our present sense of need and desire, but structurally, in the instrument of our government, one function of which is to make commitments for us that we do not have to make over and over again—to create, as it were, the conditions on which we can lead our typically more self-centered and private-valued existences. If you were to ask our citizens not whether their drug bills were a great burden to them, but whether they would like to live in a world without the kinds of complex commitments made in an enduring way by the Constitution, I hope and think that a great many would revise the judgment the Court attributes to them. In any event, a judicial opinion by the Supreme Court is the place above all at which the larger commitments and values of the Constitution should be given force, especially as opposed to unsupported judicial estimates as to the way our citizens rank their values—citizens whom it trivializes to label as mere "consumers."

Think also of the slogan "the free flow of commercial information," appearing both here and in the portion of Blackmun's opinion quoted earlier. This phrase too has the quality of cliché, obscuring both thought and reality. It takes no account, for example, of the fact that the information in question is already available to anyone who makes a phone call to the drugstore, and that, if more systematic dissemination were thought valuable, those of the plaintiffs who are not individuals but consumer groups could assemble the price data and communicate it to their members or to the public. Even more significantly, it draws attention away from the fact that the flow of information established by this decision is not really "free," since many of the speakers (that is, the pharmacists) presumably do not wish to engage in the "speech" protected here. They will in fact be compelled to speak, as a practical matter, for if one of them advertises they will all have to do so. It is not their choice that the Court is respecting; quite the opposite, the Court is establishing a regime of effectively mandatory speech, in the form of advertising, for the purpose of enhancing the recipients' range of economic choices. As a way of imagining the First Amendment, the process of speech in the world, or the reasons why speech is valuable and should be protected by the Court, the opinion is hopeless.

Living speech, in the world and in the law, requires the presence of a person in the words—the person of an author, the person of a reader. Blackmun's *Virginia Pharmacy Board* opinion erases the person, in both capacities, substituting a routine application of dead formulae. It reiterates an ideology that has no distinctive place for speech in the world it imagines—and thus cannot work as a language for thinking about a First Amendment case—and no significant place for speech in the world it enacts or performs, for the opinion cannot manifest in its own composition a conception of valuable and living speech. Although it adheres to the forms of legal thought and cites and distinguishes appropriate authority, at the deepest level it lacks the most important kind of legal knowledge. Try reading the opinion as you might read the student papers with which we began, or the speech of Polonius: as holding out a promise of a world, of a life to be lived on its terms; as an invitation to join the writer in this way of thinking and imagining, this way of writing, about speech and the Constitution—how would you respond? Blackmun, like our third student writer, is in a prison of his own, defined by the language he accepts without being able to put it into question. This means that he cannot act as a responsible and independent mind and cannot claim the authority that such action grants; it means that his writing in the deepest sense lacks the life that alone can justify its claims to power.

All this is not to say that the outcome in *Virginia Pharmacy Board* is necessarily wrong. The Court might evolve a doctrine of economic due process under the Fourteenth Amendment that would constitutionalize the market, at least to the extent of requiring the state to justify interferences with it by making factual showings that are here only presumed. This would be especially appropriate where there is a grounded suspicion that the legislation is really designed to protect the special interests of a politically distinct and effective group, here pharmacists themselves. But such a move should be made explicitly, and on due process grounds not First Amendment ones, for only then would the case be framed and argued in appropriate terms.

There remains one more dimension of this case. It is by no means easy to do what Blackmun did not attempt to do, namely to try to say why speech should be singled out for special protection, as it is by the First Amendment. Efforts to produce theories that will describe the law of the past and shape the law of the future have not worked well, to put it mildly. This fact means, among other things, that it is especially important to have what might be called performative or enacted definitions of the value of speech in the judicial opinion itself. If the real reason for the constitutional guarantee is to make possible serious and thoughtful deliberation on issues of public concern, for example, the Court itself can show us (or fail to show us) that kind of deliberation in action.

We are thus right to ask of an opinion in this field, as I have been doing, both how the Court imagines the speaking person, and the activity of speech itself, and how it engages in speech. Does the Court in its representation and performance trivialize this occasion for speech, and speech more generally, or, on the other hand, does it recognize the dignity of— or confer dignity upon—this crucial aspect of human life? Whatever the First Amendment means, it surely points in the latter, not the former, direction. Yet when we ask how speech is imagined here we can reasonably ask, How could the opinion in *Virginia Pharmacy Board* possibly recognize what is of real value in speech when it reduces speech to the transfer of information or a signal of a willingness to do business? I suggested in chapter 1 that there is a deep opposition between advertising— the world it creates, the assumptions on which it works, the activities of mind and imagination and feeling that it stimulates—and what I called living speech: speech that rewards attention and affirms the value of the individual mind and experience. The possibility of living speech is presumably one reason why speech itself is given special status and protection in our Constitution. But here Blackmun extends the protection of the First Amendment not merely to trivial or pointless or unworthy forms of expression, but to forms of expression that undermine the value of speech itself.

To turn to Blackmun's own performance of speech, we have seen that in this case he allows his mind to be taken over by a system of thought, an ideology really, in a way that leads him to slide over the issues actually presented in the case, producing a surface that does not open itself up to argument, as an opinion should, but closes it off. You either believe, as he does, in the adequacy of the formulaic language of the market to explain what is at stake here or, like me, you do not. The consequences are especially serious because of a larger cultural fact, mentioned also in chapter 1, which is that in our world at large the ideology of the market has taken over so much of public talk and action. Throughout the world, governments have given up trying to shape economic forces into socially and culturally valuable forms, instead seeing "growth" alone as their goal. Obviously economics has an appropriate role as a method of thought, but its language should always be used with caution, and certainly not as a comprehensive mode of organizing life. For economic language imagines human life in an impoverished way, as a set of choices designed to serve self-interest. It has no way to conceive of community, or collective life, except as a series of deals; no way to imagine the natural world, upon which we depend, except as a set of resources; and no way to think of speech except as a signal of willingness to deal, or as itself a commodity.[20] This is an empty way to think of human relations, human motivation, human achievement, but it is what we live with; for Blackmun to convert what could have been a moment for talking about the value of speech as such into a rote application of this ideology, which sees speech simply as an aid or adjunct to economic life, is a genuine lost moment, both for him as a writer and for us as readers.

Let me add here the important point that while the language of cliché Blackmun uses happens to be the language of economics, it would be all too possible to use the language of law in such a way, or the language of left-wing politics, or the language of religion or of human rights. The real question is whether the language and ideology in question dominate the mind and the text or whether, by contrast, the writer finds a way to assert against such forces the presence, and the value, of his or her own mind and experience.

We are all susceptible to the failure to which I see Blackmun succumb. This is the possibility against which we must work whenever we write and speak, knowing that at best we will succeed only sometimes and only in part.

---

[20] For fuller explication of this point, and for treatment of economic language as a challenge to the writer, see James Boyd White *Justice as Translation* (Chicago: University of Chicago Press, 1990), chapter 3.

Thomas v. Collins

Is it possible for a judicial writer to speak differently, or is Justice Blackmun here just an example of what we must expect? In chapter 1 we looked briefly at what Justices Jackson and Frankfurter said in the *Barnette* case, and it may be useful now to look at another passage of admirable judicial prose. Here is Justice Jackson again, this time in *Thomas v. Collins*,[21] where he concurs in a judgment striking down a Texas statute that required a labor organizer to register with a state official before soliciting memberships in a union:

> As frequently is the case, this controversy is determined as soon as it is decided which of two well-established, but at times overlapping, constitutional principles will be applied to it. The State of Texas stands on its well-settled right reasonably to regulate the pursuit of a vocation, including—we may assume—the occupation of labor organizer. Thomas, on the other hand, stands on the equally clear proposition that Texas may not interfere with the right of any person peaceably and freely to address a lawful assemblage of workmen intent on considering labor grievances.
>
> Though the one may shade into the other, a rough distinction always exists, I think, which is more shortly illustrated than explained. A state may forbid one without its license to practice law as a vocation, but I think it could not stop an unlicensed person from making a speech about the rights of man or the rights of labor, or any other kind of right, including recommending that his hearers organize to support his views. Likewise, the state may prohibit the pursuit of medicine as an occupation without its license but I do not think it could make it a crime publicly or privately to speak urging persons to follow or reject any school of medical thought. So the state to an extent not necessary now to determine may regulate one who makes a business or a livelihood of soliciting funds or memberships for unions. But I do not think it can prohibit one, even if he is a salaried labor leader, from making an address to a public meeting of workmen, telling them their rights as he sees them and urging them to unite in general or to join a specific union.
>
> This wider range of power over pursuit of a calling than over speechmaking is due to the different effects which the two have on interests which the state is empowered to protect. The modern state owes and attempts to

---

[21] 323 U.S. 516, 544–46 (1945).

perform a duty to protect the public from those who seek for one purpose or another to obtain its money. When one does so through the practice of a calling, the state may have an interest in shielding the public against the untrustworthy, the incompetent, or the irresponsible, or against unauthorized representation of agency. A usual method of performing this function is through a licensing system.

But it cannot be the duty, because it is not the right, of the state to protect the public against false doctrine. The very purpose of the First Amendment is to foreclose public authority from assuming a guardianship of the public mind through regulating the press, speech, and religion. In this field every person must be his own watchman for truth, because the forefathers did not trust any government to separate the true from the false for us. *West Virginia State Board of Education v. Barnette*, 319 U.S. 624. Nor would I. Very many are the interests which the state may protect against the practice of an occupation, very few are those it may assume to protect against the practice of propagandizing by speech or press. These are thereby left great range of freedom.

This liberty was not protected because the forefathers expected its use would always be agreeable to those in authority or that its exercise always would be wise, temperate, or useful to society. As I read their intentions, this liberty was protected because they knew of no other way by which free men could conduct representative democracy.

This passage bears on the same general question as *Virginia Pharmacy Board*, namely the role of the First Amendment in the area of economic activity, and it shows that in the discussion of ideas as well as facts it is possible to engage in thought and writing that is vivid, clear, comprehensive, and deeply meant. Jackson does exactly what Blackmun does not do, which is to think of the case in First Amendment terms; more than that, he gives a kind of performative content to the value of speech itself by the way he writes. He is obviously present before us in this prose, saying what he thinks and why, and doing so in a way that does not trivialize the activity of thought and speech in which he is engaged but, quite the opposite, confers upon it an essential dignity.

Part of the life of the opinion lies in Jackson's recognition that he is not faced with a question simply of categorization—"Is it a 'calling' or is it 'speech'?"—but a question of judgment in a case where the basic principles are in tension, shading into one another at the borderlines. The undoubted power of the state to regulate professions and employment necessarily includes the power to regulate some speech—but not all speech, as he shows with his examples of the nonlawyer speaking to issues of fundamental human and legal rights and of the nondoctor urging one or another school of medical thought. How is one to draw the line? By understanding the reasons why the state has plenary power to protect the public against "the untrustworthy, the incompetent, or the irresponsible" in the practice of callings, but not against "false doctrine," where the people, not the government, must serve as the protectors of truth.

In all of this Jackson is willing to accept responsibility for his judgment. He reasons to a coherent conclusion and in his own performance demonstrates how it is that we—the people—can indeed be "watchmen for truth." He is teaching us that we can live with the recognition that virtually anything can be contested, often by scurrilous means, yet that it is possible nonetheless to be able to speak and read and think with confidence. This teaching is not dependent upon our agreement with the particular outcome: he could have written just as good an opinion, in the sense I mean, coming out the other way. He is not in a prison either of his own construction or made by the habits of thought he adopts; he is in this sense free and responsible. Where Blackmun believes in the language and practice of economics as the ground of legal judgment and of life, Jackson believes in the human mind and character. This is judicial writing that is meant, and it encourages us to say what we mean, to mean what we say, as well.

The mind at work in this case—stating the issues, seeing the facts, defining principles, making a judgment and standing by it—is showing us a way of resisting, of not respecting, the empire of force. Jackson insists upon the value of individual judgment, in him and in his reader, in the speaker and the public, for he insists that the case make sense to him, and he invites the reader to do likewise. This is not the replication of an ideology but the opposite: thought that puts into question its own methods and materials, in the interest of reaching and explaining a judgment, defined as an individual act of mind, for which he is responsible. To say this is to say that Jackson here achieves an important kind of justice.

In this chapter I have tried to elaborate the claim made earlier, that what Simone Weil calls the "empire of force" is not simply a matter of military power, but also of language and the use of language—a matter of writing, in short. A mind like that of our first student writer—and all of our minds share this quality more fully than we should wish—is full of a repertoire of standard moves, received ideas and images, ways of thinking and writing, that it has acquired by imitation from those whose approval matters. It is full of clichés. This is not just a matter of private but public concern, as Blackmun's opinion shows, for it too is full of received and unquestioned images and phrases, not thought through. And this is how the empire of force maintains itself: through speech that is dead and irresponsible, and through the habits of acquiescence present in all of us that make such speech effective—a willingness to talk the way we hear others talk, without testing it against our own experience, our own thought.

Writing by the manipulation of expected phrases in expected ways has the effect of distancing the writer from his or her own experience, from his or her own mind, as we saw in the first and third student writers above and in Blackmun too. It closes off thought, both in the writer and in the reader, creating a false image of the world and of the mind. It creates belief in what should not be believed. All this has political as well as personal consequences, for this is how an ideology is created and maintained—an ideology that erases the experience of others, especially the poor and weak, in our country and abroad, and that makes us blind to the common humanity of all people and to our common dependence upon the natural world.

What Weil calls "understand[ing] the empire" consists to a large extent in knowing the ideologies, the clichés, the false languages, that surround us, and knowing as well our own susceptibilities to their appeal— to the pleasure and satisfaction of earning the approval of the powerful and thus having power ourselves. Knowing "how not to respect it" means knowing not only where a regime may be politically vulnerable, but, much more deeply, knowing how to resist the appeal of false language, false writing, to our own minds. In his own way Justice Jackson, in this rather routine case, finds a way to talk that resists the empire of force—resists it through the force of his own voice and presence, his insistence upon reason, his respect for arrangements external to him and to his reader alike.[22]

Without such knowledge of the empire and how to resist it, we are, as

---

[22] Or listen to the opening sentence of his dissenting opinion in *Shaughnessy v. Mezei*, 345 U.S. 206, 218 (1953), which is not without relevance for our own day: "Fortunately it is still startling, in this country, to find a person held indefinitely in executive custody without accusation of crime or judicial trial."

Weil says, incapable of justice, for we will accept false ways of thinking and imagining and talking that obscure the reality of human suffering and cruelty and greed. We will accept, for example, talk about the "national interest" or "our friends abroad" or the "evil" of those who are different or the "rising tide that lifts all boats" without examining it or the reality it obscures. If we cannot imagine the lives of others—the half of the world's population who live on less than $2 a day, for example—we cannot be capable of justice towards them, for imagination is the root of justice. And if we cannot see others as they are, and understand our own role in systems of wealth and power, we certainly are incapable of love towards them too.

CHAPTER THREE

※

The Desire for Meaning

The role of the reader in making meaning; the note on the icebox; the statute; Frost's "Road Not Taken" again; three forms of the desire for meaning; Shakespeare's Sonnet 18; the judicial opinion; desires not for meaning but for use; Francesca once more; Master Adam and Sinon.

WE HAVE JUST looked at writing by students, and writing by a judge too, that seemed in a deep sense dead: words without the presence of a mind and person to give them life. The student talking about his trip to the zoo and Justice Blackmun talking about the drug price advertisements are both in prisons of language in which they would imprison their readers as well. This is writing that denies their own humanity and that of others, including their readers.

The obvious question this presents—and it is a central question of this book as a whole—is this: What would a different and better kind of writing and speech be like? Would it be possible for a writer to master the languages of his culture rather than being mastered by them, to express his own humanity and recognize that of his reader, and in these ways to create a text that would expose and resist the empire of force? We have seen some examples, in the passages from Dante and Frost and Justice Jackson and in the student paragraph about the house martins, but we need to think much more about how such writing works, and about other positive possibilities as well. The moment of expression is the point—and really the only point—at which we can resist what Weil calls the empire of force, as it is active both in the world and in our own minds and imaginations.

In this chapter I continue to focus on the moment of expression, but I look at it, initially at least, from the point of view not of the writer but of the reader, the other necessary party to the creation of meaning. Reading is its own art, presenting its own dangers and opportunities, as Frost's poem and Dante's passage on Francesca both suggest. What is called for in the reader is of course partly a matter of skill and understanding, of alertness of mind, but most deeply a matter of desire. For like the writer, the reader can be driven by desires for the easy, the sentimental, the authoritarian—ultimately for the dead. But we may have desires of another kind as well: for facing the limits of language and the truth of our situation, for self-correction, for genuine engagement with another mind and person—ultimately desires for life and meaning.

When a reader brings to a text the desire for meaning and the writer in turn appeals to that desire—builds upon it, gives place to it, perhaps transforms it—both writer and reader are working to honor and respect the deepest center of human life. The writer confirms the value of the reader; the reader in his turn respects the importance and value of the writer's expressions, not converting them to other uses, and this is an affirmation of the value both of the writer and of himself. On the other hand, when a reader is driven by the desire to be seduced or manipulated, or to submit to a language of slogan and cliché, and when a writer appeals to such desires and confirms them, writer and reader alike are working to trivialize or deny the center of the self where meaning is made and found. This is to impair the resources within themselves and others that make possible what we mean by love and justice.

In what follows I begin by describing the three main forms or elements of the desire for meaning, and then say something about the ways in which a writer can address this desire, and a reader act upon it, in the cooperative creation of meaning, both in law and in the rest of life. I begin with a rather basic instance of reading, namely the reading of a domestic note found on an icebox; then compare what happens there with the obviously somewhat different process of reading a statute; then ask what tentative conclusions about the desire for meaning might be drawn from these examples, before considering a still more complex text, Shakespeare's Sonnet 18, and with it a larger set of intellectual and ethical issues.

READING IN ORDINARY LIFE—AND IN THE LAW

Suppose that you come back from a walk to find a note on the kitchen icebox in your spouse's handwriting containing a list, most of which you can read: "parsley, garlic, beef, oranges, onions," and then something that looks like a squiggle. It begins with an "o" or perhaps an "a," it seems to have about as many letters as "onions," but you cannot be sure of any of them. You naturally want to know whether this list is something you should act on: Are you to buy these things? Or is it rather your spouse's list for his own use? If you *are* supposed to act on it, what are you to do about the unintelligible squiggle?

You approach these questions by calling into play other things you know: your spouse's habit of leaving notes of this sort, and what that has meant in the past; what you know about his favorite beef stew—perhaps a recipe from Provence, hence the inclusion of the orange—and about his other tastes as well. Perhaps all this leads you to conclude that the squiggle should be read as "olives." Your experience is first puzzlement, then uncertainty, then tentative clarification or resolution. But you still may not know whether you are supposed to go buy these things.

For our purposes what is important here is the kind of meaning you want to discover in reading this note: first, simple intelligibility, and, through that, access to your spouse's particular intentions. You assume that he is entirely clear about what he wants—that this note is not an exercise in befuddlement for its own sake or an act of sadism, or a test, though all these are possibilities—and that he will be able to make his intentions clear when he shows up. The kind of meaning you desire, then, is the understanding of another's intention. You assume that this intention exists, is known elsewhere, and will ultimately be made plain. When it is, this aspect of the meaning of the note will have been exhausted.

Notice that meaning of this kind is not merely informational but deeply social, an aspect of a continuing relation between two people. The writing of the note and its reading, and whatever you decide to do in response, are all materials with which you and your spouse are shaping your relationship, as will be the other things that happen later: the clarification of your spouse's intention when he returns—you *were* supposed to buy these things, and the squiggle *did* mean olives; the apology for not being clearer; the other apology for not understanding what really should have been clear enough; the rush to the store before it closes; and so on. If the note were not addressed to you, you would have no interest in it at all. It would not stimulate a desire for meaning.

What happens if we turn from this example drawn from ordinary life to the reading of a legal text, say a statute? Does it work like reading the note on the icebox? Sometimes people speak as though it does, on the assumption that the task of interpretation in both cases is to determine from the words he or she has used the wishes of another person. But in the law this is not quite so, and certainly not in the case of legislation, where there is no real person with an actual intention to be discovered. A statute is a collective act, the work of many people working on different understandings and out of different motives. Some legislators may support a piece of legislation on one understanding of its meaning, others on others; still others may be motivated only by party loyalty, or by the desire for political reward. Some may have no idea what they are voting on. What we know they agree on is this, and only this: their wish to have the words in question become the law.

From the reader's point of view, this means that the desire to understand the intention of another has to work differently from the way it does in the case of something like the note on the icebox. It is present, because it is always present, but here it has the character of a fiction. The "intention of the legislature" is not to be found in the text or in the world, but must be constructed by a complex process of thought and argument that seeks to make sense of the statute in a variety of contexts: those defined by other legal texts, by the history into which they are all interventions, by the facts of the particular case one is thinking about, and so on. It is an ideal intention of an ideal legislature.

The statute has no single author, no equivalent to the spouse who can make plain his meaning when he comes home. Even when a majority of legislators wish to correct what they regard as a misreading of the words of a statute, the only way they can do so is through the form of a new statute—not by sitting as a kind of high court, approving some interpretations and disapproving others. In this sense the principle of separation of powers, central to our Constitution, is built into the idea of law itself, for the tasks of writing law and reading it are put permanently in different hands.

There is a second major difference between the note and the statute, for if he understands what he is doing each legislator—and this is true as well of the testator of a will, the drafter of a contract, the judge writing an opinion, or any other composer of a legal text—expects and in some sense intends that the text be read in a range of circumstances that cannot be wholly anticipated. He knows that he cannot think of all eventualities, all the possible contexts in which the words are to be read. This means that the kind of specific intention that lies behind the note on the refrigerator— "buy olives"—is simply missing. We can have no confidence that if we presented a hard case to the legislature its members would agree as to the proper outcome, or that the two parties to a contract would agree on the meaning of what they have said. In a real sense the author of every legally binding document thus disappears as completely as a testator who leaves a will behind him when he dies; he will not return to clarify what he means, and it is thus no longer he but the text that counts.

Because the text is meant to operate not simply on one occasion but across a range of imperfectly foreseeable occasions, it has to have the peculiar kind of meaning such a text can have, creating as it were a new dimension of reality, running across time and space, in which it aims at, even claims, a consistency of result and significance that in the nature of things cannot wholly be attained. It stimulates and works most deeply by a desire not for the discovery of actual human intention, as the note on the icebox does, or even for an ideal intention, but for a different sort of meaning: for the creation of a whole way of thinking about the world and the place we have within it and the character of our relations with each other—a desire for a general language of justice that will govern a wide range of cases in a consistent and fair way, and not just in this particular field but throughout the law.

Exactly how this general language of law and justice will in fact be put to work in any particular case, and with what effect, cannot be predicted by the legislator, any more than he can accurately predict the range of factual situations in which the statute will be invoked. The statute is not then to be read simply as an order or command, as it may at first seem—not in that sense as a rule—but as a text that is to be harmonized to the extent possible with the entire cultural and political inheritance that is the law: not only with particular cases and regulations, particular expectations and understandings, but with the most fundamental conceptions of the human actor and citizen, and of the nature of justice, that animate the whole. And the justice we invoke is itself not simply a matter of right outcomes, measured by this or that standard, but, much more deeply, a matter of right thinking and talking. The most important question for judge and lawyer is not whether a particular result is correct, but how we in the law should think and talk about that question: in what language or languages, with what respect for what authorities, with what kind of honesty, adhering to what conceptions of reason and justice—and, as we saw in chapter 2, always subject to the further question whether the person is present and responsible in what he or she says.

One way to think about the process by which ways of reading shape the meaning of a legal text would be to ask ourselves how we, as writers, would want our statute or contract read by others. This is an obviously difficult topic, but at the very least we know that we would want this act of reading to be a complex activity made up of many elements, some ethical, some intellectual. Fairmindedness, openness to the significance of context, attention to larger purpose as well as to word, sensitivity to consequence not only in this instance but in a range of instances, the wish to make this text fit with the rest of the law, perhaps fit as well with the ways we think more generally about human action and value, all these and more would be elements in our image of the good legal reading that we would want our text to receive. We would not want our statute or constitutional provision read by Polonius, or Ashcroft, or our first student writer ("nature in her full glory"), or for that matter the Blackmun of *Virginia Pharmacy Board*.

The most important intention of the author of the legal text, then, unlike that of the spouse who wrote the note on the icebox, is not so much that a particular result obtain as that the text be read in a certain way. As writers and as readers of a legal text our primary desire ought not be for the expression or discovery of an identifiable intention lying behind it but for the right thing to be done with it—that it become the occasion of a certain kind of attention and thought and conversation, in a certain community of understanding and value, which is what we most deeply and reliably mean by justice itself. It is upon the quality and integrity of that process of thought and argument that the life of the text depends. And the text does not merely depend upon that process, it contributes to it, especially by the way it invites and rewards attention. In an important sense the invocation and management of that process *is* its meaning.

THREE KINDS OF MEANING

I want now to reflect a moment on what we have done so far. What forms of the desire for meaning have we seen stimulated and responded to in the two examples I have given? As different as these examples in some respects are, in others they are alike, or at least suggestive of generalizations that can connect them.

The Life of Expectation: Completion, Surprise, and Transformation

The most basic form of the desire for meaning at work here is the desire for what in its simplest form is a kind of intelligibility. What does the squiggle mean? Or in reading the statute one might ask: Can I understand with confidence the relation between these two clauses, or these two terms? One might generalize this impulse by calling it the desire for the completion of formal expectations, a desire that is at work in our response to every human utterance. Just to begin a sentence in English, for example, raises the expectation that I will complete it, and do so in English; to break into Finnish or Turkish or Italian would be a deep frustration, as would a failure to complete the form of the sentence I have begun.

But the simple completion of formal expectations is a rather basic form of meaning, and the desire for it can in some sense be satisfied in a dead or trivial way: by reiterated clichés, for example, as in the speech by Polonius, or by the mechanical elaboration of a theory or ideology, as in *Virginia Pharmacy Board*. What we most deeply desire in this dimension is not simple completion, then, but a kind of life, as our expectations are surprised, upset, and transformed—as they are made the material of art. Think of the way in which a skillful writer will work with our desire for the completion of our expectations by first creating a sentence that threatens to collapse into syntactical disaster, then rescuing it at the last moment, or perhaps by using enough foreign or strange English terms to make us worry about its continuing intelligibility before saving it. As we have seen, Dante does much by insisting on writing his great poem in the vernacular Italian, making an extended demonstration of the resources of that language, against the expectation that high literature—literature worthy of real attention—will be composed in Latin.

At one level—deciphering the squiggle—this point is reasonably simple, but a writer can work with the desire for the completion of formal expectations in ways that are highly complex and significant. Poetry in particular puts this impulse to work in revealing ways, for it is largely built upon the formal expectations that it first creates, then modifies, confirms, or transforms. Think again of Dante and his interlocking pattern of rhymes that promises—but ultimately fails—to connect the smallest event in his poem with the largest, in a wholly ordered universe.

Or, to shift to English and a familiar example, consider a couple of small points in the structure of Frost's "The Road Not Taken." The basic meter of this poem is iambic tetrameter, a form in which each line consists of four two-syllable units, called "feet," each of which has the pattern of an unstressed syllable followed by a stressed one. As I said earlier, however, in almost every line there is an extra unstressed syllable, converting an iamb into an anapest and giving the poem something of the quality of an incantation. Here is the opening, with the double unstressed syllables marked:

> Two roads diverged *in a* yellow wood,
> And sor*ry I* could not travel both
> And be one trav*eler*, long I stood
> And looked down one as far *as I* could
> To where it bent *in the* undergrowth;

Frost thus clearly establishes the expectation that the lines will continue to have this characteristic structure; most indeed do so, but with variations that are highly significant. When he expresses the false reason why he chose the road he uses a double anapest, "Because *it was* grassy *and* wanted wear"; this is followed by a straight iambic line, "Though as for that the passing there," in this way associating the anapestic rhythm with sentimental error, the iambic with the affirmation of reality.[1]

Or consider the way rhyme works here. The opening stanza quoted above establishes a pattern of rhymes (conventionally represented as ABAAB), followed throughout the poem with great regularity until we get to the very last word:

> I shall be telling this with a sigh
> Somewhere ages and ages hence:
> Two roads diverged in a wood, and I—
> I took the one less traveled by,
> And that has made all the difference.

In a sense of course "difference" rhymes with "hence," but ask yourself exactly how you are to pronounce it. The meter of the last line seems to

---

[1] The only other purely iambic line confirms this association, occurring as it does in his statement that the roads are really the same: "In leaves no step had trodden black."

call for something like "*diff*-er-*ence*," which is awkward and forced in the extreme. The poem is built out of natural diction, and such a pronunciation would be highly unnatural, in a real sense impossible. On the other hand, to say as we normally do, "*diff*-runce," is to end the poem with a thud. What is really happening here is that Frost is using the expectations he has carefully built up, as to both meter and rhyme, to make the last word of the poem impossibly awkward. This works as a sign to the reader that something is wrong with the speaker's conclusion, and as an invitation to go back and read the poem more carefully.

The desire for the completion of formal expectations is part of the material of art with which the writer works, not only in poetry but in law and the rest of life. The danger is that it can be too easily satisfied, by routine and mechanical formulas—those of the lesser forms of poetry, or courtly love, or political debate, or sports writing, or legal argument—a danger against which the reader must himself be alert. Part of our task is to learn to make demands on the texts that we read, here the demand that something constructive be done with our desire beyond simply completing formal expectations in a regular way. What we want is the special kind of life that the expectations created by the forms of language, its modes and genres, enable a writer to achieve: not only simple completion and confirmation but surprise and transformation.

Valuable Relations with Others

A second form of the desire for meaning at work in reading the note and law alike is the desire for intelligible and valuable relations with other people in our world. One task we all face, all the time, is the definition and management of our relations with others, and every human utterance speaks to us as so engaged, holding out the possibility of valuable human connection. Often of course this possibility is rendered sterile or fraudulent—think of what in chapter 1 I called propaganda and advertising, or of the salesman who assumes a chummy familiarity with you, or of the usual political candidate seeking your vote—but sometimes it is not, and one may always hope that this moment of speech will be an occasion on which valuable and appropriate human connection will be possible.

In the case of the note on the icebox this may seem easy enough: the note asks for cooperation of a kind the reader can be assumed to understand and to be willing to give. This is partly a matter of trust and good faith, of shared understandings about food, and shopping, and notes. In a healthy relationship clarity on these matters makes clarity in the writing and reading of such a note relatively simple, for what we call the "intention" is both plain and acceptable. But in a conflicted or confused relationship that might well not be true. The note could be read as one more command in a series of commands, or as a power trip; the difficult squiggle could be seen as designed to confuse or irritate, or as just another example of carelessness; and so on. One can imagine short stories of a rather bleak kind being written about such a moment. The apparent ease with which the note assumes and manages social relations is actually an achievement reflecting a great deal of work and experience that precedes it, and upon which it relies.

That this desire is constantly present when we read, whether we are consciously aware of it or not, has the perhaps surprising consequence that every act of reading directly presents the most fundamental ethical and political questions of human life: To what kind of human relations should we aspire? When should we regard our desire for human connection as appropriately responded to, when not? There are many things to be said here—mutuality, honesty, trust, reliability, equality are surely qualities we would want—but perhaps nothing is more important, as I suggested in chapter 2, than the sense that one is genuinely connected with the mind of another who means what he says.

To think of this issue in a context familiar to lawyers, consider the difference between a judicial opinion that seems to be only a cutting and pasting of established phrases, a collage of clichés and received truths, and an opinion in which the reader has a sense that the mind of the judge is actively engaged in expressing its own processes of thought and judgment. This difference is not merely literary in kind, certainly not only aesthetic, but political and ethical, close to the center of what we mean by justice and injustice. There is a sense in which the empty or conclusory or jargon-ridden opinion, whatever its outcome, cannot be truly just, for there is no assumption by the judge and writer of the responsibility for judgment; correspondingly, there is a sense in which an opinion in which the judge does accept and face that responsibility, speaking from the center of his mind as a person present in his writing—speaking from "silence"—has an essential element of justice, even if it is in your view or mine deeply wrong in outcome. Such writing alone can call upon the reader to be present and engaged at the center, at his or her internal place of silence, below the chatter and jargon and propaganda that inhabit our minds.[2]

It is not to much to say, indeed, that the constitutional power of judicial review itself rests upon a quality of genuine judgment genuinely expressed. Certainly it is hard to imagine any reason for vesting such a power in a Supreme Court that works by cliché or slogan, by comfortable and manipulable formulations of the kind that I have called dead language. If I am right this means that the Court's authority is not established for once and for all, in a legalistic way, but must be earned over and over again, by its demonstration in opinion after opinion that it is an institution that works by the presence of individual minds struggling to express the truth as they see it and assuming real responsibility for what they say and do and are.

Ways of Imagining the World

A third form of desire for meaning at work in my examples, perhaps the most fundamental of all, is the desire to imagine the world, and ourselves within it, in a coherent way, a way that will make possible meaningful speech and action. In a sense every utterance offers us, as its readers or listeners, a way of thinking about the world and our place within it, and to this extent it appeals to the side of each of us that is constantly engaged in our own version of that activity. Of course no text does this perfectly, just as none of us can do it perfectly. To be able to imagine the world and its inhabitants in a coherent and bearable way is a central desire of the human mind, yet it is perhaps never quite achieved. Even at the moments when we come closest to success there is often an element of pathos and failure.

In the case of the note on the icebox, almost all of this is assumed: a world in which food is bought and cooked, in which one can plan

---

[2] The legal text engages in the creation of social relationships in another way too, in its definition of the institutional relation between the speaker—say the judge writing an opinion or the lawyer in a brief—and other actors in the legal universe: the legislature, the Constitution, a particular administrative agency, courts that have decided related questions in the past, the parties, future courts and lawyers and parties, and so on. Legal language creates the institutions, and the relations among them, through which the law itself must work.

a meal, in which cooperation of the sort reflected here is possible. As readers of the note we take just the first tiny step in the direction I mean when we ask whether we are supposed to act on this note, and if so when and how. Here we are really asking: What larger pattern is this part of? How do we know? In the law, by contrast, the desire for a larger vision of the world is highly prominent. The law explicitly appeals to our sense that one case can be fairly decided in light of others in a way that both reflects a coherent and manageable image of the world—of the world as a whole and of the character of human life within it—and at the same time responds to the demands and complexities of the particular facts and narratives before the court. Without a claim to coherence of this kind, challenged in this way, there can be no justice, and that is what the law promises us above all.

The desire for meaning in this expanded sense, for the location of the self and others in a coherent imagined universe, is one of the most elemental of human needs. Perhaps nothing else so clearly marks us as human, for it is the ground upon which rests our impulse to claim significance and coherence for our experience, for the shape of our lives, and it is present in some form whenever we speak or write, whenever we read. At the grandest level, this is the kind of meaning offered by Dante, who imagines literally the whole universe, and seemingly every moral and psychological human type within it, locating them all, and you as the reader too, in a structure of value and motive by which you can shape your life—yet without allowing that structure to become a version of the empire.

In my initial example of the note on the icebox, then, and in the related but much more complex example of the statute, we can see at least three different versions of the desire for meaning at work, each of which is a desire for a certain kind of life: the life that can be created by working with formal expectations, confirming them, upsetting them, transforming them; the life that can arise in a relation with another mind and person, at its best authentic, trusting, full of newness; and the life we experience when we try to imagine the world, and ourselves and others within it, in a coherent way—sometimes seeming to succeed, then recognizing failure, then, at our best, going on with a new defined sense of possibility and limit. We need now to ask more fully how those desires can be made the subject or material of art, in literature or law, and to what effect. How can a writer meet, frustrate, modify, or transform them, and to what good ends can he do so? And, on his side, how can the reader learn to understand and manage the desires he brings to reading, making them in a sense the material of *his* art?

In the sonnet by Shakespeare that follows we see how one writer works on the reader's desire for meaning, in all three of its forms and to remarkable effect.

SHAKESPEARE'S SONNET 18

Here is Shakespeare's poem:

> Shall I compare thee to a summer's day?
> Thou art more lovely and more temperate:
> Rough winds do shake the darling buds of May,
> And summer's lease hath all too short a date;
> Sometime too hot the eye of heaven shines,
> And often is his gold complexion dimmed;
> And every fair from fair sometime declines,
> By chance or nature's changing course untrimmed:
> But thy eternal summer shall not fade,
> Nor lose possession of that fair thou ow'st,
> Nor shall death brag thou wand'rest in his shade,
> When in eternal lines to time thou grow'st.
> > So long as men can breathe or eyes can see,
> > So long lives this, and this gives life to thee.[3]

Let us start with the very first line, "Shall I compare thee to a summer's day?" This line stimulates the desire for meaning of all three kinds I have mentioned, simultaneously. First, we know that this is iambic pentameter, and we expect and want Shakespeare to be able to continue that meter, with appropriate and significant variations. If we read this in a sonnet sequence, we know that he will be working within fourteen lines, and we want to see whether he can do that without straining and forcing, whether he can work with rhymes in surprising ways, and so forth. But other expectations are set up, too: We want to see how the promised

---

[3] William Shakespeare, "Sonnet 18," in *Shakespeare's Sonnets*, ed. Stephen Booth (New Haven, Conn.: Yale University Press, 1977), 19. Notes on this poem appear at ibid, 161–62. See also Helen Vendler, *Art of Shakespeare's Sonnets* (Cambridge, Mass.: Harvard University Press, 1997), 119–22.

comparison with the day will work, whether as a set of tired clichés—the equivalent of the conclusory judicial opinion—or in a way that gives this topic life. We want to see, that is, how Shakespeare will work with the various expectations created by the form and genre known as the love sonnet, asking in particular whether he will simply replicate the standard forms or work with them in meaningful ways to create a different kind of life—perhaps indeed the kind of life that puts the very conventions he employs into doubt or question.

Second, we think of this as a social document, for at least in an unconscious way we cannot help imagining ourselves as the addressee of the poem, the one who is to be compared to a summer's day. What a lovely thought, we may think, how kind of you; or perhaps at some level we feel hints of envy for the person so addressed—I wish someone would do that for *me*; but in either case we want to see how the relation between speaker and audience develops.

Third, like any text this line offers us a way of imagining the world, in this case a highly familiar one: at the beginning it consists only of the two lovers, with the summer day as a backdrop that will serve as the element of comparison. The world of the poem may remain elemental and schematic in this way, or it may develop into something difficult and interesting. We have at the moment no way of knowing, but we want to know.

In all three dimensions, then, we find ourselves wanting to go on. And as readers of Dante's passage about Francesca we know that in all three dimensions much is at stake. For it would be possible to allow the formulaic and empty language of conventional love poetry, then and now, to shape and dominate our feelings, to become the way we think of love itself. Shakespeare's first line seems in fact to point in such a direction, and one question we should have is where the poem as a whole will in fact turn out to go.

Relations with Others

Of these three forms of the desire for meaning, I begin with what I have called the social, thinking of the poem from the point of view of its imagined addressee, the beloved who is to be compared with the summer's day (whom I shall here assume to be a woman).

I am told that this poem is often reprinted or quoted on celebratory occasions, such as wedding announcements or anniversaries, or even included in wedding ceremonies, as one of the Bard's great statements of eternal love. In teaching it, I like to encourage my students to think about this use of the poem by asking them how they themselves would like to receive it as a Valentine, say. So regarded it is a very strange love poem indeed. It begins promisingly enough with a comparison of the beloved with one of the most beautiful things in the world, an English summer day, but it begins to wilt almost immediately: "Thou art more lovely and more temperate." "More lovely" is fine, though perhaps a bit generic; but "more temperate"? Perhaps that is not the quality one would most want stressed by a lover. It next turns out that the comparison with the summer's day, though still to our advantage, proceeds not by elevating the beloved above that perfection but by finding fault with the day itself: it is too rough, too short, too hot, too cloudy:

> Rough winds do shake the darling buds of May,
> And summer's lease hath all too short a date;
> Sometime too hot the eye of heaven shines,
> And often is his gold complexion dimmed;

Yet worse is to follow, much worse: actually, the beloved is told, you are not more lovely even than this highly imperfect summer's day, but in a deep sense identical with it, for as a piece of the natural world you are governed by its elemental law:

> And every fair from fair sometime declines,
> By chance or nature's changing course untrimmed:

It seems as though the poem has now got completely out of control, spinning from its praise of the beloved into a kind of metaphysical despair at the fundamental condition of human life, of all life in fact.

But here the poet claims to find a solution—perfectly timed to come at the beginning of the third quatrain—that will rescue the beloved, and all of us:

> But thy eternal summer shall not fade,
> Nor lose possession of that fair thou ow'st,

How is this to happen? Not through the force and vitality of the beloved's physical beauty, as one might think, or even her beauty of soul, but through the work and effect of this very poem:

> So long as men can breathe or eyes can see,
> So long lives this, and this gives life to thee.

So far so good. But what kind of life does "this" in fact give to "thee"? We know nothing of the beloved's form or height or hair or eyes or bearing, nothing of her character or mind or feelings, nothing of her at all, really. This "love poem" is actually written not in praise of the beloved, as it seems, but in praise of itself. Death shall not brag, says the poet; the poet shall brag. This famous sonnet is on this view one long exercise in self-glorification, not a love poem at all; surely it is not suitable for earnest recitation at a wedding or anniversary party or in a Valentine.

To put it in the terms suggested earlier, the first line stimulates in us a desire for a significant connection with another mind and person, a desire that, at least insofar as we imagine ourselves the imagined addressee, it deeply frustrates. Whether in some other way it meets that desire—and why it might be right to frustrate us as it does—are questions I shall for the present postpone.

World-Imagining

How about the third form of the desire for meaning, for a coherent way of imagining the world? This is actually the deepest subject of the poem. The sonnet starts with a conventional pair of lovers against a conventional backdrop, highly stripped down—in this respect rather like the icebox note, in fact—but in the elaboration of its initial thought something most unconventional occurs, a reimagining of the terms of comparison itself. How do I imagine you? By comparing you to a summer's day. But in six short lines I find myself facing the fact that not only the day but you, and I, and everyone—including the modern reader—inevitably decline, "by chance or nature's changing course untrimmed." All human beings are caught up in the organic processes of which we are a part, and to which death and extinction are the natural and necessary conclusion.

From an almost frivolous beginning, perhaps a kind of teasing challenge—"You say you'd like me to write a poem about you? Okay:

what shall it be? *Shall I compare thee to a summer's day?*"—the poem has moved to confront with utmost seriousness the fundamental limits of human existence. Against this background the question whether "you" are for the moment more or less lovely than a summer's day—or a rose or a rainbow—is a rather trivial one; in fact, the beloved rather drops away as the audience of the poem, to be replaced by us, its real readers.

In this context the assertion of the potential permanence of art has a wholly different significance: It is not just a selfish—or witty—turning away from the beloved to oneself, or to the poem in which she is celebrated, but an assertion of the existence of a realm of human endeavor, of imagination and creation, that resists the forces of nature that otherwise sweep us all like a river into darkness. We are all involved in the success of this poem, not just the poet, but all of us, including the beloved—though this time not as the object of praise but as human being and reader.

In this poem, then, Shakespeare offers us a series of ways of imagining the world and human actors within it: first as consisting only of the lover-poet and his beloved, with the background of a generic summer's day; then as a summer's day that suffers from the imperfections that all nature shares, most seriously the fact that it will decline into extinction, a circumstance that is now seen to include all people, including the poet and the beloved, including the reader. Against this fact there is no cure, no remedy, except for poetry itself—the very activity in which we are at this moment engaged as readers—which holds out the promise of resisting loss, potentially forever. When this poem concludes "and this gives life to thee," it has a surprising resonance, for it is no longer really addressing the beloved but the reader—and it does indeed give life to us.

This means, to return to an earlier point, that when we approach the poem not as the imagined beloved but as ourselves, it responds deeply to our desire for connection with another mind and person, for in it we are exposed to the workings of Shakespeare's imagination, as he moves from one formulation to another ever deeper into the problem that he—as perhaps no one else might—sees presented in his opening line. And to think of the poem from the point of view of its imagined auditor, the woman whose beauty is compared to a summer's day, it all works out much better than I have suggested above. This sonnet turns out not to be the conventional love poem that the speaker teasingly promised the woman in the first line. That poem dissolves into something else entirely. But if you imagine the poem as actually addressed to a real person it becomes an enormous, an astonishing compliment: she is assumed to be able to perceive and value the wit with which his empty gift of empty praise is revealed for what it is; to be able to accept the way he is teasing her for her implied and flirtatious request for a poem of praise; and to be able to see and value what the poem is most deeply about, the inherent decay of all that is natural, against which the creation, through writing, of a realm of art that can in principle last forever can be seen and felt to be the wonderful and shared phenomenon that it is. The imagined audience is herself transformed, from a person who wants a poem written to her beauty to one who wants a poem written to the truth of human experience. A love poem indeed. It might have saved Francesca's soul.

This poem shows us how Shakespeare thinks—how his mind moves—when he is working in a whole-minded way, transforming one image into another, turning a particular scene and moment into an instance of a deep and general problem, shaping thought and feeling and imagination all at once. He starts in one place and ends up somewhere else entirely. This is how we too think, at our best: Shakespeare in this sense shows us what we already do but with a depth and force and reach, as well as an explicitness, far greater than our own. One effect—one meaning—of the whole may thus lie in its teaching us something about our own capacities of mind and imagination.

Formal Expectations

What about the desire for meaning of the kind I first mentioned, the desire for the completion—and modification—of formal expectations? This may at first seem less important than the others, merely technical, but it is only in the particular details and motions of the text that its quality as art will be defined—in this case entitling the poem to the status for which it argues—and it is here, if at all, that it will make available to a reader significant aspects of the mind of the writer at work. How does this poem stimulate and address this form of the desire for meaning?

We have already seen one way in which the poem works upon formal and generic expectations, for it converts what promises to be a standard love sonnet, full of the usual gestures and images, into something quite different. But it is important that this is not only a poem but a sonnet, which in Shakespeare's case means three quatrains, alternately rhymed, followed by a couplet, all in iambic pentameter. In this poem the quatrains are in fact made the units of composition: the first sets up the comparison, the second leads us to the unexpected transformation, the third offers us the solution, and the couplet sums up. The meter and rhymes are completely regular, and the lines are end-stopped throughout. Together, rhyme and meter and the quatrain form create a kind of box in which the action occurs; but they are thematically expressive too, for these features of order are deeply related to the poem's claim to be able to resist the ravages of time and nature. It is only as a competing form of organization, with its own principles of order and meaning, that it can do this.

Within this structure, the poem sets up a series of parallels and transformations: "thy eternal summer" contrasts with the ephemeral "summer's day"; it is made permanent by the "eternal lines" of the poem itself; death's impotence to brag is contrasted with the bragging made by the poem itself; the beloved's possession of "that fair thou ow'st" picks up and transforms the legal language of "summer's lease"; the beloved's growing into time is contrasted with the decline that every fair must face; this growing takes place not in the organic realm but in the artistic one, over centuries, in the world that poetry makes; and so on. The credibility of the claim of the poem to be able to resist time is entirely dependent upon the kind of life the poem in fact creates, and this is to a large extent a matter of meeting, frustrating, and transforming formal expectations.

Transformations

The three forms of the desire for meaning I have mentioned—the desire for life-creating work with formal expectations, the desire for connection with another mind, and the desire for a coherent way of imagining the world and oneself within it—are of course deeply related. For a work to succeed it must do so in all three dimensions—good work with form would be of little value without a connection to the larger issue of the way in which the world is imagined, and vice versa; neither are really conceivable without significant connection to another mind, which in turn may be most fully realized when that mind is engaged simultaneously with the questions of form and the imagining of the world as a whole. The way a text engages simultaneously these three facets of what is at a deep level the same desire is at the heart of its meaning and value.

It is important to see that in each of the three dimensions the poem's action on the reader is truly a form of action, not simply a statement of some kind, for in each dimension the poem comprises contrasting forces—making promises and then putting them into question—in a drama leading to a resolution that is always incomplete or imperfect. An essential part of the drama is a process we might call poetic revision: putting into doubt what we first accept and thus leading us to perceptions and feelings we cannot have anticipated, into something new and fresh. You cannot say at the end of Sonnet 18, "Now I see what it is saying," and carry that away with you in a phrase or other proposition. The life of the poem lies in the shape of the gesture it achieves, or what Robert Frost once called "the figure a poem makes"[4]—the sequence of feeling and perception through which it leads the reader. What is permanent is not a conclusion but a motion with a shape.

In all of this we can perceive the poem working on our desire for meaning in all three of its forms: formal, social, and world-imagining. And in each dimension the poem is surprising, transformative, and in this sense educative, teaching us not only that our expectations about this particular "love poem" are mistaken, but that the set of expectations we bring to poetry generally, to speech generally, are limited, often self-delusive, shaped by a desire for the easy, the expected, the empty but manageable. This sonnet begins in a way that invites us to think of it as a long cliché, a standard love poem written in praise of the beloved—the kind of thing that captivated Francesca. But this beginning is wholly undone; the cliché is replaced with a serious poem about time and decay and nature and art, one that calls upon the mind and feelings in ways we could never have predicted. It self-consciously creates a dimension of life and meaning, in writing across time, that resists the relentless entropy of nature. Its voice, its humor, its feeling are as fresh and vivid now as when the words were written. In writing as he does in confirmation of the power of the individual imagination, the possibility of new and complex truth, Shakespeare leaves behind a text, an experience of mind and imagination, that still today works against the empires of force present within us and in our larger world. This poem shows us what love is not, and something of what it might be; and it expresses a vision of the human being as one seeking meaning in experience—a vision that unites us all—of a kind that makes it possible to imagine justice in a new way as well. In doing so it teaches us that our desires for meaning are not needs or impulses that can be simply

---

[4] Robert Frost, "The Figure a Poem Makes," in Robert Frost, *Collected Poems, Prose, & Plays* (New York: Library of America, 1995), 776.

met or gratified; our deepest wish is that a text will work with our desires to transform them and us, to engage us in a conversation that will teach us something about both our susceptibility to formula and delusion and our capacities of quite another kind—for the life of mind and imagination, of the inner self. Our desire for meaning is the material of the writer's art. At its deepest it is a desire for growth and life.

Poetry is in part a temporal art, the experience of movement and change. Think, for example, of the ending of this sonnet, holding out the promise that art can have a kind of permanence that organic nature cannot have. This of course stimulates the desire for a coherent form in a coherent universe; but the claim is local, founded on the motions of the mind that lead up to it, and it is specific, specific to this poem. Suppose this particular poem *is* eternal: what would that signify? Is it to be the only poem in the world? Its deepest claim is ultimately not for itself, then, but for the activity it expresses, the making of poetry; and for the claims of this poem to be realized, not only must it survive, the activity it has exemplified must continue.

Its movement is thus a call upon us to do likewise; without our response the poem must be incomplete—if we do not read it, it is not eternal—and any response we do make, however excellent in its way, will similarly be a way of calling upon others to take it up, over and over again. No stable point is ever reached. The poem calls upon us to engage in the activity of reading in a whole-minded way; it rewards that activity with an experience that teaches us something about the force of our own desires for meaning; in so doing it equips us to read more intelligently the other texts of our world (which includes reading ourselves more intelligently); and it teaches us too something about what writing and speech of the most valuable kind can be. The poem thus does not merely exhibit its processes of thought and imagination, it implicates us in them, both as the poem proceeds and after it ends.

Like all natural beings we decline; as imagining and feeling human beings, seeking in the world the kinds of meaning I describe, we participate as readers in the art that survives; but this participation is incomplete unless we ourselves speak, creating works with orders of their own that call intelligently upon the desire for meaning. The life the poem offers us lies in its way of writing, an activity in which it calls upon us to engage, from our own point of view and in our own context. In this way what we call reading becomes a kind of writing.

THE DESIRE FOR MEANING IN THE LAW

In this conception of Shakespeare's poem there is perhaps a surprising connection with the law, for, as I suggested earlier, the meaning of a statute (or contract or other legal text) can be seen to lie not in itself but in the process of thought and reading by which others engage with it. The well-written legal text, like the well-written poem, invokes this process in a deep and challenging way, and gives it shape. As the poem calls upon us to be poets, the legal text calls upon us to be lawyers and writers, to exercise the imaginative and expressive aspects of the legal mind.

Can we think of the law as working by calling upon and disciplining the desires for meaning we bring to it? At first it may seem not at all: the law is a system for official action, the exercise of state power, working through institutions or bureaucracies, and its object is not meaning but justice. Its aim is the fair resolution of disputes, the establishment of wise rules of conduct, the just distribution—and limitation—of wealth and power, the public and regular government of the government itself, and so on. What can this have to do with the desire for meaning as I describe it? Can the law be seen as capable of responding, at its best, to our desire for meaning?

Let us think about this in the context of the judicial opinion, regarded for the moment not from the point of view of a lawyer using it professionally, but from the perspective of one of the parties, or, in a case that has attracted widespread attention, from that of a member of the public. With what desires do you turn to it? How does a good opinion work with those desires?

Of course if you are one of the parties, you hope to win, and if you do you will not complain much about the opinion that achieves such a result. That is a desire for victory, not for meaning. But you know that you may lose, for everyone knows that, and if you do, you should demand a great deal of the process by which that occurs, including the opinion itself. You will want to know what it means. To use my threefold image of meaning, you will first of all find it wanting if it fails to satisfy your desire for life-creating work with formal expectations. The opinion must make sense. You will recognize, as with the poem, that this can be done in a mechanical way—the judicial equivalent of doggerel—and you will not be satisfied with that. In neither poetry nor law is it enough to establish rigid expectations which one then meets; one must come to terms with the fact that not all can be done within the form, that it must be modified to meet the appropriate demands of thought and feeling. The excellence of the text will lie in the way it does this. We all know, that is, what a judicial opinion looks like that simply recites a statute or body of judicial authority and declares that it governs the case. It meets formal expectations in a way, but a dead way. Blackmun's opinion is of such a kind, and you could imagine that a reader who was eager simply for formal completion would admire it. But it is empty. As soon as a judge begins to include more, as Jackson does, to recognize that the statute and the opinions are open to contrasting readings and that perhaps they are not the only relevant source of law—that the duty of the judge is to decide justly—the purely formal perfection of the opinion is put into danger. As with the poet, then, part of the judge's art lies in the way in which he allows the order he is asserting to be threatened, creating a kind of music of expectation, confirmation, and surprise, in the process calling upon us to come alive in response, to put the opinion to work and make it part of our minds.

As the disappointed litigant you will also insist that the opinion have a coherent way of imagining not only this case but the larger world of which it is a part, including legal precedent, other legal institutions, and the whole background of culture and value against which the case takes place. We all want a workable way of thinking about human action and responsibility, about judgment, about justice. Every opinion has a way of imagining human actors, their motives and values, their essential qualities as human beings, and this can be adequate or inadequate. An easy and incomplete coherence can be obtained by mechanical thought, by the rigid exclusion of what cannot be managed; but that will not do, and the effort to include more, to recognize more, will threaten the very coherence towards which the good judge struggles. For him, like the poet, excellence lies in the way he manages this tension. Excellence here, that is, does not lie simply in formal coherence or completeness, but in the life of the writing or speaking mind as it struggles with its materials, always imperfectly—in the life it offers to another person. What we ultimately want is a way of imagining ourselves and others and the world we share that will permit—make possible, invite—full and valuable thought, full and valuable speech.

Finally, you will want engagement with a human mind actually thinking its way through the difficulties I mention. You will not be satisfied with an official and authoritarian voice putting together propositions in what seems to be a rational manner; you want to hear the voice of a person speaking his own thoughts, for which he is responsible, as we saw Jackson do. If any of these elements is missing, you will not only be disappointed, you will feel unjustly treated and entitled to complain. If they are present, you may disagree strongly with the outcome, and argue vociferously with it; but you cannot make the complaint that the very method of thought is unjust, which otherwise you can.

The judicial opinion, then, can be seen at its best to respond to our desire for meaning in the three forms in which I have identified it: as it offers us life-creating work with formal expectations, as it establishes virtuous connection with another mind and person, and as it creates a workable way of imagining the world and ourselves within it. The creation of meaning is not incidental to its duty to do justice but central to it: if it accepts and performs its responsibility in this dimension the opinion can be seen as fundamentally just, if not, not.

All this is to think about the opinion from the point of view of the litigants, or perhaps their lawyers or the public at the time the opinion is issued. But judicial opinions have a life beyond the present case, for they constitute authority that can be invoked in later cases. Notice here an odd and interesting parallel with the poem: the opinion achieves a resolution that in a particular case has finality (subject perhaps to appeal), but at the very next moment it is only one of a series of opinions, with which it may be in tension, each of which must be read and evaluated. It will in the long run be of no greater force or value than what we call its "reasoning," which is another term for the life it creates as it works with our desires for meaning.

What is truly permanent about an opinion is not its rule or outcome, but the life of the text, if it has any; like the poem, its significance lies in its shape, in the way it manages the tensions I describe, in the specific form of the gesture it makes as it works with the desire for meaning. Like the poem it calls for the creation of other texts, in this case arguments and opinions, other instances of legal thought, each of which will have its own shape and significance. At its best, it helps teach us how our minds can work well, from the definition of a problem or issue, through its development, to a conclusion always impermanent. Success is always incomplete and imperfect, but in the good opinion it is real. Whether it can happen next time is up to us.

As we think of a judicial opinion or a statute or contract, or any other legal text, we are imagining a text existing across time, working in different contexts. The text in this way partakes of the nature of art, as Shakespeare and others have defined it, namely as a force resisting the processes of decline and decay to which we are inevitably subject. As there is a domain of human invention called art, reaching across time and space and circumstance, so there is a domain of human invention called law, which does much the same thing; as the poem works at its best not by producing a conclusion we can represent in propositional form and carry away with us, but by the quality of its life—by the character and depth of its thought, the shape of the experience it offers its reader—much the same is true of the opinion as well. Its meaning is not in its outcome alone, but in the modes of thought and imagination in which it engages, and which it teaches us. Its resolutions are temporary; what is permanent, what can make its lines "eternal," is the life by which it meets—and responds to and disciplines and transforms—the desire for meaning we bring to it.

READING NOT FOR MEANING BUT FOR USE

I have spoken of reading as an activity driven by a complex desire for meaning, with which the writer, and the reader too, can work to good ends or bad. There is always the danger, in the law and elsewhere, that we shall be satisfied with—indeed that we shall prefer—routine and dead forms of thought and expression, stereotyped and authoritarian social relations, mechanistic and reduced ways of imagining the world—satisfied by writing, that is, that cannot put its premises into question in the joint-minded relation between writer and reader.

But there is another danger, perhaps deeper, that reading for us will be driven by motives of a different kind, not for meaning in any sense in which I have been using the term but for something else entirely. Think of the lawyer or client reading the opinion not for its meaning, but for victory; this is understandable at one stage of the process, but obviously inadequate as a response to an effort by one mind to reach out to another and engage it in thought about the important questions presented by the case. Or to take an extreme case, think of pornography, read only as a means of sexual stimulation; or of other, less harmful forms of expression, such as those read only for escape, or information, or entertainment.

When a text invites us to read it for motives other than for its meaning, it may be offering us something useful, in the case of information, or relatively innocuous, in the case of escape literature; but it may also present in serious form the danger I intend to define. Take advertising and propaganda, for example: these forms invite the reader, really seduce the reader, into disregarding what the writer actually is doing with language and with the audience and into erasing the way it imagines the world as well. The danger is that this effort will be successful and affect our mind and feelings, constituting us as a consumer or as a mouther of political slogans. We can be corrupted, to some extent we necessarily are corrupted, by such productions of our culture against which we can only imperfectly defend ourselves. Yet we can defend ourselves at least a little, and the questions raised in this chapter are offered as a way of doing that. If we ask what kind of life an advertisement or political speech creates as it works with our formal expectations, what kind of relation it establishes with us, into what way of imagining the world it entices us, this may help us see it for what it is.

It is also true that wrongheaded reading can destroy the life, at least for the moment, of even the best kind of writing. In the law, think of the person who wants to reduce a case, or a class, to the statement of rule, assumed to be all one really needs to know. Or in literature, think of the person who reduces the experience of a text like Frost's poem to the cliché it is meant to criticize, or sees Shakespeare's sonnet as the generic love-poem from which it is meant to distance itself and its reader alike. We can go wrong, that is, in two ways: as we allow ourselves to be fooled or seduced or manipulated by others and as we ourselves, as readers, reduce what is in fact full of life and thought into something mindless or dead.

Francesca

Here let us think briefly once more of Francesca: she is one who reads not only without adequate critical judgment but, as I imagine her at least, out of a desire not for meaning in any of the senses in which I have defined it, but for an experience that will in a sense substitute for life, in this case for the side of life we call love. This is how she reads the literature of courtly love, presenting this literature, and herself, in a rather elegant and initially appealing way; this is how she talks to Dante and to us, and with success, for both he as traveler and we as readers are to some degree seduced by it, as she was herself seduced.

The danger of her kind of reading is enacted for us in the crisis of the story she tells. Francesca and Paolo were reading about Lancelot and Guinevere, she says, and "when we read that the desired smile was kissed by such a lover, this man here—who shall never be separated from me—kissed my mouth all trembling."[5] In reading this book, that is, they yield to it in their imaginations, accepting its image of life as a reality; perhaps indeed they bring to the reading the hope that it will stimulate certain feelings in them, in this case erotic feelings. This would be reading not for the meaning of the text but reading as an act of consumption, to satisfy another kind of emotional need or desire. ("That day we read no farther," *quel giorno più non vi leggemmo avante*.) We are to understand that Paolo and Francesca are turning to each other as a way of seeking to replicate the fantasy of the story, not acting out of love for the person the other actually is. They read this story for a simplified version of life and love—as a kind of escape from their own nature and situation—and then find that imagined story taking over their lives.

As we saw in chapter 2, Francesca's mind and feelings seem to have been formed by a certain kind of reading, one that led her to construct her life on empty and unthought principles—that "love is quickly kindled in a gentle heart," and "love will not forgive the beloved who does not return the love"—as though there were nothing more to be said. These formulas and others like them become the ground of her life. She submits to them, substituting them for the complexity and inexpressibility of real experience. It is important to see that the desire she acts on here is at work in all of us, as readers and as citizens, a desire to reduce life to the level of formula and fantasy. This is the desire that drives us to confer absolute authority upon some language that we find in the world; it manifests itself in our every acceptance of a cliché or slogan or platitude, our every appropriation of a sentimental image of life, in advertising and propaganda alike; it is the basis upon which every authoritarian system of thought and conduct rests. In the law it is present whenever one looks at a statute or judicial opinion simply as a declaration to be obeyed, or disobeyed, not as an occasion for thought and argument. What Dante is showing us is that the kind of love to which Francesca has given all is in

[5] *Quando leggemmo il disïato riso*
esser basciato da cotanto amante,
questi, che mai da me non fia diviso,
la bocca mi basciò tutto tremante.   (V, 133–36)

reality empty and misplaced. It is not love at all, really, but a dream—a reader's dream.[6]

Master Adam and Sinon

Dante presents us with another version of the perils of reading at a particularly rich moment in Canto XXX of the *Inferno*. Here Dante the traveler finds himself captivated by a brutal and apparently unending quarrel between two of the damned: Master Adam, who counterfeited the coin of Florence and was burned at the stake, and Sinon, the crafty and treacherous Greek who under false pretenses persuaded the Trojans to accept the wooden horse into their city. These two, tormented with fever and thirst, trade blows and insults, each accusing the other of his crimes, each exulting in the severity of the other's punishment.

Dante speaks first to Adam, swollen with dropsy to the point of deformation and immobility, who speaks with longing of mountain streams he remembers. When Dante asks him the identity of two souls lying nearby, Adam tells him one is Potiphar's wife, who falsely accused Joseph, the other Sinon, the "false Greek," *falso . . . greco*—adding that because of their high fever they throw off such a stink, *per febbre aguta gittan tanto leppo.* Sinon in response strikes Adam in the belly; Adam, despite his disease, manages to hit Sinon in the face with his arm, saying something like, "Although I am deprived of movement I have an arm free for such business as this!" And then they insult each other, in rough translation:

> *Sinon:* Your arm was not so available when you were being burned at the
>   stake—but certainly it was ready when you were falsifying the coin.
> *Adam:* That is true enough, but what you said at Troy was false.

---

[6] Or think again of *Hamlet*, where our capacity as readers to see the force of death at work in Polonius' speech, and the force of life in Hamlet's, is essential to our understanding of the play. It would be possible, for example, for someone to read Polonius' speech as a repository of deep wisdom and to teach it that way to his students. Or suppose the teacher who read the paper by the first student in chapter 2 ("nature in her full glory") had simply affirmed what the boy had done without seeing its emptiness, giving him an A with lavish comments of approval; or if the teacher who read the paper by the fourth student ("comosole traveler") had failed to see and respond to the vigor of the child's mind, the life of his writing. Both children, in different ways, would have by these readings been led more deeply into the domain of the empire of force.

Sinon: If I lied, you falsified the coin; I am here for one crime, you for more crimes than anyone else.

Adam: You perjurer! Remember the horse at Troy, and may it be an evil to you that the whole world knows it!

Sinon: And may the thirst that cracks your tongue, and the foul water that makes a hedge of your gut be an evil to you!

Adam: I may be thirsty and swollen, but you have a fever and an aching head, and would love to lick the pool of Narcissus![7]

Dante the traveler is simply fascinated by this and cannot tear himself away. Virgil, with uncharacteristic sarcasm, interrupts him, saying: "Now keep on looking, for I am not far from a quarrel with you!" *Or pur mira, che per poco che teco non mi risso!* Dante's response to this is of real interest: he is immediately swamped by such a feeling of shame, *tal vergogna*, that it still circles through the memory, *ch'ancor per la memoria mi si gira.* He tries, lamely, to excuse himself; Virgil in essence pardons him, saying that in the future I shall be at your side if you see people in a

---

[7]   "*Quando tu andavi*
al fuoco, non l'avei tu così presto;
ma sì e più l'avei quando coniavi."
E l'idropico: "Tu di' ver di questo:
ma tu non fosti sì ver testimonio
là 've del ver fosti a Troia richesto."
"*S'io dissi falso, e tu falsasti il conio,*"
disse Sinon; "e son qui per un fallo,
e tu per più ch'alcun altro demonio!"
"*Ricorditi, spergiuro, del cavallo,*"
rispuose quel ch'avëa infiata l'epa;
"*e sieti reo che tutto il mondo sallo!*"
"*E te sia rea la sete onde ti crepa,*"
disse 'l Greco, "la lingua, e l'acqua marcia
che 'l ventre innanzi a li occhi sì t'assiepa!"
Allora il monetier: "Così si squarcia
la bocca tua per tuo mal come suole;
ché, s'i' ho sete e omor mi rinfarcia,
tu hai l'arsura e 'l capo che ti duole,
e per leccar lo specchio di Narcisso,
non vorresti a 'nvitar molte parole."   (XXX, 109–29)

It is of interest that these two falsifiers and liars here tell the truth to each other, and not only historical truth but moral truth. In describing each other's conduct, and implicitly their own, they use the language of God.

similar quarrel, but reaffirming that "the wish to hear this is base," *ché voler ciò udire è bassa voglia.*

This passage brings to the surface a problem built into our own experience of the whole *Inferno*: that we naturally read it as Dante does this quarrel, with a kind of sadistic and voyeuristic delight in the hideous punishments with which we are regaled, and in the monstrous sins and crimes that occasion them—reading, that is, not for what I have called "meaning" at all, but for another kind of gratification altogether, essentially pornographic in kind. In this passage Dante thus stands for us, as a reader, and his correction is our own.

Both passages—Dante's fascination with the quarrel between Master Adam and Sinon, and Francesca's reading of the Lancelot story—point us towards a perversion or corruption of desire: instead of a desire for meaning, Francesca, and Dante the traveler, and we as readers all exhibit something else, a desire not to understand and respond to the text before us, as the expression of another mind and person speaking to us, but a desire to use it as an object to gratify our own desires, not for meaning but for the avoidance of life. We find ourselves functioning out of the view that the world consists of pleasures and pains, gratifications and frustrations, and that the art of life is learning to manipulate circumstances, objects, and other people in such a way as to maximize our gratification. All this is an objectification of the universe, a rejection and erasure of the voice and voices that speak to us and call upon us, offering us newness and depth of life by appealing to our desires for meaning: desires for life-creating work with formal expectations, for valuable relations with others, and for a way of imagining the world and ourselves within it in such a way as to make possible significant speech and action.

The same kind of thing can happen in other sides of life, including the law. Virtually all advertising and propaganda are aimed at gratifying a desire not for meaning, or reality, but for fantasy, for sentimentality, for a loss of self and responsibility. In the law one can sometimes see judges and lawyers alike engaged in writing of that kind, writing that seeks only to manipulate, which is in the deepest sense unmeaning and unmeant. Likewise we can sometimes see people in the law reading the authoritative texts of the tradition, the material of our thought and argument, not with an eye to what they should be taken to mean, not as expressions to which we are to be responsive, listening for voice and mind, but simply as restraints or impediments, to be got round.

Not for Use but Love: Guido del Duca

In Canto XIV of the *Purgatorio* Dante the traveler and Virgil find themselves in the realm where envy is purged. Here, as throughout Purgatory, the idea is not that the souls are punished for their vices, that is, simply made to suffer pain because they have done wrong, but that they are led into practices that will gradually free them from their vices. The focus is not on prior acts of sin, but on the disposition of their souls that has led them to sin. The correction they experience is in fact painful—here the envious are imagined as having their eyes sewn shut, keeping them from seeing the successes of others, which has been such a source of torture in their human lives—but it is nonetheless embraced by those subject to it. As an analogy from contemporary life, one might think of a person trying to free himself or herself from addiction to alcohol or drugs. The process is full of pain and suffering, yet in a deep sense he or she wants to undergo it, accepts it and embraces it; the object is a kind of freedom of the self from a desire that twists and destroys its life.

In this region the travelers meet Guido del Duca, who tells them: "My blood was so inflamed with envy that if I had seen a man become happy you would have seen me suffused with anger."[8] He goes on to say, "Of my sowing I reap such straw. O human race, why do you place your hearts there where sharing must be excluded?"[9] This remark, somewhat mysterious, is not elaborated, nor does Dante question him about it. The idea seems to be that envy destroys the possibility of partnership, of community, of human sharing, and that it is caused by a misplacing of the heart, but it is not clear how it does so, or what the alternative would be.

---

[8]   "*Fu il sangue mio d'invidia sì rïarso
       che se veduto avesse uom farsi lieto,
       visto m'avresti di livore sparso.*"   (XIV, 82–84)

[9]   "*Di mia semente cotal paglia mieto;
       o gente umana, perché poni 'l core
       là 'v' è mestier di consorte divieto?*"   (XIV, 85–87)

In the next Canto, however, these things are made the object of explicit thought and conversation. Dante asks Virgil what Guido meant when he spoke of "excluding" and "sharing." Virgil responds: "Because your desires are focussed where portion is reduced by sharing, envy moves the bellows for your sighs." But if the love of the highest sphere, that is, of God, turned your desires upward, you would be released from fear. "Because in that place the more they say 'ours,' the more each possesses of the good and the more love burns in that cloister."[10] This does not satisfy Dante, who simply cannot understand what he has been told. He thinks, as perhaps we all would, like an economist: "How can it be that a good distributed among possessors can make them more rich than if it is possessed by only a few?"[11]

Virgil explains that Dante's understanding is clouded by being fixed on earthly things, *le cose terrene*, among which he means here to include earthly ways of thinking and imagining. What Dante cannot see, and Virgil tells him, is that the infinite and ineffable good, *infinito e ineffabil bene*, races to love as a ray of light races to a bright body, that is, instantly and totally. It gives of itself as much as it finds of love, *tanto si dà quanto trova d'ardore*, and it extends itself as far as love reaches. "And the more souls there are that are beloved there, the more there are to love well and the more love is there, and like a mirror one reflects the other."[12] The idea is not that any one person (or soul) has an infinite capacity for love, but that love naturally generates love in those who are loved, then in those they love, and so on without limit or end. As we saw

[10]   "Perché s'appuntano i vostri disiri
        dove per compagnia parte si scema,
        invidia move il mantaco a' sospiri.
        Ma se l'amor de la spera supprema
        torcesse in suso il disiderio vostro,
        non vi sarebbe al petto quella tema;
        ché, per quanti si dice più lì 'nostro,'
        tanto possiede più di ben ciascuno,
        e più di caritate arde in quel chiostro."   (XV, 49–57)

[11]   "Com' esser puote ch' un ben, distributo
        in più posseditor, faccia più ricchi
        di sé che se da pochi è posseduto?"   (XV, 61–63)

[12]   "E quanta gente più là sù s'intende,
        più v'è da bene amare, e più vi s'ama,
        e come specchio l'uno a l'altro rende."   (XV, 73–75)

in chapter 2, Virgil later says in a similar vein, "Love, kindled by virtue and power, always kindles love, if only the flame be seen," *Amore, acceso di virtù, sempre altro accese, pur che la fiamma sua paresse fore* (*Purgatorio* XXII, 10–12). All this is a transformation of the language of love that leaves Francesca, and her appeal for us, far behind.

Virgil articulates here as a theological principle an elevated version of what every human being knows, that love increases love. Love is in this sense not a scarce resource but an infinitely expandable one, if we tune ourselves rightly to each other and the world. To one who sees people as in necessary and constant competition such a thought is an impossibility, unthinkable and inexpressible. To the law, which is built upon the mutual recognition of persons, upon respect for others, sometimes upon deference to them, and upon an idea of justice that includes the right to speak and be heard, to express the meaning of one's experience and claim a right for it, love is by contrast a real possibility.

CHAPTER FOUR

✠

Writing That Calls the Reader
into Life—or Death

Plato's Phaedrus, on not saying the same thing always; the conversation with the reader in William Carlos Williams's "This Is Just To Say"; the possibilities for meaning presented by the facts of Ashcroft v. Free Speech Coalition; the meaning actually achieved in the opinion in that case; Dante's Guido da Montefeltro as a legal thinker; the opinion of Brandeis in Whitney v. California.

WE HAVE JUST seen that Shakespeare's Sonnet 18 becomes a celebration—a proof—of the power of art to resist the otherwise irresistible forces of organic decay that afflict all natural beings and substances. The voice, or rather voices, of this poem are as fresh and present now as when the sonnet was first written, like coins that always seem newly minted. Much the same is true of the voices in Frost's "The Road Not Taken" and Dante's *Commedia* and in the two passages by Justice Jackson as well. Sometimes we must work to discover this freshness by learning the language in which the text is composed, and something of its culture too; but if it was once present it is always present, and we can hear it if we learn to read the text. Writing is a material art that creates a new and immaterial dimension of experience, a field of life, running across time and space, resisting the natural process of decay. And it does this not just as a matter of principle or hope, but in our daily experience.

Yet to put it this way, however true, is to simplify, for there is a sense in which the life of a text is not simply embedded within it, like a jewel in a box, but, as chapter 3 has suggested, is created by an interaction with the reader. Good writing requires good reading. Nowhere is this more obvious than in the law, where the cases and statutes and constitutions and regulations and contracts that are its material embodiment require active reading, a kind of interpretation that comes close to composition. The lawyer or judge is perpetually refashioning the material of the law, seeing it differently, claiming different meaning for it, adding to it, deleting from it, and so on. Much the same is true of the reading of Homer's *Iliad* or Shakespeare's sonnets. Great texts call for new readings, which will vary as the culture in which they are read varies over time. We can complicate one stage further: the act of reading of which I speak is not independent of the text—not a way of using it, distant from it—but a way of hearing and responding to it, and, as Shakespeare's sonnet shows us, the writing itself may do much to stimulate and shape this activity. The mysterious life of art lies not in the object, not in the reader (or viewer), but in what is created by both of them together: let us call it conversation.

In chapter 3 we saw that the desire for meaning that the reader brings to the text is really a desire for life: the life made possible by work with the generic and formal expectations that lie at the heart of language itself; the life of engagement with another mind and person; and the life of imagination through which one struggles to conceive of the world, and oneself and others within it, in such a way as to make possible significant speech and valuable action. At its best, writing can call the reader into this kind of life, always new, and in this way affirm the power and dignity of the individual mind. It can do this in a way that purely oral expression cannot, both because writing can remain as a source of potential life for centuries and because the written text can reward sustained and repeated attention in a way that oral speech cannot.[1]

---

[1] In this way writing, as we shall see more fully below, can paradoxically offer the reader a conversational life that has qualities not possible in purely oral interchange. Of course the opposite is true as well, for oral expression has its own advantages of immediacy, of the presence of the speaker in time, and so on. For a useful analysis of the difference between oral and written texts, see Jack Goody, *The Power of the Written Tradition*, Smithsonian Series in Ethnographic Inquiry (Washington, D.C.: Smithsonian Institution Press, 2000).

One perhaps surprising difference, suggested to me by A. L. Becker, is that in writing one is less constrained by one's audience. If you ask a group of people in a room each to write a sentence describing something they have seen in common—perhaps even a simple event staged for the purpose, like the instructor walking across the room and putting his books on the table—each will write a different sentence. Becker has in fact performed this experiment a great many times and says that he has never seen the same sentence twice. But if you ask people to say aloud what they saw, the first speaker will typically establish a norm to which others will conform.

This chapter explores the kind of life we can hope that writing will offer, in the process elaborating and complicating the familiar idea that writing works by a kind of conversation with the reader. My starting point is Plato's *Phaedrus*, where, in a well-known passage, Socrates seems to attack writing itself: he says that true philosophy requires the living engagement of mind with mind of a sort that writing cannot attain. Yet this is obviously a paradox, for Socrates' position is articulated and recorded by Plato in writing. How then can we make sense of what Plato is saying and doing? What kind of writing, for example, does he think he is himself engaged in? What, according to him, is good philosophical writing more generally, if such a thing exists, and to what kind of life does it call the reader?

Then I turn to a poem by William Carlos Williams, asking to what kind of life it calls its reader, what kind of conversation it begins and shapes, in the hope of giving further definition to the idea of writing, and of writing well, towards which I am working. And what about writing in the law? Here there is an evident puzzle, for writing seems necessary to what we mean by law itself, yet the cases and statutes we read are often highly ambiguous as guides to the decision of actual cases. In the terms established in chapter 3, law needs not only writing but reading—but what kind of reading does it need? As a way of thinking about these matters I turn to another case arising under the First Amendment, *Ashcroft v. Free Speech Coalition*,[2] asking what writing can achieve in this context: What is good legal writing, if such a thing exists, and what can be attained by it? To what kind of life does it call us, and what is its value? Then I examine the opinion of the Court in that case, asking how fully it has achieved the possibilities we have imagined for it.

IN PHILOSOPHY

First, then, Plato's *Phaedrus*. Towards the end of this dialogue the conversation turns from the nature of the soul and of love, its ostensible subjects, to the rather more mundane subject of writing. In this connection Socrates tells a story, supposedly from Egypt, that runs roughly this way:

The god Theuth, the inventor of astronomy and geometry and arith-

[2] 535 U.S. 234 (2002).

metic and other sciences, comes to Thamus, the king of Egypt, to offer him his various inventions. He presents them to the king, one by one; Thamus, a kind of technological skeptic, examines each, asking what it is good for and what dangers it presents, before deciding whether to accept it. The conversation is intense and extended, as the merits of each invention are discussed in detail. Theuth is perhaps a bit deflated by Thamus' critical responses, but when he comes to the gift of writing his spirits are restored: he expresses the greatest confidence that this is a great invention, one that will surely make the Egyptians happy, for it will improve their memories. In writing he has found, he says, a magic charm for wisdom and memory. But Thamus disputes this claim, saying that writing will in fact have the opposite effect from that predicted: since people will rely upon writing rather than their memories it will stimulate forgetfulness, not memory; and since they will be calling upon something external to themselves, not what is in their minds, it will create the false appearance, not the reality, of knowledge and wisdom.

Socrates then goes on to say, in his own voice, that writing is to speaking as a painting is to a person: it creates the image of meaning, but is wholly unable to answer when questioned. The written text just keeps repeating the same thing over and over, unable to adjust or respond to questions, doubts, or new ideas. For this reason, he says, we should take rather little satisfaction in what we write, even the best things we can do. This skeptical view of the value of writing is reaffirmed in Plato's seventh letter where he says that his philosophy is not to be found in any of his writings, but exists only in the living engagement of mind with mind.[3] Writing is at best a kind of play or game; the real thing, that about which we should really be concerned, lies elsewhere, in actual conversation between minds taking place in what we might call "real time."

As I said earlier, there is an obvious paradox here, for both of the Platonic strictures against writing take place in writing. Without writing, indeed, we should have virtually no access to Plato's mind, or the mind of Socrates either for that matter, or any sense of what Plato meant when he said that philosophy lay not in writing but in conversation. In fact, our best examples of the kind of living interaction between mind and mind that he admires are themselves in writing, as in this very dialogue. It is impossible to believe that Plato, one of the world's best writers, did

---

[3] Plato, *Seventh Letter*, 341C–D, 344C. (I am here assuming that the letter is authentic, a matter of some dispute.)

not value highly his achievement of this kind. What sense, then, can we make of Plato's attack on writing?

Reading the Phaedrus

A natural place to begin is with our experience of reading the text of the *Phaedrus*.[4] The first thing that is likely to leap out at one who turns to it for the first time is that this text, like so many other of the Platonic dialogues, is neither an argument written to support a particular set of propositions nor a disquisition upon a particular subject. Rather, it is a story, a drama, a conversation, beginning with the meeting of Socrates and Phaedrus outside the walls of Athens and ending with their going back into the city together. Something happens between those two points; the creation of that happening between the speakers, and the corresponding happening in the life of the reader, is certainly one aim, perhaps the true aim, of the text.

I will not try to summarize the whole thing, but it may help if I say this much about what occurs: Phaedrus and Socrates meet outside the city walls; Phaedrus talks about a party he has recently left, at which the orator Lysias read a very clever speech; Phaedrus has borrowed a copy of this speech, which he has been planning to commit to memory. Seeking a place to discuss the speech, Socrates and Phaedrus find the cool and shaded atmosphere of the river trees and comment in detail on their surroundings. Phaedrus then reads aloud the speech of Lysias, in which a seducer paradoxically argues that the fact that he is not in love is a good reason for his target to yield to his desires; Socrates, spurred on by Phaedrus, gives, in a kind of competition, a speech of his own to the same end, his point being that love is a kind of irrationality and thus inconsistent with the philosophic life. Suddenly visited by his private divine force, however, Socrates realizes that what he has said is awful, for love is a god and must be good; he then delivers a second speech, this one in favor of love, in which among other things he works out an image of the human soul as a pair of winged horses, one good, one bad, managed by a charioteer. Human souls once lived in the heavens, he says, but through mismanagement have lost their wings and fallen into an earthly

---

[4] For a fuller treatment of this dialogue, see chapter 6 of James Boyd White, *The Edge of Meaning* (Chicago: University of Chicago Press, 2001).

life. Love, Socrates says, is an experience that reminds the soul of what it once had, life in contact with beauty and truth, and it rekindles the desire to attain it. It is one of the greatest gifts of life. When Socrates has finished, he and Phaedrus speak about various questions raised by the three speeches on love, including the issue whether writing is a good or bad thing.

Even this summary should be enough to show that this dialogue is not, as I say, a sustained conceptual argument, leading by logical progression from one point to another, but a composition far more complex, in which one part answers or responds to another. Its closest familiar analogue may be a play by Shakespeare, where any position Shakespeare himself may have is expressed not by this speech or that, but by the play as a whole, by the way voice answers voice. For Shakespeare's art lies not only in the composition of the speeches but in their arrangement: it is here, in the relation of these gestures across time in the course of performance, that Shakespeare can be found. And in Shakespeare, as in Plato, one finds items of very different kinds, humorous and solemn and farcical and deeply felt.

For the reader of both authors, then, the question is not so much what this "means" in a propositional way—as if true understanding meant the capacity to utter a series of true statements that represented what Plato or Shakespeare would have said if they had been smart enough—but what it means in an entirely different way, as an experience of mind and imagination, of thought and feeling. The end is not persuasion to a set of statements, but something vastly more important and profound, a transformation of the mind and motives and understandings of the reader—the reader, that is, who learns to engage with it. This text does not work automatically, to transfer knowledge or concepts or arguments, or to serve as a set of directions, but offers the reader a complex experience of thought and judgment, an experience to which it invites and calls him but does not compel him. In this way it affirms the independence, autonomy, and value of the reader himself— his experience, his mind, his freedom.[5]

Reading the *Phaedrus* requires one constantly to ask how a particular passage is to be taken in light of other passages or other moments. Here the question of tone is crucial. For example, in the central myth about

[5] Compare Patsy Rodenburg, *Speaking Shakespeare* (New York: Palgrave Macmillan, 2002), which works out an image of the good actor as very much this kind of reader.

the soul as a pair of winged horses guided by a charioteer, part of the story is that once the soul has fallen from the heavens to the earth, the experience of physical desire for a beautiful body reminds the soul of its own earlier experience of beauty itself, in the heavens, where the Eternal Forms can be directly apprehended; the person thus touched by *eros* starts to feel the itch and pain of his feathers beginning to sprout, in the total intoxication of desire. How are we to read this? I can remember being told that this story was a perfectly serious allegory of the moral nature of the soul, and that the lesson was plain, to develop the rational faculties of the charioteer to control one's baser impulses. But this won't work at all: it is some of the so-called baser impulses that are celebrated here, and the kind of madness they bring about is far from rational control. And in any event such a lead-footed reading is totally dead to what is most wonderful about this myth: its invented, playful quality, comic even to the point of the self-consciously ludicrous, poised as it is against a kind of real seriousness. The speech is both serious and comic, both beautiful and silly, both to be believed and disbelieved.

The story about Theuth and Thamus has similar qualities. It is funny, to start with, as the resolutely practical Thamus examines the gifts of the god with a skeptical air and practical intelligence.[6] (I do not think it wholly accidental that their names, at least for me, work as a kind of tongue twister, leading me to want to lisp the second name, thus, "Thamuth.") As I suggested earlier, the apparent message of the story, that writing is bad because it will destroy memory and wisdom, is in plain contradiction to certain of the premises of the text of which it is a part. How then are we to read it?

One possibility is to start from Socrates' point that the trouble with writing is that it always says the same thing and can thus never respond to questions or criticisms, never engage in the conversational process that is the center of philosophy. In the terms suggested by my quotation from Simone Weil, the activity of writing may seem by its nature to affirm the empire of force: not to open up possibilities for the reader but to close them off; not to respond to the reader's questioning mind and feelings, not to engage him in conversation with a life and movement of its own, but to say the same thing always. Plato is perhaps here showing us why he

---

[6] This is just what Socrates in his main speech did *not* do with the gift of sexual desire, from Eros; Thamus thus stands as a mild reproach to Socrates' abandonment of reason in telling the central myth.

writes in the form of the dialogue, rather than simply telling us "what he thinks and why he thinks it"—as though such a thing could be done.

On this view, what the passage about writing suggests is that he, Plato, is trying to write a text that is different from the kind of writing he rejects and instead has some of the essential qualities of conversation. It does not simply say something, and stop; rather, it offers the reader a complex experience, in part consisting of the stimulation of questions— about the myth of horses, for example, or this very passage about reading—that the text will not in any obvious or easy way answer, but with respect to which it affords the reader material for thought, if he can grasp and manage it. Here, for example, the question, "What can Plato mean by these strictures against writing?" leads to the possibility that it is not all writing that he opposes, but writing of a certain kind—or reading of a certain kind—working on certain premises. Moreover, in the way in which Plato renders living conversation between Socrates and Phaedrus one can find some idea of what his own aim is as a writer, and the standards by which he wants his writing to be judged.

I do not want to suggest that this is where the process ends: there are other points about writing, other complications and mysteries here, but this in a sense is the main point: Plato has written a text that does not simply say the same thing always, but says different things as you bring different questions to it. Its aim is to offer its reader a disorienting experience of controlled uncertainty and thus to stimulate independence of mind, in the way that conversation, or dialectic, at its best can do. On this view philosophy, as Plato understands and practices it, is not the exposition of a certain set of propositions about the world but a mode of life and thought; its end is not a set of statements but an end of a different kind, the transformation of the mind and imagination of the reader. This is a process in which the reader is of necessity an equal partner; by its nature it has no termination until death and the hoped-for return to the world in which truth and beauty and goodness can be seen simply and clearly for what they are.

The Force and Limits of Language

One reason why Plato wrote this way, rather than proceeding as Euclid was to do in another field, from first principles, or as Aristotle did, from common knowledge, is that for Plato the language in which he thought and wrote was a major part of the subject he addressed. This was partly a matter of its particular substantive commitments, for example to an idea of justice and "goodness" that consisted mainly of the power to exercise dominion over others,[7] but partly also a matter of the nature of human language more generally—for there is no language in which the truth can simply be said, and in Plato's view we must train ourselves to accept that fact and to display our awareness of it in our speaking and our writing alike.

The point of Plato's doctrine of the Eternal Forms, at least in the *Phaedrus*, is not to assert the truth of their existence, which can after all never be observed or known while we live, but to define, by their absence, what human life lacks. It is a way of drawing attention to the important fact of actual human life that whether the Forms exist or not, knowledge of them is denied us. We must live on conditions of radical uncertainty; it is to show us how this might be done without collapsing into incoherence or despair that the dialogue exists.

The experience of reading Plato may thus provide us with a method for reading more generally, including the reading of philosophy, for it suggests among other things that the language in which philosophy—and perhaps any intellectual enterprise—is carried on can, and perhaps should always, be part of its subject. If we start to yield to the desire to create a general philosophic system, as Plato himself often did, the experience of the *Phaedrus* should check us in that course; not to prevent us, necessarily, but to slow us down. If, for example, we find ourselves talking about the "proper end of life" and defining that as "happiness," and then defining happiness in terms of the "fulfilment of human capacities," or if we find ourselves talking about the proper form of political organization and defining that in terms of "consent," and consent in terms of the "will of the majority" as reflected in the ballot, all as though those terms had meanings that were either self-evident or could be stipulated, and as though we occupied a platform somehow above history and culture from which we could speak universal truths on such subjects, the experience of reading Plato should make us pause,

---

[7] For a fine article on reading Plato as a general matter, see Hayden Ausland, "On Reading Plato Mimetically," *American Journal of Philology* 118 (1997): 371. For further discussion, see James Boyd White, *When Words Lose Their Meaning: Constitutions and Reconstitutions of Language, Character, and Community* (Chicago: University of Chicago Press, 1984), 95–98.

and ask how what we are saying might be located in one of his dialogues: poised against what counterformulations; subject to what disso-
lutions, as the terms we use are shown not to bear the weight we want
to give them; rendered to what degree incomplete or empty, as other related questions are raised to which we have no way of speaking; and so
forth. It is in fact one of the monumental achievements of Plato simultaneously to engage in the impulse to systematize and to subject that impulse to criticism.

For present purposes the main point is that Plato in this text calls his
reader into a rich and independent life. An essential part of this achievement lies in the text's perpetual frustration of the reader's natural desire
to submit to it—to find in it a set of propositions or rules or systems
which he can use and to which he can defer. In this way it calls us into
being as independent centers of meaning and judgment.

IN POETRY

The sense of writing worked out above, as an activity of mind—as an engagement with the nature of language and the limits of human understanding that cannot resolve itself into propositions assumed to be stable,
but must renew itself, again and again, whenever we speak or write—
may seem at first to be an essentially literary or poetic one. It is after all
much easier for us, in our culture at least, to see that a poem or a novel
does not simply "carry a message" than it is to read a legal or philosophic
text in such a manner; far easier to see of the literary text that much of its
meaning lies in its tones of voice and their transformations, its ways of
imagining the world and the speaker, its definition and management of
relations between speaker and audience, its metaphors and images, its
ways of meeting and upsetting expectations as to form, and so on. In particular, poetic texts are commonly seen to be founded on a tension, or a
contradiction, between different ways of thinking or feeling or acting or
imagining the world, which they may not resolve at all, or only partly. We
are ready to recognize that whatever truth such a text asserts is not reducible to one position, one voice, one way of thinking, but lies in the
fact that both opposing elements have weight and validity.

But, as we have just seen, all this can be true, perhaps should be true, of
a philosophic text, and maybe of a legal text as well. It is important to add
that while complexity, tension, paradox, and irresolution may often be

more obviously present, and of hence available to scrutiny, in literary texts than texts of other kinds, this does not mean that a literary text has these qualities for their own sake, as a way of creating an item of purely aesthetic consumption. Form is crucial to meaning in literature (and elsewhere too), but good literary writing is not simply about its form and nothing else. It has its own substantive concerns. As I hope our readings of Dante and Sonnet 18 and "The Road Not Taken" show, good poems and other literary texts are worth reading because they address and illuminate, provide ways of thinking about, the most important of questions: What kind of meaning can we claim for our experience, and how can we do it? What kind of life can we have, in solitude and with each other? What are the resources and limits of the languages we are given to use, and how can they best be managed by the speaker and writer? Can we find a way to imagine the world, and ourselves and others within it, that will make possible coherent speech and valuable action? Can we think and speak and write in a whole-minded way that is worthy of human dignity?

The poem to which I now turn is from this point of view a difficult one, for it is not obvious that it is about something important. It may not look or sound much like a poem at all, and may even seem to be reducible to a message. It is William Carlos Williams's poem about taking the plums from the icebox:[8]

> THIS IS JUST TO SAY
> I have eaten
> the plums
> that were in
> the icebox
>
> and which
> you were probably
> saving
> for breakfast

---

[8] "This Is Just to Say" in *The Collected Poems of William Carlos Williams*, ed. A. Walton Litz and Christopher MacGowan, 2 vols. (New York: New Directions, 1991), 1: 372. William Carlos Williams, from *Collected Poems: 1909–1939*, Volume 1, copyright ©1938 by New Directions Publishing Corp., reprinted by permission of the publishers, and New Directions Publishing Corporation and Carcanet Press Ltd.

> Forgive me
> they were delicious
> so sweet
> and so cold

When you first read this poem, or hear it read aloud, you are likely to have one of two rather strong reactions: either that this is a beautiful poem, special in some as yet unknown way, or that it is trivial and empty. In my own experience this was true of a group of old friends, all good readers and familiar with each other's minds, who divided in exactly that way and engaged in heated dispute over the question that divided us.

On the negative side, it seems true that the poem does not have the kind of dramatic and intense and clearly shaped imagery of a poem like Wallace Stevens's "Thirteen Ways of Looking at a Blackbird,"[9] say, which begins:

> Among twenty snowy mountains,
> The only moving thing
> Was the eye of the blackbird.

By comparison, the language "and which you were probably saving for breakfast" seems cluttered and awkward and utterly ordinary, devoid of visual force. In addition, those who take the negative view might add that this is a poem that is indeed reducible to a mere proposition: I have eaten your plums and apologize. That is all there is to it. It is just a note on an icebox.

But is that so? To test that we might ask what, if anything, the poem does that such a message does not. Here imagine that you are the poet's spouse—or perhaps roommate or partner or host—and that you found this note on the icebox door: "I ate your plums; sorry about that." How would that be different from this poem?

Part of it is formal. As one of my friends observed in the disputation referred to, there are patterns of sound that run through the poem, all leading up to a strong emphasis on the last lines, "so sweet / and so cold." "Sweet," he pointed out, picks up the rhymes of "eaten," "probably,"

---

[9] "Thirteen Ways of Looking at a Blackbird," in *The Collected Poems of Wallace Stevens* (New York: Alfred A. Knopf, 1971), 92.

and "me"; "and so cold" picks up the *d* and *l* from "delicious," the *l* from "plums," the *k* sound from the last line of each of the other stanzas, and, most of all, the enormously strong open *o*, which we have seen foreshadowed in "forgive" and "so," and less directly in "icebox" and "probably." As my friend put it, these sounds "have been laid out, given prominence, and anticipated, all as carefully as a key and scale in music."[10] This expression stimulates and satisfies what I earlier called the desire for completion of formal expectations.

But even if we assume that we could go on at length in this vein, establishing the formal complexity and coherence of what seems at first a purely ordinary statement, there remains the question to what end this formal composition exists. It could still be at bottom an empty expression, however mathematically or musically complex its organization of sounds. As the recipient of such an apology you might feel that it was ingenious, reflecting a lot of skill and effort, but still not very different in the end from "sorry about that."

This brings us to the heart of the poem, which lies in the definition of feelings and social relations achieved in its tones of voice, or what, in chapter 3, I called the social dimension of meaning. Take, to begin with, the phrase "I have eaten," which stands as its own line at the beginning of the poem. It is hard for anyone educated in the Western tradition not to hear behind this simple phrase echoes of the Garden of Eden: "And hast thou eaten of the tree whereof I commanded that thou shouldst not eat?" The significance of this allusion is reinforced by the later isolation of the word "saving" in a single line, and by the force of the phrase, again in a single line, "Forgive me," both of which resonate deeply in the language of Christianity and its emphasis on our fallen state.

What does the speaker do with this allusion? It could work in ways that are heavy-handed, portentous, mechanistic; but in fact it is quite delicate, precise, at once amusing and touching. See how it plays against the self-deprecating title—"This is just to say"—to create a real tension, between the lightness of the tone, the brevity of the poem, and the triviality of the occasion, on the one hand, and the grandness, not to say heaviness, of the theme implied in these allusions to the Fall and Redemption, on the other. In a way this tension reaches the poem itself: is it a minor, trivial, inconsequential gesture—just a note on an icebox—or is it serious, deep, solemn, maybe too solemn?

---

[10] The friend referred to is my colleague A. L. Becker, whom I thank for his help.

The biblical reference is reinforced by the fact that what is eaten here turns out to be a fruit; but at the same time it is made less merely allegorical by the fact that the fruit here is not the apple of tradition but a plum—far more delicious and tempting, yet far more ordinary at least than that traditional fruit on the tree in the Garden, in part because it is located, we learn, in the "icebox."

Despite the clarity of these allusions, a voice within us wants to say that this simply cannot be an instance of the Fall; it is far too quotidian and trivial. To think of this event in such a grand way is ludicrous. But eating an apple is trivial and quotidian too; and in the second stanza the poem makes plain that the eating of the plums was an act with real moral significance, not simply as a matter of doctrine or theology but as a matter of actual human relations, for they were not his but someone else's, and he did not eat just one but all of them. Once more we face the peculiar tension that it is the characteristic of this poem to stimulate: we are bound to feel, in part, that this is simply not a big deal, perhaps once more finding ourselves using the word "trivial"; but it is not an entirely small thing either, and if a marriage or other relation were regularly marked by such transgressions it would be full of real difficulty. (Just imagine what Jane Austen would make it mean.) And if the Fall means anything it will show up in the smallest details of life.

The speaker has in fact wronged his wife (let us assume), on however small a scale and no matter how understandable the temptation. What does he do about this fact? He acknowledges that the plums were themselves not trivial, but important to her; he also shows, especially in the "probably," that he knows her, her tastes and values. This at once makes his offense the more serious and the poem a more adequate recompense, for this is not a stereotyped apology, any man to any woman, but one addressed to her. He shows that he knows her.

His acknowledgment is the initial point of the note itself—"This is just to say." But why "just"? He is here minimizing both the expression and the wrong that gave rise to it; this is part of what leads some readers to take the poem as trivial. But this is a mistake on his part, and hence on ours, to be corrected by what follows. The speaker does not stop with the sentence begun in the title, and the sentiments upon which that sentence was based, but comes to see the need to go on, to take another step. And this is far from a small one: "Forgive me." That is either a real statement of contrition or a casual use of serious language that raises a genuine question: If he is not contrite, why is he not? Like Shakespeare's

Sonnet 18, this poem begins as something light and slight but is transformed before our eyes into quite a different work, of real seriousness and depth.

But this is still not the end. Having recognized that what he did was actually wrong, and having asked forgiveness for it, the speaker now reaffirms his taking of the plums—"they were delicious"—in part by making the temptation seem practically irresistible. The word "delicious" is an effort to elicit his reader's imaginative sympathy, even complicity, to confirm what he has done. This is also the effect of the great emphasis and intensity given to "so sweet / and so cold."

The speaker thus begins with a gesture—"this is just to say"—designed to trivialize both what he has actually done and his present communication, but he finds he cannot do this; he recognizes that the wrong, however small, was real—she was saving the plums for breakfast and he ate them all. He then asks for forgiveness, at first on the basis of his repentance. But he discovers that this too will not work, for the repentance is not and cannot be entirely sincere; he is still in the temptation and cannot deny it. Then he asks for forgiveness, implicitly, on quite a different ground, that it is his nature—and ours too: we confirm it in our response to the last line—to yield to such temptations.

The poem ends with real sweetness, in his confidence that he will be forgiven. This is an enactment of trust, part of what makes it a love poem. (The other part is his knowledge of her.) But it also ends with a real coldness, in the inescapably fallen nature of his being and ours. Yet it is this coldness that makes the sweetness possible: the sweetness is the blessing that he knows that with all his faults, he loves and is loved after all. So the ending, "so sweet / and so cold," is just right.

To return now to the questions whether this really is a poem, or really any good: you can see that I think that the answer to both questions is yes. On the other hand, the negative judgments I describe are not without basis, and the reader may be persuaded that they are right. The poem itself is perpetually creating a tension between the view that it, and the events it speaks of, are crucial aspects of eternal human truth, and the view that it is all too trivial and ordinary to count for much. The important words "Forgive me" can in our language be either expressive of the deepest sense of contrition or, in other contexts, be so slight as to be almost insignificant. Both the claim of meaning and the self-deprecation are parts of the poem, and important parts: indeed the tension between them is the center of the piece.

In this the poem captures a tension present in our own everyday lives, including as lawyers: Are the events of our own lives merely quotidian and trivial? Or do they make up a moral and aesthetic drama of real importance? The truth that grandeur can be found in the ordinary, the great in the small, is in this poem placed against the truth that the ordinary is truly ordinary; what the poem represents is thus a crucial and unresolvable uncertainty at the heart of human life. It holds itself out as a response to be imitated, finding a kind of redemption in the tones of voice with which it speaks, at once serious and comic, overstated and understated, claiming and disowning meaning, all in a gesture of love and trust.

Williams's poem can be taken as an instance of a text that does not say the same thing always, but offers its reader a drama, an experience of discovery, which like the *Phaedrus* has many of the qualities of a conversation. It calls us into a deeper kind of life—a life of thought and imagination and feeling—than we normally experience, and in doing so it affirms the value of the individual mind and individual experience, including our experience of language. Language is here used not to state a truth but to lead us into a position from which we see that none of our formulations can do justice to our situation: to our motives, to our conduct, to our relations with those we injure, and to our own desire to see significance in what we do and who we are. Like the *Phaedrus* this poem is written from a place of silence in the writer to a place of silence in the reader—a place from which our language itself can be put into question, including our own desire for simplifying formulas and clichés. I have offered one version of this poem, but it is only one version and surely not complete; what is more, I respect the views of my friends who read and judge it very differently. This poem is at heart the occasion for an activity of thought and reflection and argument, in principle not reducible to an outcome, which it stimulates and rewards. Its value is the value of that activity. In this it is like the best of philosophy and the best of law.

As a way of looking forward to my next subject, let me say that the question at the heart of this poem is also at the heart of the law. Something happens in the client's life, say an unwanted pregnancy, or an arrest for drunkenness, or a restriction on the use of his land: Does this mean anything? Does it really matter? These are the questions for the lawyer, whose task it is to see that it does matter and to give it meaning in the language of the law. We live our lives on the faith that this can be done, that law can convert the raw material of human experience—the pain, the fury, the loss—into the material of meaning, and in such a way as to permit or invite or enable meaningful action in response. Philosophy too, at least as Plato does it, lives out of such questions: Does it matter that Phaedrus is infatuated with the rhetoric of Lysias? What does it mean?

In all three fields it is a mistake—a denial of life—to try to write a text that will say the same thing always, or to read a well-written text as if that were the writer's goal. Philosopher, lawyer, poet—all three do their real work in the conversations they establish with their reader, or among their readers over time. It is the achievement of writing to make possible a kind of sustained attention, through reading and rereading, that cannot be given to purely oral expression; more than that, to make possible a conversation about the meaning of texts, itself in writing, that can also take place over space and time.

The central question is one of quality: What is the nature and quality of the conversational life to which this text or that, in philosophy, law, or poetry, calls its reader, its readers? That is where its life and meaning and value can be found. There is a side of each of us that wants to forget this, and to live in a simpler world of statements that are true or false, rules that are just or unjust, poems that are beautiful or ordinary, denying our responsibility to face the uncertainties and tensions with which even the best work—especially the best work—presents us. But this will not do: the best work in each field constantly teaches us otherwise.

LAW AS A CALL TO LIFE

What bearing if any does such an understanding of poetry and Platonic philosophy have upon the reading and writing of the law? At first it may seem none at all: the whole point of written laws in our system is that they be clear and publicly available; only then, after all, can the citizen who is subject to them conform his or her conduct to their requirements, and only then can the official who interprets and applies them be subject to the constraint we think of as government under law. Uncertainty of law is a recipe for official corruption, for the denial of the fundamental principle of notice, and for violation of the ideal that like cases are to be treated alike. We therefore demand that the law be clear, in America even making a constitutional principle of it. We in fact want the law to do just what Socrates complains that writing does, namely to say the same thing always. We do not want law to be dialectical or conversational; we want clarity, fair notice, obedience, equal treatment.

But all this is far easier to say in general terms than it is to work out in practice, as any look at a statute book or constitution or a set of judicial cases will show. The main provisions of the First Amendment to the U.S. Constitution, for example, are on the surface plain enough: "Congress shall make no law respecting an establishment of religion, or prohibiting the free exercise thereof; or abridging the freedom of speech, or of the press." When we read this we understand in a general way the values that the framers are articulating, and we know that the framers want to be read as meaning business. But as we have seen in *Barnette*, *Virginia Pharmacy Board*, and *Thomas v. Collins*,[11] serious problems emerge when it comes to the application of such a standard. Think of the religion clause quoted above, for example: Is it an establishment of religion for a legislature to begin its sessions with prayers led by a chaplain paid by tax dollars? For the armed services to employ chaplains? For a state to exempt religious organizations from its tax laws? For a city to have a Christmas display that includes a nativity scene?

Deciding such questions is not merely a matter of looking at the words and seeing what they mean, for different people will have different readings of the same language—different, reasoned, and decent readings. The question the law faces, here as elsewhere, is what to do about the fact that we do reasonably differ, including on the most important matters, and that there is no obviously right way to resolve these differences.

This means that the ideal of clear language applied the same way every time is simply out of reach. In the law the meaning of the language in which authoritative directions are given is itself always potentially in question. Much as Plato sees that the central terms of his language are uncertain in meaning and call for new definition, the lawyer should come to see that the same is true of the central terms in her discourse: terms such as "religion" and "speech" and "establishment" and "free exercise" in the First Amendment, for example. The lawyer should not

---

[11] *West Virginia State Board of Education v. Barnette*, 319 U.S. 624 (1943), was the flag salute case, discussed in chapter 1; *Virginia State Board of Pharmacy v. Virginia Citizens Consumer Council*, 425 U.S. 748 (1976), discussed in chapter 2, struck down the Virginia rule prohibiting advertisement of the price of drugs; *Thomas v. Collins*, 323 U.S. 516 (1945), also discussed in chapter 2, invalidated a requirement that a labor organizer register with the state before soliciting memberships in a union.

simply use her language as a given, then, as though its terms and formulas automatically did the work the case calls for, but see it as the proper subject of critical attention and transformation at her hands.

Likewise, the lawyer should know what Plato shows us, that there is no such thing as purely neutral, unsituated, abstract, or disinterested thought or speech: no way, except in the heavenly life Plato imagines to precede and follow our earthly one, in which one can see beauty and truth and justice for what they are, unchanging and eternal essences. Rather, every effort at thought and expression is located in a historical moment and a particular set of social relations, and these circumstances affect the meaning of what is said. This is true of the *Phaedrus* itself, which is a conversation between Socrates and Phaedrus; and it is true of the lawyer, who always thinks and speaks as the representative of a particular client—the citizen who wants the nativity scene removed, for example, or the city that wants it to remain—or, if she is a judge, as one trying to resolve the particular dispute before her by reference to the laws of her state and nation. For both lawyer and judge, the materials of meaning with which they work are to a large degree given them by others, in the constitutions, statutes, regulations, contracts, judicial opinions, and other legal texts that speak to the particular event. This material will not and should not say the same thing always; it will in fact yield different meanings to different minds in different situations, differences that themselves become the topic of thought and argument. This is part of the life a text creates when it speaks across time and culture. It is through the kind of intellectual and social experience in which we discover, elaborate, test, and for the moment resolve these differences, not through the establishment of a system of rules, that we begin to make ourselves, in Weil's phrase, capable of justice.

For the lawyer, as for Plato, every discovery, every conclusion, should be regarded as provisional, open to question and perhaps repudiation in a later conversation—think of Socrates, who in the *Phaedrus* made one speech against love, another one in praise of it, and then changed the subject entirely. It is common for a Platonic dialogue to end with Socrates in a kind of perplexity—or if not that, by reaching a conclusion that is still, in the terms established in the dialogue itself, open to doubt, and thus leaving the reader in perplexity, even if Socrates seems not to be. So too in the law: though each performance is the best we can do at the time, it is always open to revision—by appeal, by distinction, by overruling, by amendment.

The life of the law, like the life of philosophy, lies in the activity by which a problem is defined and approached, not in any permanent solution to it. This activity is what we learn and what we teach. The part of this activity that we call "reading" has much of the character of a conversation with the ruling texts of the law, and "writing" takes the form of conversation too, between judge and lawyer, among lawyers, between lawyer and client, and so on.

Ashcroft v. Free Speech Coalition: The Case

Let me give an example of what I mean by turning to a somewhat simplified version of an actual case, *Ashcroft v. Free Speech Coalition.*[12] This case involved the validity, under the First Amendment, of a statute passed by Congress in 1996 to prohibit the possession or sale of what is called "virtual" child pornography. The statute, entitled the Child Pornography Prevention Act, is directed both at representations of people having sex who are in fact over the age of majority but look younger and at digitalized images that look like children having sex (usually with adults) but are actually computer creations. In the first case, someone is actually having sex, but he or she is not, as it appears, a child; in the second case, no one is having sex, but the video or photo looks just like a video or photo of a child or children doing so. The statute is thus intended to reach not only movies and photos of children actually having sex but certain representations that look like, perhaps exactly like, children having sex. The language the statute uses to achieve this result prohibits the possession, distribution, sale, or reproduction of "any visual depiction, including any . . . computer-generated image or picture" that "is, or appears to be, of a minor engaging in sexually explicit conduct."[13]

The case arose in an action to enjoin its enforcement brought by certain publishers and film producers and distributors. This procedure was itself somewhat extraordinary, for normally one may challenge a criminal statute only defensively, that is, when one is prosecuted under it. The idea of this requirement is that it will ensure that judicial time is not wasted on hypothetical cases and that, when the matter does come before the court, it is embedded in a factual context that will both shape

---

[12] 535 U.S. 234 (2002).
[13] 18 U.S.C. Section 2256 (8).

and inform the process of reasoning. Where the conduct in question takes the form of speech, however, the Court sometimes permits a potential defendant to attack the statute directly, "on its face," not requiring him to publish and be prosecuted first. The reason for this doctrine, technically called "overbreadth," is that the very existence of a statute that threatens protected speech will lead people who are thinking of speaking or writing on the borderline of protection to refrain from doing so, skating safely away from ice they think might be thin. This results in a "chilling effect" that may interfere both with the legitimate interest of the speaker in uttering protected speech and with the interest of the society as a whole in having it available.

On the other hand, under the overbreadth procedure the case must be decided without the full development of facts. The lawyers do not have actual photos or videos or other materials upon which to base their arguments, and the judges lack the benefit of the development of a full factual record. The case is decided abstractly, the question being, in the jargon of the law, whether the statute is "facially invalid," not whether it is "invalid as applied" to particular facts. As we shall later see, this circumstance will affect the character of the opinion and perhaps the outcome of the case.

1.

How should this case be thought about and argued? What are the critical issues, and how should they be analyzed?

To start with, it is obvious that one cannot find the answer to the question of the statute's validity in any simple way "in" the First Amendment itself. The amendment's language could of course be regarded as "plain," but that position would be highly artificial and conclusory, as a moment's thought will show. In this case, for example, one side might focus on the plain meaning of the word "speech" and argue that the term obviously does not reach purely filmic representations at all; the other side would focus on the language declaring that Congress may "make no law abridging the freedom of speech" and argue that this creates an absolute right to self-expression that cannot in any way be curtailed by the state. Both conceptions of the First Amendment have in fact been argued, but as a matter of our history, both have been rejected. No one now thinks that the amendment is limited to words or that the right it defines is absolute.

In the present case, then, the language of the amendment does little or nothing to resolve the dispute as to its interpretation. It just sits there, as

Plato says, reiterating itself and unable to respond to the questions we have of it. As readers, we are very likely to have strong instinctive feelings about the merits, feelings that are not shaped by the legal materials but arise from within ourselves: that of course child pornography of all kinds ought to be beyond the protection of the First Amendment, for example, or that of course it would be wrong to prohibit the publication of any text or film that did not inflict actual injury directly on actual human beings. The reality of such strong and opposed feelings in the audience and in the Court is part of the material with which the opinion should ultimately work.

But in the law we have more than the language of the First Amendment and our strong reactions to the issue: we have the cases decided under it, which together create what might be called a culture of argument, a way of thinking and talking, that one can learn and use. If you were to examine the relevant part of our tradition, you would find something like the following. It has been agreed by nearly everyone on the Court for fifty years that "obscene" forms of erotic representation are simply beyond the protection of the First Amendment. After some period of uncertainty as to the proper test for the definition of "obscenity," the Court in *Miller v. California*[14] pronounced the following rule, which is still regarded as the law: speech is "obscene," and beyond First Amendment protection, only if it appeals to the "prurient interest"—that is, if it is sexually arousing; if it represents sexual activity in a way that is patently offensive in light of community standards; and if it lacks serious literary, artistic, political, or scientific value. None of these terms is given much definition, either in *Miller* or in subsequent cases, in part because the question of "patent offensiveness under community standards" is held to be a question of fact for the jury, and thus reviewable only for unreasonableness. On the face of it the statute at issue here fails to meet the *Miller* test for "obscenity," because it does not require "prurient interest" or absence of expressive value, and because it determines offensiveness not in a case-by-case way under "community standards," but by a conclusive statutory presumption against any depiction that "is, or appears to be, of a minor engaging in sexually explicit conduct."

But *Miller* does not deal with child pornography, as this statute does, and in *New York v. Ferber*[15] the Court held that the *Miller* requirements

[14] 413 U.S. 15 (1973).
[15] 458 U.S. 747 (1982).

did not apply to photographs of children having sex. The obvious reason is that the state's interest in protecting against this kind of child abuse outweighs whatever marginal expressive value such photos might be thought to have, and does so whether or not they appeal to the prurient interest and whether or not some literary, artistic, political, or scientific value can be claimed for them.[16] Photos of children having sex with adults, or each other, that appeared in a scientific journal or social work textbook would thus be unprotected, and rightly so. For sex with children is a serious crime of undoubted constitutionality, and the state is entitled to punish the possession, sale, and distribution of photographs of that crime.

But this situation leaves open the following problem, to which the Child Pornography Prevention Act is addressed: What if a pornographer produces a movie of two people having sex, one of whom is actually over the age of eighteen but looks much younger? Or suppose a pornographer makes use of computer technology to produce a movie with digitalized effects to make it look as though a child were having sex with an adult, or with other children, though in fact no such act took place? (Assume that no real child's face is used.) Are these productions punishable only if they meet the *Miller* standard, or can they be punished outright as the statute attempts to do?

2.

There is no obvious right answer under the cases. The Court must decide whether the right of the state to suppress child pornography is limited to representations of actual children actually having sex or whether some simulations are punishable as well. This is itself a challenging question: If no children are actually involved in sexual conduct, why should the representation be beyond First Amendment protection? Is the argument that the availability of simulated child pornography would lead to acts and patterns of sexual abuse? With what degree of certainty must the state establish this? Or is simulated child pornography itself directly punishable as a moral evil? Or is it punishable perhaps because it would be deeply disturbing to people of normal sensibilities and will as a matter of practical fact be inflicted on unwilling viewers? (If that is the rationale, is the state entitled only to prohibit such infliction, not possession or production?) Or

---

[16] It may also be a factor that proof of "prurience" is more difficult where the material appeals to a perverted sexuality of a kind that the judge and jury will usually not share with the users of the material, at least not in an intense enough form to make it clear to them what the material means to those who use it.

consider this possible argument in support of the statute. If technology can make the digitalized process so realistic that one cannot tell whether action in the film was simulated or real, it will be far more difficult to prosecute those who produce films of actual sexual exploitation because it will be hard or impossible to demonstrate whether any particular film is real or simulated. Can technology in fact do this? If so, is that a reason for construing the First Amendment more restrictively in this field?

In addition to all these questions there is another: What weight should the Court give, or should regard itself as required to give, to judgments made by others, especially, in this case, judgments made by the United States Congress? To what extent, for example, do answers to the questions raised above properly depend upon estimates of social facts and probabilities that Congress can make much more reliably than the Court? (An example would be the judgment that "virtual" child pornography, in which no child is actually injured, is likely to lead to the molestation and abuse of real children.) And, to return to the overbreadth aspect of this case: Is the Court right to think of this as a case that can be decided in the abstract, as it were, in order to prevent the chilling effect the statute would create if left on the books until an actual case arose, or should the Court require, as it normally does, the elements of a full case and controversy based upon an actual dispute on particular facts?

To think still more broadly, there is at work here the basic First Amendment question how the reasons for according special protection to the activity of speech bear upon virtual child pornography. Is the amendment to be read as resting on a faith in a marketplace of ideas, a sense that freedom of speech is essential to democracy or to autonomy, a deep skepticism as to our capacity to make reliable judgments of value in this field, or what? If freedom of speech is normally to be valued so highly, why should there be an exception for certain kinds of erotic expression, and how should that exception be defined?[17] What bearing should our answers to these questions have on child pornography of the kind defined by the statute?

---

[17] Beyond such questions as these are those relating to the control of obscenity, or pornography, in the first place. On what view of the First Amendment, and the value of speech, should one ever be permitted to produce and sell pictures of people actually having sex, including adults, at least where there is no other evident purpose or value to the film? Why, for example, is this not a kind of aiding and abetting prostitution? It is sex for money: the only difference is that in the usual prostitution case it is one of the parties to the sex act who pays, whereas here it is a third party who hopes to profit from it.

In a legal composition addressing this case, whether a lawyer's brief or judge's opinion, these questions should all be considered, and not in isolation but in an important way together. For the good lawyer recognizes that a case is not a collection of discrete issues, each of which can be addressed and answered in the abstract, but an opportunity for complex and interactive thought about the decision of a whole case. The task of a lawyer or judge is to create a text that does justice to the importance of each issue, and to the force of arguments both ways, and also weaves the issues together into an order or shape that has a meaning of its own, the ultimate point of which is to explain why this or that result is the right one, under considerations both of law and justice. This is the life to which the case calls the legal mind, and it presents a challenge and opportunity worthy of any mind, any character.

Ashcroft v. Free Speech Coalition: The Opinion

I turn now to the opinion actually written in *Free Speech Coalition*, with the question: How far does the opinion rendered here realize the hopes we can have for such a moment, such an occasion? To what kind of conversation does it call us? Since this is a First Amendment case, we can also ask of it a series of more particular questions arising from that fact. How does this opinion imagine the activity of speech itself, and its value? How does it imagine the First Amendment, its purposes and meaning? How does it imagine and justify its own role, both in relation to Congress and to the reader? How does it define the value of speech performatively, in its writing, in the conversation it establishes with its reader? In all of these contexts we can ask whether it trivializes speech, and the Constitution, and its own role and that of its reader, or finds a way to conceive of these things in a way that gives them value and dignity.

1.

As I said earlier, the key provision of the statute prohibits "any visual depiction," including films, photographs, videos, and computer-generated images, that "is, or appears to be, of a minor engaging in sexually explicit conduct."[18] The phrase "sexually explicit conduct" is defined in the statute as "actual or simulated . . . sexual intercourse, including

---

[18] 18 U.S.C. Section 2256 (8).

genital-genital, oral-genital, anal-genital, or oral-anal, whether between persons of the same or opposite sex; . . . bestiality; . . . masturbation; . . . sadistic or masochistic abuse; . . . or lascivious exhibition of the genitals or pubic area of any person."[19]

There are, as usual, two questions: How should the statute be interpreted? So read, is it constitutional?

With respect to the first question, the opinion of the Court, by Justice Anthony Kennedy, observes that the statute does not require that the offending depiction appeal to the prurient interest, lack serious social value, or patently offend community standards, as required by *Miller.* The statute would reach images that did not appeal to the prurient interest, the Court goes on, such as those appearing in a "psychology manual" or a movie depicting the "horrors of sexual abuse." It would prohibit representations that would not violate community standards, for example some "pictures of what appear to be 17-year-olds engaging in sexually explicit activity." And it might prohibit speech that had serious value, for example certain imagined productions of *Romeo and Juliet,* or the movies *American Beauty* and *Traffic.* The Court tells us that the "literal terms" of the statute would "embrace a Renaissance painting depicting a scene from classical mythology."

With respect to the constitutionality of the statute so construed, the Court holds that the *Miller* standards do indeed apply and strikes down the statute, rejecting the argument that this situation should be treated differently (under *Ferber*) because it involves representations of children. The Court says that the reason for the outcome in *Ferber* was that in that case real children were actually involved in the sexual activity that was the subject of the offending photographs. Accordingly, "the fact that a work contained serious literary, artistic, or other value did not excuse the harm it caused to its child participants." In *Free Speech Coalition,* by contrast, the statute is designed to reach depictions that do not involve actual children engaged in actual sexual conduct. Therefore *Miller,* not *Ferber,* governs the case and requires the Court to invalidate the statute.

This all makes a certain kind of sense, but the opinion is nonetheless a real disappointment, and this is so whether or not one ultimately agrees with its outcome. For it does not really consider any of the large issues the case seems to present: why the First Amendment protects speech in the first place, why "obscenity" is unprotected, how the statute should

[19] 18 U.S.C. Section 2256 (2).

be interpreted in light of the evils against which it is directed, whether the costs of the injunction procedure authorized by the overbreadth doctrine outweigh its benefits in this case, whether *Miller* or *Ferber* ought to be in any way reconsidered, and what weight ought to be given the determination by Congress that the kind of depiction it prohibits is likely to stimulate or facilitate actual child molestation and abuse. Instead, *Miller* is reduced to its rule, requiring prurient interest, patent offensiveness, and lack of redeeming value; *Ferber* is reduced to its facts, which involved photographs of actual sexual conduct (in this case masturbation) by real children; and the whole process is reduced to a mechanistic matching of the facts of the case to prior texts, the meaning of each of which is assumed to be plain and to say the same thing always.

a.

Let us first consider the statutory issue raised in *Free Speech Coalition*. Ought the statute be read to reach the movies, plays, Renaissance paintings, and pictures in psychology manuals of which the Court speaks? It is true that the statute does not in explicit terms require the three elements of the *Miller* test—prurience, lack of value, and contravention of community standards—but might it not be possible, and perhaps correct, to read the operative language as reaching only depictions that in fact meet those requirements? This is the argument in essence advanced by Chief Justice William Rehnquist in dissent, and it has merit.

The technical question is the meaning of the phrase "appears to be" in the statutory language, "is, or appears to be, of a minor engaging in sexually explicit conduct," and the word "simulated" in the definition of sexually explicit conduct as "actual or simulated . . . sexual intercourse." It would be possible to read this language to reach, as the Court does, a movie in which minors are shown wrestling erotically under a blanket ("simulated" sex) or a person plainly over the age of eighteen actually having sex but pretending to be a child ("appears to be" a minor). But you could also read both provisions, and the statute as whole, as reaching only representations that are virtually indistinguishable from depictions of actual minors actually engaging in the prohibited sexual acts. With respect to sexual intercourse, for example, on this reading the statute would not reach blanket wrestling, or an innuendo plainly meant to suggest that the teenage lovers had sex offstage, but only representations of actual sexual intercourse by persons who are visually indistinguishable from minors.[20] The force of "simulated" would only be to say that physical penetration would not be required, so long as the effect of the depiction was indistinguishable from actual sex; and the force of "appears to be" would be to say that the statute reaches only cases in which the visual representation is indistinguishable from actual children actually having sex.

The statute can, not surprisingly, be read either way—it does not say the same thing always—and a responsible opinion would seek to justify its interpretation, not just to assert or assume it as the Court does. The Court does not support its reading by reference to the purpose and tenor and language and context of the statute; rather, it claims to be reading its "literal terms," though the dissent directly challenges the majority on the point. This is a failure to engage with the central problem of meaning that the statute presents. Perhaps the Court is right, perhaps the dissent, but in any event the Court has not discharged its responsibility to read the statute in a comprehensive way; the opinion does not call the reader to life, inviting her to face complexity and importance, but simply tells her how things are, on the assumption that the language of the statute has a plain and obvious meaning that says the same thing always. In this it is a performance of the empire of force.

The reasoning of the opinion and its writing have throughout a certain thinness, a sense that words are being replicated, or moved about on the page, without real thought. Think back for example to the "Renaissance painting depicting a scene from classical mythology," which the Court said the "literal terms" of the statute would embrace. But the Court says nothing to specify the images it is imagining in this hypothetical painting, which could be relatively modest or extremely explicit. Rather, in an unexamined way it seems to be trying to enlist the prestige of Renaissance painting to support its as yet unarticulated view of this case.[21] Or

---

[20] 535 U.S. 234, 269 (Rehnquist, C.J., dissenting): "Read as a whole, however, I think the definition reaches only the sort of 'hard core of child pornography' that we found without protection in *Ferber*, 485 U.S. at 773–774. So construed, the CPPA bans visual depictions of youthful looking adult actors engaged in actual sexual activity; mere suggestions of sexual activity, such as youthful looking adult actors squirming under a blanket, are more akin to written descriptions than visual depictions, and thus fall outside the purview of the statue."

[21] The use of the word "literal" is a giveaway, for here, as usual, it obscures the fact that a claim is being made about the meaning of the language, a claim that like all such claims needs to be justified; the vagueness of the image referred to makes the claim all the more unreasoned.

consider its instances of pictures that might appear in a "psychology manual" or in a movie depicting the horrors of sexual abuse. But what kind of "psychology manual" would present images of children having sex with each other or with adults? And who is to say that such images would not stimulate the destructive erotic response covered by the phrase "prurient interest"?[22] As for the horror movie supposedly intended to portray the horrors of child abuse, could that not have the effect of legitimizing what it seems to oppose? Indeed the makers could even have such an intention. Think of tobacco advertisements, allegedly designed to dissuade children from smoking, but which according to at least one study have the opposite effect, namely to encourage them.[23] The examples given by the Court are presented as though they will be clarifying and persuasive, but they are in fact unspecific images that have not been thought about, let alone thought through. They are the equivalent of slogans or clichés.

b.

The Court's treatment of the constitutional question in *Free Speech Coalition* has a similar mechanical and forced quality. Of course *Ferber* involved a case in which actual children were engaged in actual sex, and this presents obvious evils that the material at issue here does not; it also true that the Court there indicated that if an artist were prevented by that case from producing something of real value, simulation of some sort might be a solution.[24] But it is plain that the Court in *Ferber* did not think very much about the kind of situation the present statute addresses, which has to do with the bearing of the First Amendment on "virtual" child pornography. While both *Miller* and *Ferber* can help us to think about that question, in neither case did the Court really address it. This means that in *Free Speech Coalition* the Court should not slavishly follow

[22] Is the Court here saying that the test of prurience is not effect but intention? If so, why should that be? Perhaps it is the right rule, but the Court gives us no reasons to support it.

[23] See Matthew Farrelly et al., "Getting to the Truth: Evaluating National Tobacco Countermarketing Campaigns," *American Journal of Public Health* 92 (2002): 901.

[24] 458 U.S. 747, 763. The Court said: "A state judge in this case observed, if it were necessary for literary or artistic value, a person over the statutory age who perhaps looked younger could be utilized. Simulation outside of the prohibition of the statute could provide another alternative."

the rules of those cases, as it understands them, any more than it should slavishly read the statute. It should think freshly about the First Amendment, and the cases interpreting it, in the new context of this statute and the issues it addresses, and this it does not do.

The mechanistic quality of the Court's mode of thought leads among other things to blindness to the genuine human problem at which the legislation is aimed: the terrible wrong of sexual abuse of children, and the ways in which that practice can acquire legitimacy, indeed become eroticized, through publications and movies, whether or not they meet all of the criteria of *Miller*. Perhaps the First Amendment should be read to tolerate that damage, but the harm should not be erased, as it is throughout the opinion, with the use of legal clichés like "the prospect of crime . . . does not justify laws suppressing protected speech"[25]—a phrase that of course buries its conclusion in its premise that the statute would reach "protected speech."

c.

A fundamental question presented by *Free Speech Coalition*, and not addressed by the Court, is whether some forms of speech can be prohibited or controlled not because of their tendency to produce physical or even psychological injury but because they themselves in some way corrupt or pollute the public mind and world. Racism and anti-Semitism do this, one could argue, and so may pornography, especially pornography involving children or the images of children, for it stimulates a way of imagining life, of directing one's erotic desires, of thinking of others, that is fundamentally corrupt. Milder forms of this corruption can of course be found throughout our advertising culture, which works on the assumption that human happiness and fulfillment are not to be found in meaningful engagement of person with person, or in human action directed at significant ends, but in the use of the productions or person of another to gratify one's desires, whatever they may be. But the fact that we tolerate one form of this evil does not mean that we are compelled to tolerate it in all forms. What would happen if we were to think of the kind of child pornography protected here as a kind of advertising, that is, as the simultaneous stimulation of desire for and legitimation of actual child abuse? Has this argument no force? Businesspeople certainly

---

[25] 535 U.S. 234, 245

think advertising works in other contexts, from soft drinks to fast food to autos and tobacco and real estate firms, and the Court need not close its eyes to such effects.

At work in the opinion here is the unexamined assumption that speech can only be controlled if it injures or threatens an interest independently recognized by the law, such as that of bodily integrity, reputation, or economic value. This assumption is widespread, and perhaps the Court is not to be faulted for not taking it on. On the other hand, the representations involved here—images of child pornography that look real but are not—present perhaps as strong a case for rethinking it as anything we could name. The question is whether the Court should recognize that some speech can inflict some serious harms that do not injure such established "interests" but are nonetheless of first importance. This would mean recognizing that some evils are peculiar to speech, just as some good things are, and that these evils might justify regulation even where more traditional nonspeech analysis would see "no harm." Here the Court would recognize that images that appear to be of children engaged in explicit sexual conduct are not themselves valuable speech; that they are produced for sexual use, not for their meaning; and that the moral consequence of a widespread acceptance of the taste or preference for these images could be a serious and sustained corruption of mind and feelings.[26] Their meaning is death, not life. Some might say that the judgments this course of action and thought would require are impossible for the Court to make, but I do not think that is so. In refusing even to think about these questions, the Court in effect erases the entire world of the imagination as of no consequence or significance—though it is the imagination that gives any facts, or harms, or actions their meaning.

Of course the Court might after thought conclude that "virtual" child pornography, in some of its forms, is protected speech, and it could reach the same conclusion about racist speech as well. But that is not the only possibility. Other democratic and civilized governments restrict racist speech without giving up on free expression as a deep social norm and value, and might well do the same with "virtual" child pornography. Maybe we are right not to do these things, but if so, at least the hazards

---

[26] I am assuming here that the depictions were not merely suggestive but actually showed minors, or those who appeared to be minors, actually engaged in sexual relations of the sort prohibited by the statute, or in activities that appear to be actual sexual relations. The blanket scene, the embrace on a bed, would of course not be included.

of the course we have chosen should be honestly addressed, not brushed aside with slogans.[27]

The Court does not face such questions in a grown-up and responsible way. Instead, in this part of its opinion and indeed throughout it engages in analysis at the level of what I call formula or cliché. It is the stuff of law school outlines, not a distinguished judicial opinion. Think of this sentence, for example: "The prospect of crime . . . does not by itself justify laws suppressing protected speech." Of course not: but the questions here are whether this speech is or is not protected and why, questions the formulaic language evades. Or: "As a general principle, the First Amendment bars the government from dictating what we see or read or speak or hear." Of course, of course; who would say otherwise? Or: "It is also well established that speech may not be prohibited because it concerns subjects offending our sensibilities." Or: "The Government cannot ban speech fit for adults simply because it may fall into the hands of children." Or: "The mere tendency of speech to encourage unlawful acts is not a sufficient reason for banning it." Or: "The Government may not suppress lawful speech as the means to suppress unlawful speech."[28] Or think again of the unargued conclusion with which the opinion disposes of *Ferber*. "*Ferber*'s judgment about child pornography was based upon how it was made, not on what it communicated."

There is here an absence of thought, a reduction of analysis to the

[27] The Court should also have thought about its relation to the other actors in the legal world, especially to Congress. What weight should it give the congressional judgment that the kind of depictions prohibited by this statute will encourage child molestation by stimulating corrupt desires and making their gratification seem imaginable and legitimate? Or that this kind of child pornography presents the danger that it will be used to seduce children? Or that technology has advanced to the point, or soon will, where it can produce completely digitalized pictures that are visually indistinguishable from actual films of actual molestation? (As I said above, the danger is that prosecution for actual films will be made more difficult, because offenders can make the claim, hard to disprove, that their films are only "virtual" images of this sexual crime, not actual images.) Determining the proper degree of deference is a difficult matter, but it is important that the Court engage in the process, especially when it strikes down a federal statute, as it does here. For the legitimacy of its exercise of the power of judicial review depends not upon any explicit provision in the Constitution but on the quality and fairness of its reasoning, especially with respect to its relation to an equal branch of the federal government.

[28] In one sense this sentence is a truism, but it is also misleading, for the judgment as to whether speech is protected is normally not made in the abstract but in a particular situation; what is permissible in one place or context is often not permissible in another.

empty and mechanical, that is all too familiar to law teachers; the opinion presents a plausible surface, but does not come to terms with the fact that the task of the lawyer and judge is to think responsibly about difficult problems, a kind of thinking that cannot be reduced to imitation or to the manipulation of forms. What this opinion does here matters, a very great deal, for it enacts an image of speech, and of the First Amendment, that is empty and trivializing. Instead of calling the reader into life and thought of a deep and engaged kind about the First Amendment, about obscenity and pornography, about the relation between the Court and Congress, and about the propriety of the overbreadth procedure in general and in this instance, it calls us to a kind of death and thoughtlessness. In erasing the life of the law, and the mind of the reader, it erases at the same time the social reality with which it deals: the life-scarring experience of child abuse; the corruption of forms of expression that stimulate, validate, and authorize it; and the judgments of the legislators, and their constituents, that lie behind the statute. It defines law, and the Constitution, as a set of rigid and basically empty phrases.

2.

In the shading and nuance of its language the *Free Speech Coalition* opinion is even more disturbing than I have suggested. Consider the following, asking yourself first with which of these assertions you, or anyone, would disagree, then why you think they are included in this opinion:

> The statute proscribes the visual depiction of an idea—that of teenagers engaging in sexual activity—that is a fact of modern society and has been a theme of art and literature throughout the ages. . . . It is, of course, undeniable that some youths engage in sexual activity before the legal age, either on their own inclination or because they are the victims of sexual abuse.
>
> Both themes—teenage sexual activity and the sexual abuse of children—have inspired countless literary works. William Shakespeare created the most famous pair of teenage lovers, one of whom is just 13 years of age. In the drama, Shakespeare portrays the relationship as something splendid and innocent, but not juvenile. The work has inspired no less than 40 motion pictures, some of which suggest that the teenagers consummated their relationship. Shakespeare may not have written sexually explicit scenes for the Elizabethan audience, but were modern directors to adopt a less conventional approach, that fact alone would not compel the conclusion that the work was obscene.

Contemporary movies pursue similar themes. Last year's Academy Awards featured the movie, Traffic, which was nominated for Best Picture. The film portrays a teenager, identified as a 16-year-old, who becomes addicted to drugs. The viewer sees the degradation of her addiction, which in the end leads her to a filthy room to trade sex for drugs. The year before, American Beauty won the Academy Award for Best Picture. In the course of the movie, a teenage girl engages in sexual relations with her teenage boyfriend, and another yields herself to the gratification of a middle-aged man. The film also contains a scene where, although the movie audience understands the act is not taking place, one character believes he is watching a teenage boy performing a sexual act on an older man.[29]

The Court's remark that one of the lovers in Romeo and Juliet was "just 13 years of age," while true in the imagined world of that play, seems to be included as a way of suggesting that at least some films of thirteen-year-old girls graphically simulating sex, or films of people who are in appearance and presentation (though not in fact) no older engaging in actual sex, would be constitutionally protected from legislative control by our Constitution, and that Shakespeare himself would have approved. When the opinion says that while Shakespeare may not have written "sexually explicit scenes," and goes on to argue that a "less conventional approach" ought not be automatically beyond the protection of the First Amendment, it seems not merely to protect but to validate or authorize not only "sexually explicit scenes" but such scenes involving girls the presumed age of Juliet. The phrase "less conventional approach" establishes a coy and allusive relation with its reader, working as a kind of verbal wink that hints at unnamed but delicious possibilities.[30] Compare the sentence later in the opinion: "The second flaw in the Government's position is that *Ferber* did not hold that child pornography is by definition without value." At the end of the passage quoted above, the Court goes on to

[29] *Ashcroft v. Free Speech Coalition*, 535 U.S. 234, 246–48 (citations omitted.) Look at the first sentence: "The statute proscribes the visual depiction of an idea—that of teenagers engaging in sexual activity—that is a fact of modern society and has been a theme in art and literature throughout the ages." But the kind of exhibition with which the statute is concerned is the visual presentation of sexually explicit conduct by minors. To call this an "idea" is to erase the whole world of the image, of the performative, of art itself, in an uncomprehending way. Is all "speech" the communication of "ideas"?

[30] The statute of course does not purport to punish a "less conventional approach" but only depictions meeting the statutory standard.

say: "Our society, like other cultures, has empathy and enduring fascination with the lives and destinies of the young." Ask yourself this: Exactly how does that sentence function in this opinion that strikes down the Child Pornography Prevention Act?

3.

What I miss most of all in this opinion is the presence of a mind actually engaged with a difficult problem of understanding and judgment. The opinion reads, as I suggest above, rather like a brief, identifying the contentions of the Department of Justice in defense of the statute only to knock them down. But this is a difficult and important case, presenting serious questions regarding the relation between the Court and Congress, the nature and ground of judicial review, the meaning of the First Amendment, the propriety of categorical reasoning, and the evils of pornography, especially of child pornography. Yet it reads like an empty exercise, a law school memo or moot court brief, in which nothing, absolutely nothing, is talked about as if it mattered—to the writer, to the reader, or to anyone else. Left out entirely are the children who may suffer life-destroying trauma as a result of it.

The opinion makes the whole process in which it is involved seem easy, mechanical, boring. No one could mean this kind of thing; and no one could read it with any interest except an interest in pathology, for it is written without interest. It is, to say the least, not written out of silence, out of the silent place within, nor is it written to the silent and thoughtful part of its reader.

To return to the first topic discussed above in connection with this case, the overbreadth doctrine, it may be that the Court's biggest mistake was to hold that doctrine applicable at all. If the Court had waited for a real case, it would have been much harder to dispose of it in this mechanistic way, as though it were only a law school hypothetical. The Court would have had before it actual films against which the state had chosen to proceed, and it would have been far harder to treat the whole business in this airy and abstract way. What of the "chilling effect" of a decision to wait? If only those publications consisting of borderline child pornography would realistically be deterred it is hard to see this as a major First Amendment loss.

There is a more general point as well. As *Virginia Pharmacy Board* used the First Amendment to protect what are really economic interests, a case like *Free Speech Coalition* can be read to use the First Amendment to protect what is really an interest not in speech but in sexual privacy or autonomy, and so can what might be called the "naked dancing" cases.[31] A similar point can be made about *Buckley v. Valeo*,[32] which struck down the federal campaign finance law on First Amendment grounds, for this is really a case about the use of wealth to influence elections, not a speech case. In my view it depreciates and trivializes both the First Amendment itself and the kind of meaningful speech it should be read to protect when it conceives of commercial advertising, commercial sex shows, and the spending of money for elections as lying within the purview of the First Amendment. One of the major aims of this book is to suggest a way of thinking about speech and its value that would help the Court and its critics read the First Amendment with an eye to what is distinctive about the activity of "speech" that the amendment protects: not speech as commodity, or speech as information, or speech as spending, or speech as sexual arousal, or speech offered for use in other ways, but speech as the way in which human beings seek to claim meaning for their experience and to establish trusting relations with others.

It may for many reasons be wrong for the Court to uphold congressional efforts to suppress speech, even pretty poisonous speech, simply on the grounds that the speech in question is thought by the Court to be evil. But there is no reason for the Court not to make every effort to attain the highest quality of speech in its own work, and thus to establish something of a standard by which other forms of speech may be judged. The trivializing force of the opinion in *Free Speech Coalition*, and others like it, has the effect of weakening the First Amendment itself, by belittling what can be achieved by speech. It makes it too easy to think of really destructive forms of speech—those that trivialize human experience and capacity—as not so bad after all, for such is the effect of this opinion. If the First Amendment calls upon us to tolerate what this statute

[31] See *Barnes v. Glen Theatre, Inc.*, 501 U.S. 560 (1991), and *City of Erie v. Pap's A.M.*, 529 U.S. 277 (2000), in both of which the Court, while upholding restrictions on nude public dancing, stated that this form of activity had at least some value of the kind protected by the First Amendment. But what would that value be? To speak loosely about the expressive nature of the art form we call dance hardly addresses the situation of women stripping naked in order to display their bodies to men drinking in a bar. The *Barnes* Court speaks of an "erotic message," 501 U.S. at 570, but is there any self-expression here at all, and if so, on the part of whom? The women earning their living this way? The bar owner? Is there any political statement? This seems rather to be simply a form of virtual prostitution, the sale of the sight of a body for purposes of sexual arousal.

[32] 424 U.S. 1 (1976).

prohibits, let that judgment be made in an opinion that recognizes the evil of the speech protected, and counters it by calling upon the dignity and self-respect of its readers. It is possible for writing in the law, as in other fields, to call the reader into life, life with language and life with other people, and hence into a world in which love and justice are possibilities. It can resist the forces of death and empire—of advertising and propaganda, of cliché and commodification—by insisting upon a kind of speech that speaks from person to person, mind to mind, and recognizes that in all our language uses we are claiming meaning for the experience of ourselves, and others, meaning for which we are responsible.

GUIDO DA MONTEFELTRO

In a passage in Canto XXVII of the *Inferno*, Dante speaks to the question of legal—or legalistic—thought in a particularly rich and compelling way that bears on what I have just said about *Free Speech Coalition*. Here Dante the traveler meets Guido da Montefeltro, a soul who inhabits the same region of hell as Ulysses, that of the false counselors. Like the spirit of Ulysses, Guido's spirit lives embedded within a constantly burning flame.

This is how Guido first tells his story, very succinctly: "I was a man of arms, then wore the cords of a friar," *Io fui uom d'arme, e poi fui cordigliero,* "believing myself, so restrained, to make amends," *credendomi, sì cinto, fare ammenda* (67–68). He is saying, that is, that he led a life of sin as an active soldier and statesman for much of his existence—you can think of your own modern analogues; then he changed course and became a monk, with the idea of making up for what he had done. He does not say anything about exactly what sinful conduct he supposedly repents—the implication is apparently that it is something that somehow naturally goes with the life of arms—or about what kind of "amends" this strategic decision could be thought to make. In fact, as we shall learn, his plan did not work, but—as he sees it—not because of any defect inherent in it but because he was foiled by someone else, the "grand priest," or pope, who seduced him to return to his evil ways. "And my belief would have been fulfilled," *e certo il creder mio venìa intero,* he says, "if it were not for the grand priest, may ill take him! who set me back to my first sins," *se non fosse il gran prete, a cui mal prenda! / che mi rimise ne le prime colpe* (70–71).

After this summary of his story, he tells it more fully. In life "my works were not those of the lion, but of the fox; I mastered all wiles and secret ways, so well that the fame of them went out through all the earth. When I reached the age when a man should furl his sails, I made myself penitent and confessed."[33] (Is this a real confession and repentance? We do not know, but in what follows it still sounds as though it were purely strategic.) "Alas for me, this would have worked," but for Pope Boniface, the prince of the Pharisees. "He needed my counsel to win a local war against Penestrino and asked for my assistance, telling me not to mistrust him, *tuo cuor non sospetti.* 'I absolve you from this moment, if you teach me how to throw Penestrino to the ground,' *finor t'assolvo, e tu m'insegna fare / sì come Penestrino in terra getti* (100–102). 'I have the keys that lock and unlock Heaven, as you know.' Pushed by these arguments to a place where silence seemed the worst, *là 've 'l tacer mi fu avviso 'l peggio,* I said, 'Father, since you wash me of the sin into which I must fall, *Padre, da che tu mi lavi / di quel peccato ov' io mo cader deggio,* I will give you my advice, which is: long promise and short performance, *lunga promessa con l'attender corto,* will give you what you want' " (107–10).

Guido's twice-told story, then, is that he had successfully confessed and repented his sinful life, and would have been saved had the pope not seduced him into sin once more by his promise of absolution—a promise reinforced by the implicit threat in the pope's claim to have the power to lock as well as to unlock heaven. Guido believes, that is, that the pope has the power both to admit and to exclude him from heaven. But both positions are wrong, as Guido should have known. Salvation cannot be bought or bargained for; it is the work of each individual soul to struggle towards it. In yielding to the claims of the pope, Guido was submitting

---

[33]   *Mentre ch'io forma fui d'ossa e di polpe*
    che la madre mi diè, l'opere mie
    non furon leonine, ma di volpe.
    Li accorgimenti e le coperte vie
    io seppi tutte, e sì menai lor arte,
    ch'al fine de la terra il suono uscie.
    Quando mi vidi giunto in quella parte
    di mia etade ove ciascun dovrebbe
    calar le vele e raccoglier le sarte,
    ciò che pria mi piacëa, allor m'increbbe,
    e pentuto e confesso mi rendei;
    ahi miser lasso! e giovato sarebbe.   (XXVII, 73–84)

to the empire of force, and for a reason that is by now familiar to us, that he wished to evade the individual responsibility for judgment that is every human being's simultaneous gift and duty.

When Guido died, he found that Boniface's absolution was of no value. As the fiend who seized him said with impeccable logic: "Who does not repent cannot be absolved; and it is not possible to repent and will [the same wrong deed] at the same time, since the rule against contradictions will not permit it."[34] "I was then sent down here," says Guido, "where now you see me lost, and so robed, *sì vestito*, going in bitterness" (128–29). (He has changed his friar's robes for those of the flame in which he is perpetually punished.)

Guido's view is that it is not really fair that he be punished for the sin of giving Boniface advice to make false promises, since he did this only because he was tricked by Boniface with his false promise of absolution. But this will obviously not work. For one thing, Guido could have repented the false counsel after giving it, instead of relying on the supposed absolution; for another, the counsel itself does not amount to much—it is a cliché of its own; in a way still worse, Boniface shows that he already knows it, and in the most telling way, for he makes to Guido himself a "long promise, with short performance."

What really rankles Guido—and makes him in an earlier passage reluctant to talk, for fear of infamy if the truth be known on earth—is not that he gave the false counsel for which he is punished but that he, the fox, *volpe*, was outfoxed by Boniface. Indeed it may be, since the advice was so redundant, that the whole transaction was a way in which Boniface, to satisfy his own evil and destructive impulses, rather gratuitously, and successfully, secured Guido's damnation.

But this of course does not excuse Guido, who could have repented, had he any real idea what repentance was, what sin was. The real reason he is in the Inferno is the way he imagined the whole world, including the moral and religious law of God. He saw the moral injunctions, enforced by future punishment, as a system of deterrence and incentives, essentially manipulative in kind and inviting a manipulative reading on his part. His reading is not pornographic, like Dante's involvement in the quarrel between Master Adam, the counterfeiter, and Sinon, the false wit-

---

[34] *ch'assolver non si può chi non si pente,*
      né pentere e volere insieme puossi
      per la contradizion che nol consente.   (XXVII, 118–20)

ness, but it shares something with pornography: it is reading for use, not meaning; a reduction of speech and speaker alike to objects to be managed, not an expression of a person to be heard and understood; and this is a perversion of the human mind and spirit as a general matter and a perversion of law in particular. He tells us twice that he thought his stratagem of conversion would have worked, if it had not been for Boniface. But in fact we know it would not have worked, because it was not genuine. He did not repent, did not confess, from his heart, as we know from his conduct after his supposed absolution; these were empty gestures, engaged in to earn him what he thought they would bring. But empty gestures bring only emptiness. To count at all, one must mean what one says. Guido cannot see the meaning of anything that is said to him, nor can be truly mean anything he says. For him the language of sin and repentance is a set of empty phrases, calling him not into a life of thought, and self-examination, and growth—not towards love and justice—but into a kind of legalistic death. This is how he reads what he has been told, and he replicates this understanding—this misunderstanding—in his writing.

Guido's view of the law may remind us of that of the Court in *Free Speech Coalition*: for him it is a set of requirements that have no real subject, no real purpose, no person behind them, and do not call for understanding, thought, and judgment but ask only to be read in "literal terms," and put together in an apparently coherent, but in fact deeply incoherent, whole. For him, as for the Court, the law does not demand or make possible responsible judgment but is to be read as a cluster of empty forms. And it is not only Guido and this opinion that take such a manipulative and strategic view of law; it is in some circles orthodoxy.

In the dramatic scene described above Guido is carried off to the Inferno by a fiend who demonstrates the logical impossibility of Guido's strategic repentance. This is appropriate, for Guido himself has lived by a false logic, putting his trust in a legalistic view of the power of the pope. Yet the reasoning the fiend employs was available to Guido all along, as it is to us, and should have been no surprise at all. It springs nothing new on anyone who thinks in a purposive and substantive way about what should be meant by "repentance." Guido's failure of soul expresses itself in a failure of intellect. This fits with Virgil's prediction at the gates of hell, when he said to Dante the traveler: "We have come to the place of which I have told you, where you will see the miserable people, *le genti dolorose*, who have lost the good of intellect, *c'hanno perduto il ben de l'intelletto*" (III, 17–18).

For Dante the failure of sin is in part a failure of mind, which means that the work of the mind can uncover something of sin's nature and force, and guard against it. This is crucial to understanding the poem's relation to its readers, for the poem assumes that we still have the good of our intellect, can still see the force of reason and can learn from what we see and hear—as Dante the traveler also learns. Thus, at first the reader might look with sympathy on Guido's situation, accepting his legalistic view of the world, and say: If you cannot rely on what the pope tells you, what can you rely upon?[35] The poem's answer is for the purposes of the present book enormously significant: among human things, at least, you can most rely upon being a good reader, a reader of the kind this poem teaches you to become, one who can respond to the call to engage in living conversation with another mind; this requires you to be a good writer as well, one who can create sentences and compositions and gestures that express your mind at its deepest and best and call others into a life you can share. This is what Dante does and shows us how to do.

Guido and Boniface imagine the world as an empire of force and act on its premises. You can see the kind of false, seductive, manipulative conversation that they invite, full of trickery and deceit. Dante calls us to a very different conversational life indeed, of which these pathologies, and their opposites, are the subject, but which itself works in utterly different ways: open, engaged and engaging, corrective and self-corrective, an effort to speak from silences within to silences without, to achieve and manifest the deepest value of speech itself. The question for us, in life and in the law, as people and lawyers and judges, is whether we shall speak in empty, strategic, manipulative ways—ways of death—or find a way to call our readers to a conversation that offers them, and us, life.

---

[35] One might think here also of Queen Semiramis, who appears in the region of the lustful, where we saw Francesca. Semiramis had the power of lawmaking and used it to validate her incest with her son. "She was so broken to the sin of lust that in her law she made what she wanted legal, in order to remove the blame she had incurred" (V, 55–57):

> *A vizio di lussuria fu sì rotta,*
> *che libito fé licito in sua legge,*
> *per tòrre il biasmo in che era condotta.*

But her reliance on the law was of no more effect than Guido's reliance on the pope.

BRANDEIS IN *WHITNEY*

As a kind of antidote to Guido and *Free Speech Coalition* alike, let us turn to a famous passage that sets forth a different vision of speech, a different vision of human life. This is Justice Louis Brandeis in *Whitney v. California*:[36]

> Those who won our independence believed that the final end of the State was to make men free to develop their faculties; and that in its government the deliberative forces should prevail over the arbitrary. They valued liberty both as an end and as a means. They believed liberty to be the secret of happiness and courage to be the secret of liberty. They believed that freedom to think as you will and to speak as you think are means indispensable to the discovery and spread of political truth; that without free speech and assembly discussion would be futile; that with them, discussion affords ordinarily adequate protection against the dissemination of noxious doctrine; that the greatest menace to freedom is an inert people; that public discussion is a political duty; and that this should be a fundamental principle of the American government. They recognized the risks to which all human institutions are subject. But they knew that order cannot be secured merely through fear of punishment for its infraction; that it is hazardous to discourage thought, hope and imagination; that fear breeds repression; that repression breeds hate; that hate menaces stable government; that the path of safety lies in the opportunity to discuss freely supposed grievances and proposed remedies; and that the fitting remedy for evil counsels is good ones. Believing in the power of reason as applied through public discussion, they eschewed silence coerced by law—the argument of force in its worst form. Recognizing the occasional tyrannies of governing majorities, they amended the Constitution so that free speech and assembly should be guaranteed.[37]

Brandeis here invokes the framers nearly as demigods, confidently asserting what they thought and meant by the First Amendment itself. From one point of view this is a kind of fantasy, for we know that the framers were not superhuman beings, that they were not united but divided in their attitudes, that in any event the society out of which they

---

[36] 274 U.S. 357 (1927).
[37] *Id.* at 375–76 (citations omitted).

functioned was unjust, and so on. From another point of view, however, this act of imagination or something like it really is essential to the task of lawmaking that is the Court's responsibility. For the words of the text alone do not mean much, nor do they carry much force even if understood; the kind of knowledge we need includes the capacity to imagine the author of the text, and ourselves, in such a way as to make possible an intelligent reading of the text itself, and this is an act of creation.

The heart of Brandeis's achievement here is to imagine the First Amendment as based upon the recognition that speech as such can have unique value, both in the life of individual people and in the life of the community as a whole. He imagines the world as made of people speaking to each other, and speaking well; at stake are the deepest qualities of the human being—"thought, hope, and imagination"—and the deepest qualities of democratic communal life as well, in which the "fitting remedy for evil counsels is good ones." The First Amendment for Brandeis is not based upon a radical skepticism, as it is, say, for Holmes—a sense of the impermanence of value—but upon an image of human life as thoughtful, expressive, engaged in the individual and collective effort to claim meaning for experience, and finding a permanent value in what that image represents.

Brandeis does not merely say these things, he enacts them before our eyes. Take the structure of the two long sentences at the center of the quoted paragraph, for example: they are built as a string of clauses connected by semicolons, a style that gives a sense of connectedness and sequence among different thoughts, or different aspects of the same thought. Not as in a logical outline, in which one first asserts premises then deduces conclusions, nor in the usual inductive structure, in which one first presents factual details then asserts a conclusion that flows from them. Rather, Brandeis is showing what it is like to think, as a whole mind, all at once, the way we really do think. What he says is not reducible to a tag—say, "the education for democracy rationale" of the First Amendment—nor is it translatable into a series of propositions set forth as a theory. The words work here the way they do in ordinary speech and literature alike, not by the stipulated definitions necessary for a certain kind of rationality but in a process of continual and reciprocal redefinition. Speech, and safety, and fear, and hatred, and reason, and discussion, and government, all these terms interact to create a whole language, a way of talking and thinking.

It is a language we can learn, but not by simply repeating the phrases, just as we cannot simply point to the passage with a word or two or think of it as a theory in the form of a set of propositions. We must make it our own, and in doing so we shall change it. For this passage is written in Brandeis's own voice, alive, speaking the truth as he sees it; not in clichés, or in forms simply lifted from the past, or from others, but as a writer does these things, transforming the materials he has inherited; and it invites us to do these things too. This passage enacts or performs its meaning; it represents to us, in the way it captures the movements of the mind of the writer, what it means to engage in the kind of thought and speech he describes and in the processes of self-government through discussion that he celebrates. It cannot be translated into other terms, and its meaning lies in large part in that fact—in what an attempted translation would leave out or distort. It calls upon us to speak not by repeating his words, but by doing in our own way what he has done; it invites us to assume the responsibilities he has assumed, for conceiving of the value of speech at its best and for demonstrating that value, as far as we can, in our own expression. The life to which it calls us is a writer's life.

One way to read this opinion is as giving Brandeis—and us—a certain kind of character, one that is secure in its education, its intellectual capacities, its depth and breadth of mind, and therefore has no fear of speech that does not meet its standards.[38] Brandeis is using his mind to make him and us strong, unafraid, able to face and live with what we despise—with what we are right to despise; part of the strength of what he achieves lies in the confidence with which he asserts his commitment to the mode of life and thought he enacts.

[38] See Vincent Blasi, "The First Amendment and the Ideal of Civic Courage: The Brandeis Opinion in *Whitney v. California*," *William and Mary Law Review* 29 (1988): 653.

ⱳ

Human Dignity and the Claim of Meaning

Athenian tragedy and the judicial opinion compared; Aeschylus,
The Oresteia and The Persians; Sophocles, Oedipus at Colonus and
the Ajax; Justice Harlan in Cohen v. California; the relation be-
tween the claim of justice and the claim of meaning, especially in
Dante's treatment of Virgil.

AT WORK IN THIS book from the beginning has been the striking fact
that sometimes we feel that something we are reading—or watching or
hearing—trivializes or degrades human experience, reducing life to existence without significance and in this way stimulating a kind of cynicism
or despair; and that on other occasions we have the opposite feeling,
that the expression to which we are exposed—the Bach cantata, the
painting by Vermeer, the poem by Keats or Dickinson—dignifies or ex-
alts the human being and his or her experience, and marks out possibilities of significance in life, in our lives, that can serve as a ground of hope
in a universe otherwise replete with confusion and suffering. We cannot
easily explain how it happens, but in the first case we come away somehow ashamed of being a human being, in the second glad and proud to
belong to such a species. The crucial difference between these two kinds
of expression is that the one finds a way to recognize, the other denies,
the fundamental human capacity for claiming meaning for experience. It
is in this capacity that our deepest dignity resides, and upon its erasure
that the empire of force always depends.

In what follows I try to give fuller content to what I have just said, and
greater complexity too, starting with an examination of the fundamental
elements of Athenian tragedy, a genre that perhaps as much as any other
body of literature in the West has been seen to express the essential dignity

and value of the human being. My question is how it does this. I then turn to the law from this perspective, for in our readings of the opinions by Frankfurter and Jackson (and perhaps even more tellingly in the hopes we brought to the opinion in *Free Speech Coalition* and which were so profoundly disappointed by it) we have a real basis for thinking that the judicial opinion can in its own way be the occasion for a kind of speech that dignifies humanity and human experience, rather than trivializing it. My example in this chapter is the opinion of Justice John Harlan in the well-known First Amendment case *Cohen v. California*,[1] of which I ask as usual both how he imagines the activity of speech in the world—the speech that the First Amendment protects, or does not protect—and how he defines the possibility of valuable speech in his own performance.

All of this leads naturally to a comparison, of a rough kind at least, between the cultural form of Athenian tragedy and that of the American judicial opinion. The idea is not to draw abstract lines of similarity and difference between these two genres of thought and expression, but to try to capture something that is at work in both institutions, in fact essential to what each at its best achieves: to show how it is that the best instances of both forms resist the ever-present impulse to erase and trivialize human experience and instead confer upon the individual, and his or her struggles in the world, an essential dignity.

BRINGING THE REMOTE INTO THE CIRCLE OF ATTENTION

The Tragic Theater

First, some background about Athenian tragedy. In Athens the performance of tragedy was a highly public and intensively competitive event that occurred in its full grandeur only once a year, at the great festival of Dionysus. Only three dramatists were permitted to compete; they were chosen several months ahead of time and given that period in which to perfect the performance of the four-play sequences they had submitted. What we might call "rehearsal" was no small or casual matter; it cost roughly as much to train a chorus for a single set of plays as it did to keep a warship at sea for a year, and rich men were called upon by the state to bear this burden. The plays were performed at the Theater of

---

[1] 403 U.S. 15 (1971).

Dionysus, next to the Acropolis; they were then judged, by officials or by the crowd, and assigned prizes of great honor for the best play, best actor, best chorus, and so forth.[2]

The tragic theater was a cultural form, an occasion for the making of public and shared meaning, which had certain standard elements and ways of working. These were naturally realized differently by different playwrights and in different plays, but there are three important strands running through this body of work that, as we shall see, have perhaps surprising analogues in some of the best opinions of the Supreme Court.

Let me begin with the great trilogy of Aeschylus called the *Oresteia*. The first play, *Agamemnon*, tells the story of that hero's return to Mycenae from the Trojan War, and how he is shamefully killed—in his bath—by his wife, Clytemnestra, and her lover, Aegistheus; the second tells how her son, Orestes, commanded by Apollo to avenge this murder of his father, kills his mother; the third brings on stage in pursuit of Orestes the Eumenides, the dreadful Furies who punish the shedding of kindred blood. Orestes finds refuge in Athens, where he is tried for his act by a court and jury established for the purpose. He is acquitted, for in killing Clytemnestra he was acting under divine compulsion in the form of explicit orders from Apollo. The trilogy ends with the establishment of courts of justice in Athens. The idea is that these courts will, in the future, break a chain of vengeance, such as that which plagued the house of Atreus, by imposing sanctions for homicide that themselves do not occasion blood guilt, for they are the actions not of individual people—whose mixed motives necessarily include a desire both for revenge and for justice—but of the collectivity, represented by the jury, which is imagined to be capable of impartial judgment on the merits. One real subject of the trilogy, then, is the invention of law.

The *Agamemnon*, and with it the trilogy, begins with a watchman in Mycenae waiting, at dawn, for the beacon of light that will announce the victory at Troy—for Clytemnestra has arranged for fires to be lit on mountaintop after mountaintop to bring this news across the sea in

---

[2] For a brief account, see the articles on *choregia* and Greek tragedy in Simon Hornblower and Antony Spawforth, eds., *The Oxford Classical Dictionary*, 3rd ed. (Oxford: Oxford University Press, 1996), 323–24, 1538–42. See also Peter Wilson, "Powers of Horror and Laughter: The Great Age of Drama," in *Literature in the Greek and Roman Worlds*, ed. Oliver Taplin (Oxford: Oxford University Press, 2000), 88–132. For more about Aeschylus' *Oresteia*, see chapter 8 of James Boyd White, *Heracles' Bow: Essays on the Rhetoric and Poetics of the Law* (Madison: University of Wisconsin Press, 1985).

a single night. Next, in a song about the events that have led up to the present, the chorus alludes in a dark and frightened way to the fact that, when the Greek fleet was held in harbor by adverse winds on its way to Troy ten years earlier, Agamemnon sacrificed his daughter, Iphigenia, to persuade the gods to let the ships go—a terrible crime that Clytemnestra will later invoke as a justification for her own terrible crime. Soon after, a messenger arrives to describe the sack of Troy, in his vivid account bringing directly before the other characters in the play—and before the audience in Athens, too—these remote and perilous happenings.

In all of this the drama brings into the space we call the theater, and before the minds of the people of Athens, imagined events that are distant in both time and place. Here, for example, the audience is asked to imagine Mycenae at the time of the fall of Troy, Troy itself, the chain of mountaintops running from Troy to Mycenae, the sacrifice of Iphigenia ten years earlier, and so on.[3]

In an age of television, movies, newspapers, and the internet, it may be difficult to see this for the surprising and powerful cultural phenomenon it was, for we are besieged with communications that seem to invite us to imagine the remote and distant. But these plays took place in a different kind of world, one in which this was a real invention. In bringing on stage, and into the conscious imaginings of the people, events that were remote in time and space, the drama invited the audience to connect themselves to the distant. This was one of the central functions of the Athenian theater, and it had a perhaps surprising political and ethical significance.[4]

Think, for example, of another play by Aeschylus, *The Persians*. This tells the story of the great naval battle at Salamis, at which the Athenians destroyed the Persian invaders. Writing only ten years after the battle,

---

[3] More precisely, the audience is first asked to imagine that the space before it, the theater, is of a different time and place, in this case Mycenae; then, by speech and song, events in places and times remote from that one are brought into its field of attention.

[4] Of course, there were other forms that did something like this, especially the *Odyssey*, one of the foundational texts of this culture, which invited the audience to imagine both the world of Odysseus and then, through his speeches about his travels, a world beyond that. But the drama does this in a much more immediate way, inviting the audience to believe that what they are seeing and hearing in real time, on this spring morning, are the events of long ago or far away. The *Odyssey* told of remote events; the drama acts them out, in real time as it were, through what Aristotle called "spectacle."

Aeschylus surprisingly locates the action of his play in Persia itself, where we see the royal women of Persia awaiting news of the expedition. The audience thus sees these events not from the point of view of Athens, as a wonderful triumph, but from the point of view of the Persian women, for whom it is a disaster, and the audience is invited to sympathize with their suffering. Of course, the audience is Athenian, so they actually see it both ways at once—they are forced to do so—and that double vision is a central part of the meaning of the play.

At the climax of *The Persians*, a messenger reports the story of the battle itself, to which he was an eyewitness—telling how the Persians were tricked into rowing around the island of Salamis all night, then penned into a narrow bay from which they could not escape. These events in fact took place just a few miles away from Athens—the audience can see the mountains of Salamis from their seats—which means that in this play, occurring in Athens but set in Persia, Athens itself is brought on stage, simultaneously into the imagined world of Persia and the real world of Athens itself. The play thus makes Athens look at itself as it appears to others.

In setting the play up this way, Aeschylus is talking to his fellow citizens about their own history, simultaneously stimulating pride in their great victory and disciplining that pride by the recognition of the terrible loss it brought to others. He is also warning the Athenians that they should guard against the heady overconfidence that might otherwise naturally arise from the victory. In a real sense this play is thus a teaching play, teaching the public something crucial about its moral situation, as the *Oresteia* taught it something about its central institutions—in both cases, by bringing to awareness what is distant in time and space, and morally distant too. Both the *Oresteia* and *The Persians* in this way work to counter or erode what are likely to be the first reactions of the audience: that of course injury calls for revenge and that of course the victory over the Persians is the occasion for unalloyed triumph. The clichés of the culture are complicated by the presentation of competing points of view— those of Agamemnon and Clytemnestra and Orestes; those of the Athenians and Persians—that challenge them, in a sense make them unsayable, at least in the old way. In this way the plays resist simplified modes of thought and expression upon which the empire of force always depends and extend the realm of the human against forces that deny it.

It is not just that the theater carries distant events before the consciousness of the people. It brings into the light of day facts—or forces or ideas or impulses—that are normally repressed or hidden: the reality of the experience of the Persian women, for example, or of the murdered Iphigenia, or the psychic and moral forces represented by the Furies in the *Eumenides*—monstrous deities who usually live out of sight, underground, so hideous in the performance, says one account, that women miscarried at the sight of them. Perhaps the most famous example of this habit of bringing on to the stage what in a deep sense is felt to belong off it is the *Oedipus Tyrannos* of Sophocles, where, as Freud helped us see, some of the most profound and disturbing of human psychological forces are brought directly into the consciousness of the audience, as it contemplates Oedipus' violation of the central taboos against incest and patricide.

Another striking instance of this impulse can be found in the theater's treatment of women. In the world of Athens, women had a legal and social position mainly as the possessions of men, whether fathers or husbands; even in procreation women were imagined to contribute nothing to the child except a kind of oven in which the male seed could grow; and they themselves had essentially no property and no civil rights. Yet by all three of the great dramatists of Athens they are represented on stage as psychological and moral actors who are in every sense (except power) the equal of men. It may be indeed that such figures as Antigone and her sister, Ismene—and Phaedra, Medea, and Alcestis too—are the most deeply and fully realized women in Western literature until Shakespeare, perhaps even Jane Austen. It is hard to know how to explain this phenomenon fully, but I think it is another expression of the general impulse to put on stage what is real but unseen—a part of life that is normally excluded from the vision of the male citizens who made up most of the audience.[5]

In all of these ways the drama works as a way of expanding and intensifying our sense of what it means to be human, making it possible to pay attention to what we had not fully seen before. This kind of drama is not merely a kind of entertainment, not an item of consumption, but a major public and political event, one of the purposes of which, at the hands of the three great geniuses whose work we have, is educative and transformative, bringing its audience to a new kind of life.

---

[5] For an account of the ways in which such characters can nonetheless be seen to serve the needs of a male-dominated culture, see Helene P. Foley, *Female Acts in Greek Tragedy* (Princeton, N.J.: Princeton University Press, 2001). On the place of women in the theater, see Wilson, "Powers of Horror," 127–32, note 2 above.

The Judicial Opinion

When we turn to the contemporary form of expression and life we call the judicial opinion, especially the opinions of the U.S. Supreme Court, we find that there are, despite obvious differences, significant and illuminating parallels between this cultural form and that of the Athenian tragic drama. What we call the Supreme Court is in an important sense not the nine men and women who sit on the Court, or even all those who have done so in the past, but an entity that exists primarily in cultural and imaginative and political space. It is a public arena, bounded by its own structures and rules, one function of which is to bring certain stories and the problems they present into public attention, not for the sake of entertainment but in some sense for education or enlightenment. Likewise, it has its own sense of time, in which the remote is brought into the present, perhaps especially when its own decisions—some of them very old—are treated as speaking with direct authority. The time and space it creates and within which it works are in a sense of its own making, for it is the Court itself that gives significance and reality to these dimensions of its existence; and it does so in the form that its great Chief Justice John Marshall did much to invent, the opinion of the Court.[6]

Like the ancient theater of Athens, the Court is an institution for the making of shared and public meaning that regularly brings into the circle of public attention events and people and places that are normally overlooked or excluded or just not seen. It does so with the object of complicating and ultimately transforming the expectations—the ways of thinking and talking—that the culture has trained us to bring to

---

[6] That it is through the form we call the judicial opinion that the Court does these things is too obvious for argument. Imagine, for a moment, that the court had been forbidden to write opinions and that its judgments had to stand on their own, undefined and uninterpreted.

This would destroy the possibility of law as we know it. Of course, a case matters in part because of its outcome, especially to the parties; but to the rest of us this outcome matters largely because of what it is made to mean, in the first instance by the Court that decides it, then by later courts and commentators. The case does not have a meaning automatically, that is, but is given meaning through the opinion that describes, explains, and justifies the outcome. As a teacher once said to a writing class, "The facts do not 'speak for themselves.' You have to speak for them." So too is it with the results reached by the Supreme Court. It is the opinion that gives significance. For elaboration of this point, see James Boyd White, "What's an Opinion For?" in *From Expectation to Experience: Essays on Law and Legal Education* (Ann Arbor: University of Michigan Press, 2000).

whatever kind of issue the Court is deciding. In this way the good opinion, like the Attic theater, resists the language of cliché and slogan and insists instead upon recognizing the pressure of real and surprising human experience. This is in fact one of its central functions.

For a particular instance, let us consider the well-known First Amendment case *Cohen v. California*. The facts of the case, reflecting the era of the Vietnam War in which they occurred, were these. The defendant, Paul Robert Cohen, wore a jacket bearing the words "Fuck the Draft" while walking down a corridor of the Los Angeles municipal courthouse. He was then arrested and convicted of violating a California penal statute that made it an offense to "maliciously and willfully disturb the peace or quiet of any neighborhood or person . . . by . . . offensive conduct." The state court imposed a penalty of thirty days in jail. The Supreme Court, in an opinion by Justice Harlan, reversed the conviction.

The judicial process here brings into a zone of public awareness material that is normally unseen, most obviously and dramatically, and perhaps a bit embarrassingly, in the use of the word "fuck"—a word that, although known to almost all English speakers, is even today, let alone in 1971, typically used only on certain kinds of occasions, with certain kinds of audiences, and is definitely excluded from most formal discourse, certainly the discourse of the Supreme Court of the United States. Justice Harlan marks the distance between this term and the language of the Supreme Court—and the decorous conversation he seeks to establish with his readers—by the way he recites the facts of the case, not in his own words but in those of the California court: "On April 26, 1968, the defendant was observed in the Los Angeles County Courthouse in the corridor outside of division 20 of the municipal court wearing a jacket bearing the words 'Fuck the Draft' which were plainly visible."[7] He thus uses the word, but distances himself from it, burying it between two sets of quotations marks, in this way at once confirming and violating the expectation that he would never use such a word in this context. This stimulates in the reader a kind of embarrassed uncertainty, which offers her a direct experience of the substantive question at the center of the case: What should we do about the complex set of feelings, both repressive and liberated, that are triggered by the use of this word in such a place?

[7] 403 U.S. at 16.

This is not the only way in which the repressed or unknown is brought by the opinion in *Cohen* into a public place, where it can be seen and thought about and responded to in a new and deeper way. Until the law acted on it, Cohen's story was from almost all perspectives a rather trivial one, a minor skirmish in the national war about the war. He was not, so far as I know, otherwise an important person in the world, but just a young man opposed to the draft. This was a case of no political or public significance until the Court made it so, claiming that despite the apparent triviality of the event the issues presented here—presented, that is, by the lawyers, and seen and articulated by the Court in this very opinion—are "of no small constitutional significance."[8] This case is thus a piece of the world that the national public would normally never see or think about, brought before it as a way of saying, "This too is real and requires attention." To do this puts into question the habits of thought and speech that run through our minds without our being aware of it, the slogans and clichés we carry with us about the war, or protesters, or free speech, or the use of crude talk.

Notice, too, that the imagined world in which this story is placed reaches far in space and time alike. In space, it reaches out to Los Angeles and the county jail, to bring what happens there into the circle of public attention that the Supreme Court defines. As we shall see, it reaches back in time, too, when the Court tries to explain its decision, as it must, in the terms and understandings established by earlier decisions. Everything the Court has ever done is of potential relevance; that inheritance must be examined, thought about, and reorganized into a system of thought that will give appropriate and tolerable meaning to the events before it.

This process—giving significance to the apparently insignificant—is a major part of what the Court regularly does. Think, for example, of a case like *Powell v. Texas*,[9] where an alcoholic pauper was thrown into jail overnight to sober up, then charged with public drunkenness, to all the relevant actors as minor and routine an event as occurs in police work. The Supreme Court made this the object of learned, and contrasting, reflections on the conditions upon which the state may punish conduct as criminal, especially conduct arising from disease, in a set of opinions

[8] *Id.* at 15.
[9] 392 U.S. 514 (1968).

that might have remade criminal law in this country.[10] In this case—as in every criminal procedure case, in nearly every First Amendment case, and throughout the law, really—the unimportant is made important. This has its own political meaning, for it says that there is no case too small, no person too insignificant, to be worthy of potential attention. Here and elsewhere the Court makes big law by attending to small events. No one is excluded on principle.

When a playwright invokes what is physically or morally distant, we naturally ask what he will make of what he brings before us: What meaning will he claim for the story of Iphigenia, say, or the looting of Troy, or the events at the Persian court? The answer of course lies in the particularities of his writing and of the actors' performance. In the same way, when Cohen's story is brought into the theater of the courtroom, we ask what it will be made to mean by the lawyers and by the Court, and this, too, is of necessity a highly particular matter, tied intimately to the facts of the case and to the language of the First Amendment that is brought to bear upon it. For, as every lawyer knows, we do not and cannot know ahead of time the cluster of arguments on both sides by which the law will work in a particular case, which the Court must in turn resolve, and which it will use and transform in its own opinion.

This process requires a kind of attention, makes possible a kind of invention, different from the kind of talk usual in political or theoretical debate. What is happening in the *Cohen* case, from one perspective, is just another event in the long struggle over the meaning of the Vietnam War. But the law cannot think in such terms; it must fashion itself to meet the particularities of the case as these emerge in thought and argument that are themselves shaped by the particularities of prior cases, prior arguments. When the bright light of attention is focused on what we have not seen, or not seen clearly, it almost always reveals a complexity and richness of significance that we had missed, thus putting in question, among other things, our own prior habits of mind and imagination. It frustrates and educates our expectations. In the *Cohen* case, the large issue—that of the draft, and the war itself—is, of course, on everybody's mind and the source of deep, sometimes violent, internal national conflict. What the law does here is take a tiny fragment of that larger story, this simple act

[10] I say "might have" because, in the event, the Court later backed away from the possibilities opened up in *Powell*. Nonetheless, that case had real force in focusing thought on the problem of criminal responsibility, and doing so in a highly constructive way.

of protest, and examine it not in the terms of the national political debate—prowar or antiwar—but as a constitutional problem, to be analyzed, argued, and decided in the terms established by this branch of the law. This means, as we shall soon see, that an essential part of the opinion will be a delineation of these terms, an account of the universe of meaning established by the First Amendment and the cases decided under it.

Like the drama, then, the opinion brings before us what is remote in time and space and in doing so creates a world of imagination, simultaneously drawn from the world we otherwise know and an alternative to it. The idea in both cases is not to offer the audience an escape into fantasy, but to create an imagined reality that can run against that other imagined reality we call the "real world," both to test it and to be tested by it. In both forms, particularity is essential to the art; and in both forms, the created order is at once final and tentative: final because it reaches a conclusion, comes to an end; tentative because the rest of life continues, creating an ever-changing context that will challenge or confirm the imagined order in new and different ways. Both forms thus work to resist and complicate the simplified forms of thought and speech that we of necessity normally use to imagine our world and to shape our judgments and conduct within it—the forms of thought that characterize the empire of force and give it power.

MOVEMENT TO DISCOVERY BY DRAMATIC OPPOSITION

Perhaps a more obvious feature of Greek tragedy is that it lives and works dramatically, by the interaction between different characters speaking out of their respective situations in different voices. This is of the essence of drama as we think of it, but originally it was a real invention. The earliest forms of Greek drama were purely choral performances; at first one actor was added to the chorus, then another, then, finally, by Sophocles, the third.[11]

The opposition of character to character is so much the soul of what we think of as drama, then and now, that it is hard to appreciate the force and originality of the invention. Think, for example, of the opposition between Creon and Antigone over the relative authority of the city's decrees and that of the timeless and unwritten laws that the young

[11] See Aristotle, *Poetics*, 4,10–17.

woman invokes; or of the confrontation between Orestes and the Furies at his trial for the murder of Clytemnestra; or, in the play that bears her name, of the intense struggle between Medea and Jason. Or, to shift nearer our own world, think once more of Shakespeare's *Hamlet*, which can be seen as a set of antagonistic conversations between Hamlet and others—Gertrude and Claudius and Polonius and Laertes and Ophelia—each defining somewhat differently the meaning of the past they share and of contemplated future action too. The question the drama characteristically presents is, What kind of sense can be made of a world defined by such contrasting possibilities of speech and meaning?

It is equally obvious that, with us at least, the law works in a similar way: by the opposition of character against character, plaintiff against defendant, each representing a different vision of the world—and of the law—and seeking to establish his or her own as the dominant one. The central legal institution we call the hearing works by a disciplined opposition that is intended to lead—and sometimes does so—to deeper understanding, indeed, to the revelation of central questions theretofore obscured by our ignorance, or by our habits of thought and imagination.[12] It is not simply that play and trial work by opposition, but that the opposition leads the participants and the audience out of their accepted habits of mind and imagination into new discoveries: about what has happened and what it can be said to mean; about what ought to happen; about who these people are and ought to be.

As the play often takes as its subject a familiar story from mythology or history, which is told in such a way as to reveal for it new possibilities of meaning, so the hearing often begins with a set of preconceived ideas—in the parties, judge, and lawyers alike—about the facts and their significance, about the law and its bearing upon them, which are tested and complicated in argument and sometimes completely transformed. When the play and the hearing work well, they both carry us by the force of opposition from a position defined by our preexisting expectations into quite different and often surprising terrain. This happens in *Cohen* itself: like the *Free Speech Coalition* case discussed in chapter 4, *Cohen* is a case to the facts of which lots of people, including judges and lawyers, would have highly predictable responses, pro or con, and one of

---

[12] In this connection, see Robert P. Burns, *A Theory of the Trial* (Princeton, N.J.: Princeton University Press, 1999); Milner S. Ball, "The Play's the Thing: An Unscientific Reflection on Courts under the Rubric of Theater," *Stanford Law Review* 28 (1975): 81.

the functions of the opinion is to complicate these responses, perhaps beyond recognition, by the discipline of the body of thought and law developed under the First Amendment. The formulas and clichés expressing
our knee-jerk reactions one way or the other are, at the best, converted
into other forms of speech and thought, forms that one hopes will be
worthy of the problems and of the minds that are addressing them. Of
course that does not always happen, as we saw both in *Virginia Pharmacy Board* and *Free Speech Coalition*, but it is what we can hope for.

Notice that in *Cohen*, as is usual in American law, the lawyers for the two
sides create a drama of opposition that the Court will in turn address, but
that Cohen himself is not a participant in this conversation. His original
speech—the slogan on his jacket—is reported by others, but he himself
has no opportunity to say what it should be said to mean in the language
of the law. That is the task in the first instance of the lawyers, then of the
courts. Unlike Orestes or Oedipus, Cohen is a real flesh-and-blood person, with his own ways of talking, his own vision of the meaning and perhaps the necessity of what he did, and neither the reality of his experience
nor his way of claiming meaning for it is present in the legal argument,
especially on appeal. Our law—unlike other systems of law, perhaps most
notably that of ancient Athens itself[13]—is in this way built upon an imposed silence, a silence that makes possible another kind of speech.

For the law works by providing a second language, into which the
languages and experiences of ordinary life must be translated. The people of the law will locate and define what happened in the real world in
these terms, placing what Cohen himself actually said and did in a
larger context, which will in turn do much to shape the kind of meaning that can now be claimed for Cohen's words. The law is in this way
a cultural process, working on the raw material of life—the injury to
the body or the psyche, the failed business, the broken marriage, the
vulgar words in the courthouse—to convert it into something else,
something of its own: the occasion for the assertion of a certain sort of
meaning in the created dimension of legal speech and writing, running
over centuries and, in the case of the common law, over much of the

---

[13] For two useful and contrasting accounts of the way Athenian law worked, see Dou-
glas M. MacDowell, *The Law in Classical Athens* (Ithaca, N.Y.: Cornell University Press,
1978); and Steven Johnstone, *Disputes and Democracy: The Consequences of Litigation in
Ancient Athens* (Austin: University of Texas Press, 1999).

globe. It is a kind of translation, and like all translations entails a necessary loss.

One of the striking features of the opinion in *Cohen*, and one of its great merits, is that it acknowledges this fact about itself: the difference between ordinary language and legal language, between Cohen's speech and Harlan's, is not erased or elided, as such differences often are, but made inescapably prominent. This means that in addition to the usual dramatic opposition between the lawyers there is another overt tension, between two registers of discourse and between the people who speak in these different ways: between Cohen, wearing his jacket with its blunt-spoken legend in the municipal courthouse, and Justice Harlan, speaking as he does in elaborate and sophisticated legal terms about that event. On one side, we have the crude and simple phrase, a gesture of contempt and defiance that seems to express the view that nothing else need be said—to claim that this is a wholly adequate response to the issue of policy it addresses, indeed the only proper response. On the other side, we have a mind of great fastidiousness and care, defining, by the way it works through the issues, a set of crucial cultural and social values: the values of learning, of balance and comprehensiveness of mind, of human intelligence, of depth of understanding. Nothing could seemingly be farther from the mind exemplified in this elegant, complex, civilized composition than the kind of crude speech it protects.[14] By creating in his own voice a tone that respects ordinary canons of decency in expression, then incorporating this vulgarism within it, Justice Harlan performs, at the level of the text, just what he says the First Amendment requires of society in places like the courthouse: the toleration of what we normally exclude or suppress.

In this way, while protecting the speech of Cohen, Justice Harlan distances himself from it, defining himself and the Court as different from, indeed opposed to, the values—the sense of self and other, the idea of public thinking and speaking—expressed by it. It is this distance that enables him credibly to say at one point that the tolerance of "cacophony" required by

---

[14] I have spoken as though Cohen's gesture were simply a crude vulgarity, and the question were whether or not to tolerate it. This is, in a sense, of course true, but there are also respects in which his utterance was in its own way highly mannered. In a footnote, Justice Harlan explains that Cohen went into a courtroom where a trial was proceeding and, before he did so, took off his jacket and folded it up so that the slogan was not visible. Whatever his feelings may have been, from an objective point of view this was an act of respect for the courtroom and the judicial process. A policeman present suggested that the court hold Cohen in contempt, but the judge sensibly refused (403 U.S. at 19 n.3).

the First Amendment may be a sign of strength, not weakness, in the society that is capable of it, for he is himself demonstrating the strength and security of his own way of talking in tolerating one that he has defined as cacophonous. This is a message that he does not merely articulate but performs or enacts throughout the whole opinion, for he simultaneously protects Cohen's speech and exemplifies ways of thinking and talking that are, in one sense at least, at the other end of the spectrum. One ought not imagine from this opinion that one might be well advised to use language like that on Cohen's jacket in addressing the Supreme Court, or that to display such a jacket in a courtroom might be immune from sanction.

In the terms suggested in chapter 1, the kind of speech that Harlan himself exemplifies and values in his own performance is not "free speech" but a kind of valuable speech that depends for its very value upon the fact that it is highly regulated and constrained: by the principle of judicial authority, which requires serious attention to earlier cases and to the tensions among them; by a conception of excellence in legal thought, which shapes the kind of attention Justice Harlan gives to those cases; and by canons of civilized and rational discourse, including grammar and syntax, that govern the forms of expression.[15] It is, in fact, this very

[15] In this context consider the way in which Harlan, having quoted the lower court's statement of the facts, reproduced above, goes on to define the procedural posture of the case, including the jurisdictional question it is said to present, all in a way that defines and exhibits his commitment to the highly restrained and effective language of the law:

> In affirming the conviction the Court of Appeal held that "offensive conduct" means "behavior which has a tendency to provoke *others* to acts of violence or to in turn disturb the peace," and that the State had proved this element because, on the facts of this case, "[i]t was certainly reasonably foreseeable that such conduct might cause others to rise up to commit a violent act against the person of the defendant or attempt to forceably remove his jacket." 1 Cal. App. 3d, at 99–100, 81 Cal. Rptr., at 506. The California Supreme Court declined review by a divided vote. We brought the case here, postponing the consideration of the question of our jurisdiction over this appeal to a hearing of the case on the merits. 399 U.S. 904. We now reverse.
>
> The question of our jurisdiction need not detain us long. Throughout the proceedings below, Cohen consistently claimed that, as construed to apply to the facts of this case, the statute infringed his rights to freedom of expression guaranteed by the First and Fourteenth Amendments of the Federal Constitution. That contention has been rejected by the highest California state court in which review could be had. Accordingly, we are fully satisfied that Cohen has properly invoked our jurisdiction by this appeal. 28 U.S.C. § 1257 (2); *Dahnke-Walker Milling Co. v. Bondurant,* 257 U.S. 282 (1921). (403 U.S. at 17–18)

quality of Harlan's opinion, its regulated and shaped nature, that makes its protection of Cohen's slogan so significant and important: it is protecting something very different from itself, and in doing so it defines the kind of toleration the First Amendment has at its center. Yet at the same time it recognizes, almost of necessity, that this other utterance has a force and value that may be missing from the opinion itself; indeed, it almost necessarily suggests that there may be times when the right response to a political situation is not more reason, not more civilization, but the kind of verbal gesture one cannot quite imagine Justice Harlan, as he defines himself here, ever making.

For there are points in this opinion at which one might be less inclined to call Harlan's manner of speech "elegant" or "sophisticated" than "stuffy" or "stilted"—as, for example, when he says that we should remember that speech "conveys not only ideas capable of relatively precise, detached explication, but otherwise inexpressible emotions as well," and goes on to add that the Constitution should not be assumed to have little or no regard for this "emotive function," which "may often be the more important element of the overall message sought to be communicated."[16] When I read this, I have the feeling that I am in the presence of overformal speech, the product of a mind that is at the moment constricted by its own commitments to a certain kind of thought, here a mechanical view of language as the vehicle for the transmission of ideas and feelings. But this very fact has its dramatic and literary meaning, for it enacts for us what it might mean to insist, as California wants to do, that Cohen should be compelled to translate his utterance into more formal and generally acceptable speech—this would make him sound like me, Harlan is in effect saying, and it would bleed what he says of its life and vigor.

We can see now that the other impulse I mentioned, the bringing on stage of that which is unrecognized or alien or perhaps taboo, is at work through the entire opinion. Harlan brings on this phrase, this moment, not only to protect it but to establish a dramatic tension with it, a tension that validates it as well as tolerates it. One is reminded of Shakespeare's capacity to see the world from every point of view, in this sense to humanize every monster. Even Caliban, the subhuman creature who tries to rape Miranda and destroy Prospero, is given his moments of sympathy, and more than sympathy—of unique and beautiful expression. So here, where there is no monster, but a person speaking crudely

<hr>

[16] *Id.* at 26.

but forcefully about a crucial public issue, Harlan can see value in language he would not use.

CLAIMING MEANING FOR EXPERIENCE

In addition to its way of imagining the distant and remote, and its way of working by dramatic opposition, Greek tragedy has a third feature, harder to define than the others but no less important, not only for Athens but in its consequences for the literary and dramatic imagination ever since—as we can see in Dante's great poem in particular. What I have in mind is the sort of speech in which a speaker looks back over his experience as a whole—and thus our experience too, as readers—seeking to find a meaning in it, to claim a meaning for it, and such a meaning as will enable him to shape his future speech and conduct in a coherent and valuable way. This, you will remember, is the third kind of meaning discussed in chapter 3, which I there called "world-imagining."

Not all speech in Attic drama has this quality. Much of it consists of simple response to events, in the form of lamentation or the expression of joy or worry; some of it consists of denunciation, or manipulation, or planning, or the giving of orders—think of Creon speaking to Antigone—or the pursuit of clarification, as in *Oedipus*. All of these gestures can, of course, be ways of giving meaning to experience, but they have not the quality I seek to define, which includes a kind of summing up, a self-consciousness, an effort to imagine the whole world and oneself and others within it, to see one's story as a whole and place it among other stories. It is the full performance of a gesture that is begun over and over in human experience, both in our own lives and on the stage, but rarely taken to completion.

Oedipus and Ajax

Let me give two brief instances from Athenian tragedy. In *Oedipus at Colonus*, the blind and aged man after years of wandering finds at last a home in the sanctuary of Colonus on the edge of Attica. The townspeople in the chorus are afraid of him and wish to drive him off; Creon, his brother in-law, comes from Thebes to seize him and bring him back to that city, to ensure that he will be buried there and thus to confer on Thebes the benefits that an oracle has promised to the place that receives his body. Oedipus himself is filled with a sense of cost and loss, an awareness of his own status as an object of fear and taboo, but he also displays a remarkable serenity, reflecting an essential integrity of mind; towards the end, in an argument with Creon, he surprisingly asserts his fundamental innocence. He looks back over his entire life and claims new meaning for it. He was, he says, the object of a divine decree from birth, which required that he should do these unspeakable things—how, then, can it have been his fault? He did not know who it was he killed, or who it was he was marrying; when he did kill he acted in self-defense. He has—and he knows it—violated the deepest of taboos and is by this fact eternally marked; but he also sees that in another and deeper sense he is innocent as well (lines 960–999). The action of the play confirms this sense of his own deep innocence, in two ways: first, in Theseus' expulsion of Creon and acceptance of Oedipus into the territory of Athens; then, in Oedipus' own apotheosis, his conversion by divine power on his death into a kind of quasi-deity himself.

In accepting the facts of his conduct, yet asserting his fundamental innocence, Oedipus puts together the central and seemingly irreconcilable facts of his life: that he was an immensely competent man who outwitted the Sphinx, saved his city, and pursued with intelligence and vigor the discovery of the pollution that was destroying it; yet that he was also the murderer of his own father, the husband of his mother, and the father of children who were also his half-siblings, a kind of monstrous violator of the order of nature. The coherence he creates is not one he can possibly have learned or copied from his culture, for his situation is utterly unique; it had to be his own discovery and creation. Sophocles presents Oedipus in a life situation the only possible meaning of which seems to be utterly intolerable; this is what Oedipus is expressing when at the end of *Oedipus Tyrannos* he blinds himself—death would be too easy; yet at the end of his life in *Oedipus at Colonus* he finds a way to tell the truth of his life that makes it not only tolerable to him but magnificent: for now he represents all of us, all of us who are like him in that we too, in our own lives, contribute to the making of a story that has a meaning we cannot know until the end.

For another instance consider Sophocles' *Ajax*. This story takes place during the Trojan War, just after the death of Achilles. The marvelous armor of Achilles, made for him by Hephaestus, has been given by the expedition leaders, Agamemnon and Menelaus, not to Ajax, who is sure he deserves this mark of honor, but to Odysseus, in what Ajax regards as an act of fraud. Filled with helpless fury at this injury, Ajax sets forth at night to kill Odysseus and the two leaders, the only response he as a man of war and honor can possibly imagine. But the goddess Athena sees him set out to do this and deludes him into thinking that a herd of sheep are the enemies he seeks; he slaughters them, delighted at his revenge; but then he gradually returns to sanity, surrounded by the corpses of these animals, a laughingstock to the whole world, utterly humiliated. The course for him is plain, and he faces it clearly and with characteristic courage: "It's a contemptible thing to want to live forever. . . . Let a man nobly live or nobly die."[17] The meaning of his situation is that he should die and be done with it.

Tecmessa, the captive woman with whom he lives and by whom he has had his only son, pleads with him not to end his life, for at the moment he dies she and their son will become slaves of others, which will be horrible for themselves and a humiliation both to Ajax' parents, who are still alive, and to his own memory. Ajax at first rejects her claim, but he is in fact affected by what she says, and when he returns to the stage after a choral ode lamenting his decision, he speaks in a wholly different way, not from inside his misery of the moment but from outside, at an enormous distance, philosophical or religious in kind.

> Strangely the long and countless drift of time
> Brings all things forth from darkness into light,
> Then covers them once more. Nothing so marvelous
> That man can say it surely will not be—
> Strong oath and iron intent come crashing down.
> *My* mood, which just before was strong and rigid,
> No dipped sword more so, now has lost its edge—
> My speech is womanish for this woman's sake;
> And pity touches me for wife and child . . .   (644–54)

So, he says, he will go to the shore of the sea and purify himself, hiding his sword in the sand.

---

[17] Lines 473, 479. All quotations from *Ajax* are from the translation by John Moore, in *Sophocles*, ed. David Grene and Richmond Lattimore (Chicago: University of Chicago Press, 1957) 2:7–62.

From now on this will be my rule: Give way
To Heaven and bow before the sons of Atreus.
They are our rulers, they must be obeyed.
I must give way, as all dread strengths give way,
In turn and deference. Winter's hard-packed snow
Cedes to the fruitful summer; stubborn night
At last removes, for day's white steeds to shine.
The dread blast of the gale slackens and gives
Peace to the sounding sea; and Sleep, strong jailer,
In time yields up his captive. Shall not I
Learn place and wisdom?   (667–79)

This is an extraordinary speech. It represents an enormous shift of mind
and feeling, from a self-centered despair to an acceptance of his lot, which
is in turn based at least in part on a recognition of the claims and experience of others. Ajax can now see Tecmessa not merely as a possession
but as a person with whose experience he can sympathize. His virtue has
so far been to be without pity; now he can pity. What is more, he now
sees his present defeat not as a single, unique, and humiliating event but
as part of the larger order and process of the world, in which all dread
and powerful things give way in the end: winter, and night, and storms,
and sleep, and wakefulness. We live amid cycling emergences and with-
drawals, dominances and submissions, of which this event is only one.
His humiliation is thus stripped of social and moral significance and
made a fact, a fact of nature, like death itself.

This speech is, therefore, an answer to a central question the play
presents, which is how one can possibly live in a world in which life is so
utterly subject to chance, even to malicious destruction. The answer is
ultimately a matter of voice and character, of imagination and speech.
Ajax lives in a world of uncertainty and destruction; but he can see that
and say it, and in doing this can see himself not as a unique heroic ego
but as part of a set of processes larger than he is; and all this enables him
to accept his life and its conditions.

Or so it seems. For despite what he says in this speech, Ajax shortly
afterwards retires to the seacoast not to bury his sword, as he here declares, but to fall upon it as a suicide. How, then, are we to understand
the remarkable speech we have just heard? Does his suicide mean that
the speech was simply a deception, meant somehow to placate for the

moment Tecmessa and the chorus of sailors from Salamis, his country-men? So some would take it, but this would be extremely odd in a per-son as direct and forthright as Ajax is throughout. Yet how then is one to explain his self-destruction? One possibility is to see it as the continu-ing work of Athena's hostility. On this view the speech is sincerely meant when given; its intention is later undone by Athena's curse of madness.[18] But this would reduce the meaning of Ajax's suicide by making it invol-untary, eliminating his status as a responsible actor at this crucial mo-ment. And who could imagine him actually submitting to Menelaus and Agamemnon? A third reading has been suggested, namely that the first part of the speech quoted above is actually a soliloquy, without an audi-ence on stage; in it Ajax truly articulates his view of the way the world is; but this is not a vision he accepts, quite the reverse of that. The lan-guage about revering the Atreidae shows how impossible that would be. The speech in this way confirms his resolve to leave this impossible life.[19] One might add a fourth possibility, which sees Ajax himself undergoing a change in the course of his speech: his suicide is no longer caused by the humiliation that has been his torture, of which it would have been in fact an intensification, but by the dawning recognition that there is in this world no place for him, no place for a person of his character and values. His suicide is not madness, not a response to humiliation, but a sensible response to the fact that he has no place in this culture. This read-ing will later be borne out by what we see of Agamemnon and Menelaus when they come on stage, for they are brutal, cynical, manipulative, true figures of the empire of force. It is not humiliation but the loss of the very kind of meaning Ajax has been trying to claim that makes further existence worthless to him.

My own preference is for the last interpretation, but it is not necessary here to try to resolve the tensions among the competing understandings of the text. All of them see the speaker as struggling to imagine the world, and himself within it, in such a way as to make possible meaningful speech and valuable action, and this is for our purposes by far the most

[18] Soon a messenger will report the words of Calchas, a seer, that if Ajax can be kept within his tent for this one day, Athena will harass him no more (lines 758–59). But this of course does not happen.

[19] See Bernard Knox, *Word and Action: Essays on the Ancient Theater* (Baltimore: Johns Hopkins University Press, 1979), 134–41. For other views, see C. M. Bowra, *Sophoclean Tragedy* (Oxford: Oxford University Press, 1967), 39–46; and R. P. Winnington-Ingram, *Sophocles: An Interpretation* (Cambridge: Cambridge University Press, 1980), 46–55.

important fact about the passage. It expresses a desire, an impulse perhaps first made part of the Western inheritance here in the tragic drama of
Athens: the impulse to stop, to sum up life as a whole and to try to make
sense of it, to claim a meaning for it; to try to imagine the world and oneself within it in such a way as to make meaningful action possible—
whether that action is the kind of suicide upon which Ajax first resolves,
and later, perhaps still under the destructive spell of Athena, commits, or
whether it is the kind of life in connection with others that he, in this
speech, for a moment, imagines, but then rejects as impossible.

This kind of speech is essential to what may be the deepest contribution of tragic drama, which is to give dignity to human life by recognizing
and enacting the possibility that the human mind—the self or soul—can
maintain its integrity even, or especially, at the moment of its dissolution. It is such an act of character and imagination that enables Oedipus
to overcome and transform what he has done in marrying his mother
and killing his father; that enables Prometheus, chained to the rock in
Aeschylus' play named for him, to maintain a moral and psychological
superiority to the Zeus who tortures him; and that enables Ajax, for a
moment at least, to accept and live with the humiliation thrust upon him
by fate and the gods. This is what I have in mind when I say that it is in
the human capacity for speech of a certain kind that human dignity most
deeply resides: speech that invokes what is distant and remote and brings
it before the mind, where it can provide material and a point of view
from which the culture, and the self, can be criticized; speech that
moves, as the play and trial both do, by opposition and contrast into
new perception and understanding; and speech, like that of Ajax or
Oedipus, that seeks to sum up experience and claim a meaning for it.
This is speech that resists the empire of force.

Harlan's Opinion in Cohen

To return once more to *Cohen*, I want now to suggest that in writing his
opinion for the Court Justice Harlan is expressing very much the same impulse, in a different context, that we saw at work in the speeches of Ajax
and Oedipus: the desire to sum things up, to tell again the story of the
past, to imagine the world and its people, all in ways that will make possible coherent speech, intelligible and appropriate action. Part of the duty of
the Court is to say how this case should be talked about in the language

the Court has made—in this instance, the language made in cases decided under the First Amendment. To do this, it must attend to the entire authoritative past created by the Court and do so with the duty of resolving so far as it can the tensions it discovers within it, with the aim of asserting, for the moment, that justice has been done. It must use this language to make a claim to coherent speech and appropriate action, while subject to a double fidelity: to the "law," as that is defined by prior cases and the larger legal discourse, and to "justice," as that is defined by our deepest sense of right. You could say that Harlan's task, in the terms of my epigraph from Weil, is to demonstrate in his writing that he can "be just."

1.

Here is a brief outline of what might be called the argumentative structure of Justice Harlan's opinion, suggesting how he attempts to do these things.

He begins a bit like a modernist painter sculpting out negative space by telling us what, in his words, this case "does *not* present" (emphasis in original). First, he says this is a case in which the state seeks to punish not conduct that is associated with speech but speech itself.[20] Likewise, the case involves not a statute directed at the special need for decorous speech and conduct in the courthouse or its precincts, but one of general applicability. This means that no special deference is due any judgment of the legislature as to the proper control of speech in the halls of a courthouse, for no such judgment has been made.[21] And, despite the sexual vulgarity of the central term employed, this is not an obscenity case, for the expression is in no way erotic.[22] Furthermore, the phrase in question

[20] This is not self-evident, for one might easily think the Constitution could draw a line between speech, say, on a street corner, or in a newspaper, and speech that takes the form of slogans emblazoned on a jacket and displayed in a courthouse. But that is actually part of Harlan's point, for in the latter case the state would be punishing the manner of speech, not its content or substance, which, if defined as a communication that opposes participation in the Vietnam War or the military draft, is immune from suppression. The question, then, is whether this is an appropriate time, place, or manner regulation.

[21] What is more, there is no notice in this statute that the courthouse is a special place, governed by special rules. "No fair reading of the phrase, 'offensive conduct', can be said sufficiently to inform the ordinary person that distinctions between certain locations are thereby created" (403 U.S. at 19).

[22] He puts this point as a question of fact: "It cannot plausibly be maintained that this vulgar allusion to the Selective Service System would conjure up such psychic stimulation in anyone likely to be confronted with Cohen's crudely defaced jacket" (*id.* at 20).

does not qualify as the sort of expression the Court has termed "fighting words," unprotected by the First Amendment, for it was not a "direct personal insult," nor is this a case of a speaker "intentionally provoking a given group to hostile reaction." Nor is a prohibition of this phrase justified by the fact that it was forced upon "unwilling or unsuspecting viewers," as a "captive audience"; to justify suppression on such grounds, the government must show that "substantial privacy interests are being invaded in an essentially intolerable manner," which is not the case here.[23]

Justice Harlan thus runs through nearly the entire body of potentially relevant First Amendment law, only to put it aside on the grounds that it does not bear on the case before him. That is, he simultaneously admits the surface relevance of the arguments he states and denies their force in this case, creating a space for real thought, his version of the space of silence from which the best speech emerges. He is here addressing and resolving the sort of argumentative opposition between lawyers I referred to earlier. It is important to add that none of the points he dismisses is without some merit, none of his own positions beyond argument. He recognizes what can be said the other way but is, at the same time, exercising a power—the power of a language-shaper—to determine its scope and basis and reach. This is to expose himself to potential criticism, both intellectual and ethical, for if his summary of the law is not fair, he can be accused of failing to account for countering arguments and thus of speaking in conclusions, as we saw Attorney General Ashcroft do in the passages quoted in chapter 2. If Harlan's summary is fair, however, it is a gift not only to the student but to the law, a way of bringing order out of confusion. Moreover, on any particular point he can be challenged in future cases, especially since what he says here is background, not part of what lawyers call the "holding of the case."

---

[23] The phrase on Cohen's jacket is not comparable to "the raucous emissions of sound trucks" outside one's residence, for "those in the Los Angeles courthouse could effectively avoid further bombardment of their sensibilities simply by averting their eyes" (*id.* at 21). Harlan concludes that this is no basis for suppression, especially where there is no evidence that "persons powerless to avoid appellant's conduct did in fact object to it" (*id.* at 22), and where the legislature has not focused attention on the issues presented by the captive auditor but "indiscriminately sweeps within its prohibitions all 'offensive conduct' that disturbs 'any neighborhood or person'" (*id.*). Here Harlan does find a way to give force to objections that might have been made to the statute on its face, but he does this not in an abstract way but in the context defined by the particulars of this case. The statute may thus be valid in other cases, but not as applied to this conduct in this case—at least not without a showing of a legislative judgment made on the issues presented here.

2.

For Harlan all this is a kind of brush clearing that brings into the open, where it can be seen and thought about, what he regards as the real issue in the case, which is whether California may "excise, as 'offensive conduct,' one particular scurrilous epithet from the public discourse." It cannot do so, he first says, on the theory advanced by the lower court, namely that it is "inherently likely to cause violent reaction," for there is no evidence to support that contention.[24] But there is a second theory supporting the conviction, which to Harlan's mind commands more respect and attention: that the states may suppress this "unseemly expletive" in an effort to "maintain what they regard as a suitable level of discourse within the body politic."[25] He here recognizes the reality and significance of a question that, as we saw, is also at the heart of *Free Speech Coalition*, but completely ignored by the Court in that case: may the legislature's regulation of speech be based only on material interests, such as the interest in preventing violence, or may it also be based on the quality and nature of the speech itself?

Harlan begins his examination of California's argument at a highly general level, reimagining as it were the first premises of the legal universe. First, he says, we must make this judgment with an understanding of the purpose of the constitutional right of free expression: "It is designed and intended to remove governmental restraints from the arena of public discussion, putting the decision as to what views shall be voiced largely into the hands of each of us, in the hope that use of such freedom will ultimately produce a more capable citizenry and more perfect polity and in the belief that no other approach would comport with the premise of individual dignity and choice upon which our political system rests."[26] This is a lovely and economical statement, drawn as Harlan's references make clear from a more extended one, the famous concurrence

---

[24] *Id.* at 22–23. He makes this point—in the first instance, at least—as a question of fact, and finds the government's case wanting. "We have been shown no evidence that substantial numbers of citizens are standing ready to strike out physically at whoever may assault their sensibilities" by such "execrations." But he quickly moves to a normative position: there may be some people "with such lawless and violent proclivities," but that does not constitute a sufficient basis for the regulation of speech. To hold that it did would amount to the "self-defeating proposition" that to avoid censorship by a "hypothetical coterie of the violent and lawless" the state may impose that censorship itself (*id.* at 23).

[25] *Id.*

[26] *Id.* at 24.

of Justice Brandeis in *Whitney v. California*, discussed in chapter 4. The result of this freedom, Harlan goes on to say, "may often appear to be only verbal tumult, discord, and even offensive utterance."[27] But these are side effects of what a broader debate enables us to achieve, and "that the air may at times seem filled with verbal cacophony is, in this sense not a sign of weakness but of strength."[28]

In turning to the particulars of this case, Harlan makes two central points. First he says that the result contended for by the prosecution would confer "inherently boundless" powers on the state. If this word can be excised from public speech, where is the power to stop? There is simply no principled way to distinguish between this particular term and other vulgar words. Harlan's view here rests on an important under-standing of the nature of language, namely that words cannot be sorted like peas or bolts, according to size or weight. They have a life that is more mysterious and multidimensional, more context dependent, than such a view would allow.

Second—and central to the ultimate meaning of the case—Harlan says that to force a translation of Cohen's utterance into more socially pre-sentable speech would strip it of much of its significance. For human speech, he says in a passage I quoted earlier, "conveys not only ideas ca-pable of relatively precise, detached explication, but otherwise inex-pressible emotions as well"; and we cannot believe that the Constitution has "little or no regard" for this "emotive function which, practically speaking, may often be the more important element of the overall mes-sage sought to be communicated." And even if this is not true, he thinks that it would be too facile to assume that one "can forbid particular words without also running a substantial risk of suppressing ideas in the process."[29]

Note a tension here. First Harlan says that speech does more than express "ideas" and that what he calls its "emotive function" is crucial to its value; then he returns to the topic of "ideas" once more, saying that we cannot be confident that the suppression of vulgarity would not involve the suppression of "ideas"—all as though ideas are the important things after all. He thus reaffirms the distinction between ideas and feelings he

---

[27] *Id.* at 24–25.
[28] *Id.* at 25.
[29] *Id.* at 26.

has just criticized; but the earlier criticism—insisting on the value of emotive expression—continues to work, transforming his point from its rather crude statement about "ideas" to a crucial recognition that our language about language is itself inherently limited and constricting. What unites his two perceptions, despite the tension between them, is his sense that we cannot be confident that we can know how the meaning of language works, certainly not so confident that we can inflict surgery on an utterance without running the risk of destroying its life.

This is the most important part of the meaning of the Court's opinion: a sensitivity to the fact that meaning and form are inseparable. It is a familiar truth of literary criticism that the meaning of a poem or a play or a novel, or any other work of art, lies not in any restatement of it into other terms—in any message or idea—but in its performance, in the life and experience it creates for its audience or viewer. In adopting and performing this position in the law, Harlan takes an enormously significant step away from the view that the First Amendment should be held to protect only speech that contributes to the "marketplace of ideas," and especially of political ideas. Of course Cohen's own speech is deeply political; but the way the Court imagines and resolves his case makes the amendment reach much farther, to the protection of art—and perhaps to a dissolution of the simple distinction between political and nonpolitical, as the opinion dissolves the distinction between ideas and feelings.

There is thus this additional connection between the opinion in *Cohen* and the Greek dramas with which we began, that *Cohen* provides a language and an authority for the protection of these plays and others like them. It is not only itself a drama; it is a way of thinking about drama.

I think that the desire for meaning of the kind that is reflected in the speeches of Ajax and Oedipus, and stimulated in the audience or reader, is the deepest impulse from which the best literature comes; what is more, it lies at the heart of our hopes when we approach a judicial opinion, especially a Supreme Court opinion. But the impulse is even more general than that, for we ourselves participate in it in our own lives and imaginations. Every human being has the desire to find a way of describing and claiming meaning for his experience, for the narrative of his life, partly shaped as it is by forces outside himself, partly by his own choices. At the most general level, this is a desire for a way of imagining the world, and himself and others within it, that will make possible coherent speech and valuable action, even in the face of the deep uncertainties and injustices life necessarily presents.[30] The process is never complete, for the future lines of the story we are telling are necessarily unknown to us; but we do know that when they come they will certainly, like the murder of Agamemnon or the madness of Ajax, give new meaning to what is past. As we do this, we work against two deep fears: that the story we shall then be able to tell will have a meaning that is intolerable to us—or no meaning at all.

To discover shape and coherence and significance in a work of art—or law—presents us with an acute form of this problem, for it simultaneously stimulates the desire for meaning of the kind I mean and reminds us that our experience, our story—like that of Agamemnon—is necessarily incomplete. In this way it is one function of art, and law too, to challenge life at its imaginative center.

Imagine for the moment that we could not claim meaning for our experience, and that all our speech was reducible—as, indeed, certain strains of thought in our own world would reduce it—to something called information. Under these conditions, instead of what we call meaningful speech, we would send signals that communicated particular desires or aversions, expressed a willingness or a refusal to engage in a course of conduct, and so on. We could perhaps make offers, pay bills, get the car fixed, go to the hairdresser, buy a suit, order a dinner, arrange for sexual gratification, even watch or play baseball, but we could not say what any of these things means to us. We could not justify our decisions, or explain our preferences, we could only act on them; we could not engage in the kind of conversation by which we discover who we are, what we do desire and should desire, what kind of life we live and want to live. Life would go on as a series of exchanges, and expression as a set of signals that make the exchanges possible.

Such an existence would in the most important sense not be human, for it would omit the most deeply human form of speech, which is the effort to define our experience and claim a meaning for it. Description, explanation, justification: these are for us essential activities of mind and language. And they all take place in the human relation that is created by speech between or among human beings who are conceived of as centers of value and imagination, inherently equal—as people who can be called, as they can call others, into deeper forms of life and thought. These

---

[30] For earlier statements of this theme, see James Boyd White, *The Edge of Meaning* (Chicago: University of Chicago Press, 2001) especially 1–9, 55–56.

activities resist the objectification of others that is the hallmark of the empire of force.

As we have seen, the form we call the opinion of the Supreme Court—like the drama—is a cultural institution that works to teach the public, in part by bringing into the zone of collective attention that which is distant or remote, unseen and particular; in part by the way it works through dramatic opposition, with character poised against character, voice against voice; in part by the way it seeks to give meaning to the events thus examined, locating them in a larger context and a larger story, running back in time and including, potentially, all the elements of its institutional memory. It does this in a language fashioned for the purpose, in which the Court—like Ajax or Oedipus—claims, or struggles to claim, that it can describe, explain, and justify its decision in an appropriate way, one that will make possible coherent speech and meaningful action in the future. Like the drama it has the potential—realized in cases like *Cohen* and many others, though certainly not in all—to enhance our sense of the dignity of human life and experience, in resistance to those forces, in this and every age, that would trivialize these things.

In the judicial opinion and the drama alike, we are thus exposed to imaginations that, at their best, confront the deep uncertainties of the world, of language and the mind, but nonetheless create orders, in language, that run against those uncertainties. In each—the speech of Ajax in the play that bears his name, the opinion in *Cohen*—the order is necessarily tentative, temporary, soon to be replaced by others, or redefined as the context that gives it meaning changes. In this way, both forms call upon us, as readers, to engage in our own versions of this fundamental activity of imagination and language: become a maker of order yourself, they tell us, become one who claims meaning for our shared experience, or the possibility will be lost.

THE CLAIM OF JUSTICE AND THE CLAIM OF MEANING

In a sense not only human beings but all creatures need to have a coherent way of imagining the universe. The butterfly can feed on the nectar of the lily only if in some way it knows that lilies have nectar; terns can migrate from one end of the Americas to the other only if the magnetic field they use for navigation is reliable; bats can feed despite their visual blindness only if their echo system for locating prey will work. Each creature has its own way of perceiving the world, what naturalists call its *merkwelt*, and it has to be able to rely on its perceptions or it is headed for disaster. Our need for coherence in this sense goes all the way down to the roots of animal life. But as human beings we have a need that other animals do not seem to have, namely to tell the stories of our life in a way that makes sense of them, that yields a tolerable meaning. For us an essential question at work in every such story is justice—the justice of what some person or government did or failed to do, the justice of the gods, or of God, perhaps the justice of the universe. We want to be able to affirm the justice of what has happened to us, and of what we see around us; in default of that we need—our integrity demands it— to be able to express our sense of injustice. This need is essential to the dignity and value of human life. Indeed, to make a claim of justice—or injustice—is a large part of what language is for: language seen not as a system of signals, or an instrument for the exchange of information, but language as a way in which we claim this kind of meaning for our experience.

Such a concern for the claims of justice is another element that unites the Greek tragedies I have discussed and the judicial opinion, as represented here by the *Cohen* case. Certainly *Ajax*, the *Oresteia*, and *Oedipus at Colonus* are in different ways all about the question whether the world is just, or simply indifferent or malign; *The Persians* too is radically concerned with justice—the justice of the victory at Salamis, and of the Athenian response to it, and of what might happen to Athens if it allowed itself an inappropriate sense of triumph. And of course justice is at the center of the *Cohen* case: Harlan's claim is not merely to imagine the world coherently, but to do so in a way that permits him to claim that justice has been done in this case.

Even more important than our judgment whether the world, or a part of it, is in fact just is the question whether the claim of justice itself has standing and intelligibility, a grounding in our nature, or is seen by contrast as simply empty. This is a topic in philosophy from ancient days until our own: two of Socrates' interlocutors, Callicles in the *Gorgias* and Thrasymachus in the *Republic*, take the view that all talk about justice is inherently vacuous—at worst mere sentimentality, at best a cynical way of manipulating a crowd—a position both Socrates and Plato strongly resist (though of course the definition of justice itself eludes them). Like these last-named philosophers, Job in the Hebrew Bible insists upon the legitimacy of a claim to justice, in this case a claim that his unjustified suffering demonstrates that the God of the universe is not just. Job insists and insists upon the injustice of his suffering; in a sense he has a heroic call to speak for all humanity in protest against injustice—until, at last, he comes to perceive the equally unjust suffering of others, of widows and orphans, and to find himself in the actual presence of the Holy One, when his own immediate concerns dissipate almost entirely.[31]

The universe and its rulers may be unjust, but if they are, as Job shows, we have the right to call them that. An essential ingredient of our humanity lies in our capacity to make that charge or claim, and the denial of that capacity is the essential foundation of the empire of force in all its forms. Nothing would suit the empire better than a way of viewing the world in which justice was no longer to be a topic, but was replaced by a language of objectification, gratification, self-interest, instrumentalism, or mere causation.

In this context let us think once more of Dante's great poem. Its central concern, both in its grand design and in its particular parts, is with the meaning of human experience, constantly presenting the question whether it is possible to claim meaning for our lives. It is common for a soul with whom Dante speaks, in each of the realms of the afterworld, to tell the story of his or her life, and to claim significance for it. In the *Inferno* these stories are invariably misleading, in the *Purgatorio* sometimes distorted but always sincerely meant, and in the *Paradiso* always resonant with truth, though sometimes beyond our comprehension.

In the poem as a whole Dante sets forth a vision of the universe and of human life that makes a certain kind of meaning possible and in so doing grants dignity to human beings and to human experience. His vision is comprehensive, running from the beginning to the end of time; it promises to make sense of our experience, including our experience of ourselves, and of our deepest longings; it offers a way of imagining the world that makes possible coherent speech and action; and at its center is the question of the justice of God. But Dante's vision is not of an authoritarian system, asserted to be just and presented as though the human mind could grasp it all, human language express it all. It is articulated in a created relationship between author and reader in which both his and our ignorance, and weakness, and skepticism too, are all given a

---

[31] For striking development of this last point, see Gustavo Gutiérrez, *On Job: God-Talk and the Suffering of the Innocent*, trans. Matthew J. O'Connell (Maryknoll, N.Y.: Orbis Books, 1987).

place; in this way his poem creates the tensions and uncertainties, described in chapter 1, that have the effect of calling upon the reader to assert himself as an independent center of thought, experience, and judgment, a necessary step if he is ever to understand, and not respect, the empire of force. Dante's vision is presented in our immediate experience as well, the experience of reading that works through time to transform our minds, bringing us at the end to see what cannot be seen, to hear what cannot be heard.

In all of this Dante makes the justice of the universe he is representing not only a crucial topic of his own but a fundamental and explicit problem for his reader. To start with, the whole idea of eternal punishment for human wrong is likely to seem to us wildly excessive and deeply unjust; in addition, the assignment of many of the individual souls to their designated regions in the Inferno is likely to seem to us wrong on the merits, as I have suggested we are likely to think with respect to Francesca and Ulysses; finally, and perhaps most salient, it will seem to us both cruel and unfair that Virgil, of all people, should be confined to Limbo, living huddled by the fire in the dark with the other figures of the classical past.

Here I shall consider only the problem presented by the treatment of Virgil, postponing until chapter 6 the other two questions of justice (relating to eternal punishment itself and the selection of those who suffer it). As I suggested in chapter 1, Dante makes the fate of Virgil unavoidably problematic. When we get to Purgatory, for example, we find that the gate is guarded by Cato, the great Roman republican. Like Virgil, Cato lived and died before Christ and was to boot a suicide—which is of course a sin, perhaps the only sin one cannot normally repent, and a sin for which a special place is reserved in the Inferno. In addition he was an implacable opponent of Caesar, the founder of the empire, so in a sense he was both a traitor and an enemy of empire. We cannot help asking: What is Cato doing here in Purgatory, when Virgil is in Limbo? A similar problem is presented part way through Purgatory when Dante and Virgil meet Statius, a poet who lived after Christ but is now to be saved, we are told, because he became a secret Christian. This conversion is a patent authorial ruse, for there is no other evidence for it; what is for our purposes perhaps more poignant, Statius attributes his conversion to a famous passage in Virgil's *Fourth Eclogue*, one that had been widely read to foresee the birth of Christ. He tells Virgil, "By you I became a poet, by you a Christian," *per te poeta fui, per te cristiano* (*Purgatorio* XXII, 73). So Virgil can convert others to Christianity, others who will end up in

Paradise, while he remains in Limbo. One necessarily feels that this cannot be just.

Finally, in Canto XX of the *Paradiso* we are told of two more saved pagans: Trajan, who was by legend allowed through the prayers of Gregory the Great to return briefly to life so that he could convert and be saved, and Ripheus, of whom we only know that he is briefly referred to in the *Aeneid* of Virgil (!) as the most just of men, *justissimus*. The explanation given by the authoritative speaker in this Canto, the Eagle of Empire, roots this exception in the "warm love and living hope which conquer the divine will," *da caldo amore e da viva speranza, / che vince la divina volontate* (95–96). It is good to hear that love and hope can conquer rigid justice, but why should Ripheus be the object of such special treatment? Because, we are told, he "directed all his love to righteousness," *tutto suo amor là giù pose a drittura* (121) and "by grace upon grace, God opened his eye to our future redemption, and he believed in it," *per che, di grazia in grazia, Dio li aperse / l'occhio a la nostra redenzion futura; / ond 'ei credette in quella.* (122–24). This is all lovely, and teaches that the apparent rigidities of doctrine, and of the Divine will, are only apparent. But when the reader recalls Virgil's fate he cannot help asking, How, then, can the treatment of Virgil possibly be just?

Dante's treatment of the pre-Christian Jews, perhaps surprisingly, also reinforces our awareness of this problem. We are told in Canto II of the *Inferno* that when Beatrice was visited by Lucia—the emissary of Mary, who urged her to act to save the lost Dante—she was sitting beside Rachel, as if that were perfectly natural. But what, the reader will sensibly ask, is Rachel doing in a Christian heaven? This question itself is rather quickly answered when we are told, in Canto IV, that Christ rescued some of the most illustrious of the Old Testament Jews during the Harrowing of Hell (his time spent there between the Crucifixion and the Resurrection). Thus Adam, Abel, Noah, Moses, David, and Rachel, and many others, were all saved (*Inferno* IV, 55–61). In terms of Dante's system of belief this all looks like an extraordinary dispensation, to say the least, though it is apparently limited to the greatest figures of the Old Testament. But when Dante the traveler has his final vision of the heavenly court, with the souls arranged in ranks and rows on two sides of Mary and Christ, in a kind of cosmic football stadium filling the sky, we are told that half of these souls are Jews from the time before Christ, half people saved the Christian way, by baptism and a life of faith. All this is glorious and beautiful, a wonderful acceptance of what to Dante were the people of the Old Covenant, another performance, in Dante's eyes, of the immense generosity and love of the Ruler of the Universe.[32] But when one returns to the treatment of Virgil, it makes what happens to him seem still more singular and odd.

Dante the traveler seems to accept Virgil's fate as a doctrinal matter, without explanation, but the poem certainly makes it an issue—as indeed it also does with the justice of eternal punishment for anyone, for anything. The effect of this is to compel the reader to assert his own judgment about the matter, thus constituting him as an independent mind, forcing him to think things through in a way for which he will himself be responsible. The poem thus seems written to express and celebrate orthodox Christian views, but to resist authoritarian and empty ways of conceiving of them. Theologically speaking, we can read this as an enactment of the premise that the individual soul, in this case that of the reader, cannot be saved by empty compliance with rules, or empty affirmations of belief—think of Guido da Montefeltro, for example—but must itself engage with the fundamental issues of doubt and belief, including facing the apparent fact of the radical injustice that is a feature not only of Dante's imagined afterworld but human life itself. Any human being with experience of life knows deeply that the world is not what it ought to be; it is Dante's surprising achievement to replicate that feature of our experience in his account of the regime of the Deity—at least so far as we can understand it—where we might expect it to be missing or resolved. His poem is thus not a way of escaping or evading the problem of justice at the center of our own experience of the world; quite the opposite, he forces it upon us.

The crucial thing is that Dante presents the question of justice as a real and valid one, the nerve of human life; for the purposes of the poem this is far more important than whether we are persuaded that this or that action of his imagined, or real, God is in fact just. In this Dante is telling us, showing us, that in the face of injustice we have a claim of justice—against the universe, or its God, or the state—a claim that asserts the core of the human being and his or her experience. To have a view of the

[32] This generosity does not extend to persons of the Jewish faith who adhere to it after the life and death of Christ. Wrong as this may seem to you and me, to Dante this does not present a problem of justice; it simply makes sense as the consequence of a deliberate refusal to accept what is offered. Dante was not, that is, a religious pluralist; but in that he was not alone, and that not only among Christians but Muslims and Jews as well.

universe, as some do, that stripped us of this claim would be to strip us of our deepest humanity.

Perhaps something could still be said to justify the treatment of Virgil, and perhaps Dante the poet would even agree with it.[33] But the poem as written does not say such things; equally important it does make us feel,

[33] Here is something that might be said in response to our feelings of outraged justice—not that it will justify the treatment of Virgil exactly, but it may complicate our response to it. What the souls in Limbo suffer, Virgil says, is that we live in desire without hope, *che sanza speme vivemo in disio* (*Inferno* IV, 42). To the Christian mind this is not a rare or odd condition for a person who lived when Virgil did, but is rather the necessary state of humanity from which the entry of Christ into the world rescued or redeemed it. What is more, the real-world Virgil himself did in fact suffer from a kind of desire without hope, as his poetry, full of a sense of cosmic sadness and loss, makes plain. *Sunt lacrimae rerum*, he says in a famous passage, tears are in the nature of things (*Aeneid* I, 462); perhaps nothing so marks the *Aeneid* as the sense of an unbridgeable gap between the way things should be in the world and the way they are, a gap that fills Virgil and his reader with sympathy and sorrow.

When Christ comes to save humankind, why can he not save those who have lived and died before he arrived? The answer the Christian mind would make is that human beings live, and always have lived, in linear time, in history. It is only possible for Christ to enter history and redeem humanity—to make everything different—if in fact there is something to redeem us from, a real condition of limitation. If there is such a condition, Christ's entry cannot simply reverse it for it is a fact of the world. It cannot be the same for those who come before and come after, or Christ's entry into history works no real change. For Dante those who come before Christ live in a world without Christ, which means without the possibility of the three theological virtues—faith, hope, love—and the kind of life they make possible.

This is not a state of sinfulness or evil, and Virgil is not being punished; it is rather that he represents a historical state in which people's minds and imaginations and hearts were limited in a way that Christ's presence into history would change. Virgil is not blamed in any way: he achieves all the happiness of which human beings are capable without redemption through love.

Such are the things that can be said, and perhaps they will persuade, perhaps not. There is still the question of Ripheus and Trajan and Cato. It is part of the teaching of the poem as a poem that such efforts to intellectualize and rationalize all run out in the end, as they do in the Book of Job as well. We have before us the imagined life Dante presents, full of uncertainty, full of at least apparent injustice, to which it is our task to respond as well as we can, as it is our task to respond to life itself.

One final note on Virgil, which both confirms our sense of injustice and holds out the possibility of something else. In Canto II of the *Inferno* Virgil tells us what Beatrice said to him when she sent him to rescue Dante. She concludes this way: "I am Beatrice who bids you go; I come from a place to which I desire to return; love moves me, and makes me speak. When I am before my Lord, I will praise you often to Him." (70–74).

repeatedly and acutely, that Virgil's treatment is unjust. As I say above, this works as an insistence that we be responsible and independent, capable of our own thought and judgment and shaping our own moral destiny. It is in this way that Dante writes a poem about an empire, the empire of the whole universe in fact, without becoming an apologist for it. The cry of injustice is the first, last, and deepest insistence by the human being upon his or her own value, and the value of humanity itself. It is the center of our capacity to claim meaning for experience, and the center of our resistance to the empire of force.

> I' son Beatrice che ti faccio andare;
> vegno del loco ove tornar disio;
> amor mi mosse, che mi fa parlare.
> Quando sarò dinanzi al segnor mio,
> di te mi loderò sovente a lui.

Why will she praise Virgil often? She must have a hope that something will at last be done for him; this, as I say, at once confirms our sense of radical injustice in his treatment and gives a hope of its correction. After all, when Mary sent Beatrice to Dante it was not because he was deserving but because of her compassion for him; this results in a "hard judgment in heaven being broken" (*Inferno* II, 96).

> Donna è gentil nel ciel che si compiange
> di questo 'mpedimento ov' io ti mando,
> sì che duro giudicio là sù frange.   (94–96)

The compassion of Mary works, that is, as an exception to justice, which indeed is the purpose and effect, in Dante's religious view, of the life and death of Christ himself. None of us deserves salvation, which is always an act of unmerited grace, a fact that suggests the possibility that it might be extended, in our imagined version of the eternal world, to Virgil as well.

CHAPTER SIX

❦

Silence, Belief, and the Right to Speak

Living speech; trivializing and degrading speech; silence and mean-ing among the Quakers; the law as an institution built upon speech that claims meaning for experience; belief beyond language, in life and law; Dante; justice and love; Simone Weil.

IF WE ARE ALIVE, we look at the world and listen to what we hear around us, and say, "How am I to live in such a place, speak such a language?" We look at ourselves, at our own tendency to use the sentimental and au-thoritarian languages and locutions we hear, and say, "How can I possi-bly find a way to live and speak decently and well?" In our world the strong forces of advertising and propaganda constantly work to trivialize our language and experience, to infantilize us as political actors and thinkers, and to reduce us to consumers and voters with defective minds. How to resist these forces, ultimately forces of death, and to assert the re-ality and power and life of the human mind and spirit in ourselves and others is, in my view at least, both the central question of individual life and the largest cultural and political issue of our era.

Consider the experience of commercial television. The ideology is that the viewer is being "entertained" or "informed" at the price of being ex-posed to advertisements. But in fact the driving purpose of the networks is the advertising, for that is where their revenue comes from; the motive of the "entertainment" or "information," then, is actually not to entertain or inform but to collect an audience for the advertisers. In a real sense what we call the "shows" are thus also a form of advertising: advertising to the advertisers to persuade them to sponsor the program. Despite what he is told, and his own impressions, the viewer is not so much being entertained or informed by television as becoming a part of it and the system of life it creates. This is a system of politics, for it is based upon a view of the good human life, individual and collective, which it constantly urges the public to pursue; and it is based upon a kind of language, empty and manipulative, that would be the death of democracy if it became the standard form of political thought and debate in our country.

At the individual level our aim should be to resist the empire of force by refusing to be the kind of person and mind it requires us to be. If we could do it, this would be an achievement with its own value for each of us who did so; to multiply and generalize such an achievement would have great consequences for the whole world. For us to show that we understand the empire of force, with all its seductive allure and power, and know how not to respect it—and to insist upon respecting instead the center of the human mind and soul, where meaning is claimed and made—is the only way in which our world can be transformed for the better. It is the only ground of hope.

Such a transformation would have political consequences of the most radical kind, for it would be based upon the view that our first collective aim should be the creation and maintenance of the conditions, both cultural and material, on which meaningful speech and action would become possible for every person. Perhaps the worst thing a person can suffer is not simply deprivation of this or that material good, or as Ajax shows us even life itself, but the lack of a language in which to talk about his or her experience, including injuries and losses, in a way that will effectively assert its meaning. To ensure these conditions requires wise economic and institutional policies, but the motive and aim would not be economic or institutional; rather the liberation and education of the human spirit.[1]

In a sense this book thus has a deeply political purpose. Yet I have not here engaged in debate about questions defined as political by our

[1] For people to have equal opportunities to develop their minds and imaginations in ways that will enable them to speak effectively as centers of meaning, and to respond to others when they speak in this way too, of course entails economic support, but it is not about economics. It is about libraries and schools and prenatal health and safe streets and a social and cultural environment that respects the individual person. It requires that the polity be concerned with the state of its own culture: Does our culture invite, reward, make possible genuine and valuable speech, or is it dominated by the forms I have been calling advertising and propaganda, which diminish and infantilize the human actor and his mind, corrupting his language? All this is a way of imagining democracy itself as a form of conversation, as Dewey claimed when he said, "Democracy begins in conversation" (*Dialogue on John Dewey*, ed. Corliss Lamont [New York: Horizon, 1959], 58). Not in the form of a national town meeting, for that cannot exist, but world in which we all stand up for the importance of speech that is deeply meant, and seek to engage in it ourselves.

contemporary discourse: the tension between the economy and the environment, say, or the proper relation for our country to have with other nations or with international organizations, or the propriety of a particular act of war, or the wisdom or justice of our tax policies, or the meaning of abortion or the death penalty. This is not because such issues are not important to me, for of course they are, but because I think that wise and decent thought on these questions requires first of all, before anything else, a sense of how to put them into living speech—speech that can avoid the trivialization and emptiness of so much of what we hear and say, and instead confirm the essential dignity and value of human life and experience. This kind of speech both expresses and enacts—it makes real in the world—a way of being human that can in turn make possible a healthy community. I cannot predict exactly what policies a democracy that was characterized by speech of this kind would adopt, but I am confident that they would be fundamentally respectful of self and others and that the community so defined would be one to which I would be glad to belong.

Similarly when I have talked about law I have not for the most part asked what rules or principles of decision the courts ought to use in deciding First Amendment cases, or how particular cases ought themselves be decided. This has been deliberate on my part. Of course it matters, enormously, what outcomes are reached in particular cases and what principles are used to decide them. But my focus has been on something prior to that, namely how we should talk about these properly contested matters. Unless we have the right image of the kind of speech we should be most interested in protecting, and why it is valuable, and unless we can find ways to talk that way ourselves, we shall not be able to think well and confidently about the cases and principles in the first place. So this is indeed a book about law, but it is not meant so much to be a contribution to existing legal debates about particular rules and outcomes as to focus on an earlier question: How, on what understandings of the nature and value of speech, should people in the law, whether judges or lawyers or law teachers, think and speak about the human activity of speech? How should they speak themselves?

SILENCE AND MEANINGFUL SPEECH

When Quakers gather for silent meeting for worship, they are not simply being quiet. They are waiting for one of their number to be moved to speak, as they would say, by the Spirit. This should happen only from time to time for any one person. Those who feel an inclination to speak to the Meeting should engage in lengthy self-scrutiny before breaking the silence, in order to be as sure as they can that it is indeed the Spirit that is moving them to speak—not their own need for attention, or their desire to be heard, or the pleasure of telling others how things are and what to do. What one says should come from the center of the self, not the surface where our clichés and formulas cluster. One should not simply blurt out whatever comes to mind but reflect upon it, trying to recast it in ways that will make it both briefer and more resonant for others. It is to be both deeply meant and shaped by art.

This means that the silence that fills the room is not passive but full of expectancy and activity: people are reflecting and imagining and thinking, listening for a voice within; deciding whether they are truly called to speak; casting what they might say first this way, and then that; listening for signs that others may speak, and preparing to pay deep attention to what they say if they do. Sometimes the process is so intense as to manifest itself in bodily tensions and movements, a kind of twitching or quaking, a version of what in the seventeenth century gave rise to the name by which the community is known.

Among traditional Quakers there are no priests or pastors, for the basic premise is that there is "that of God in every person," and accordingly it is not just through people set aside by ordination or special training that the Spirit will speak, but through anyone. It is this central part of the person that is called upon to speak, and when it speaks it should be listened to—and listened to with attention, over time, in silence. The essential principles of Quaker ethics, including nonviolent social action, rest on the same basic image of the person: it is because there is "that of God in every person" that every person should be treated as equally and uniquely valuable. Violence and brutality obviously break this principle, as does any erasure of the autonomy and reality of another person, especially of his or her deepest self.

Quaker practices of political resistance similarly work by appealing to "that of God" in the other person—in the angry segregationist, the officious colonel at the nuclear missile site, the hard-hearted CEO, the self-satisfied university teacher or administrator, the curious passerby—and in oneself and one's friends as well. This kind of resistance is of course not magical, and often has no immediate success. But over time, who can say?

I have been saying something similar throughout this book: that each person is uniquely valuable because each is a unique center of meaning and a source of value. It is this, for example, that makes the birth of a child such an astonishing and wonderful event: here is a new person who will be, from this moment on, the center of a world of significance and meaning; she will have her own experiences, never fully shared or share-able with others, of which she will have to make sense her own way; she will live in a set of relations with other people, and with the culture, that are replicated nowhere else in the universe but are unique to her. In all of this she should have—and it is our duty to see that she does—the capac-ity to speak and write in ways that claim for her experience the meaning she finds or creates within it.

This image of human uniqueness and possibility is the opposite of the image of humanity upon which advertising depends. Advertising typically assumes that the images with which it works—of a sunset on the beach, or of two people about to have sex, or a cold beer after work, or of the Marlboro Man—are the same for everyone, or at least for everyone in its target audience. The message is, smoke Marlboros and you—all of you—will be like this rugged man on horseback, tough, experienced, outdoors, manly; drink Miller and you will join with other men in hav-ing the universal feeling of a job well done, now rewarded by the beer; buy a Chevrolet and your life will be like a sunset on the beach; use Old Spice and you will find women, here presented as beautiful, irresistibly drawn to you—and what could be better? Life itself is turned into a se-ries of stereotypical moments, into which you are invited to convert your own experience, by buying and using the advertiser's product.[2] In this way advertising constitutes a force that denies and resists the natural movement of the human soul into ever deeper uniqueness of thought and

---

[2] The premise of the culture of advertising, as I have said, is that human fulfillment consists of the gratification of human desires. The happy person is the one who has what he wants. The satisfaction of human desire is the highest good. But, as any experience of life teaches, our own frustration, disappointment, loss, and ultimately weakness and death are essential parts of life, not only factually but normatively: it is, as the chorus in *Agamemnon* says, suffering that brings wisdom (Line 177). This is what the other Greek plays we looked at, *Oedipus at Colonus* and *Ajax*, also teach. It is often our greatest disappoint-ments and losses that are in the end best for us. Think of children you care about: of course a part of you wants to spare them all distress, but if you succeeded in doing so they would never become fully human, capable of growth, and understanding, and depth. They would become exactly what the world of advertising constantly tells them to become, ignorant of yet subject to the empire of force.

experience. The aim of advertising, and its cousin propaganda, is the creation of a population that will live in a displaced zone, not in the world or in their own minds, but in a fantasy land where all is reduced to images that make a false claim to universal meaning, and at the price of the erasure of their own experience, their own souls.

The discourse of advertising and propaganda regularly presents images not only of what it conceives to be the good life, but of those who do not participate in it: "other people," who are lumped together as different from us, yet themselves somehow all the same. This is true of outsider figures in advertising, those with whom the audience is not invited to identify, whoever lacks the appearance and social position held out as valuable: the geek at the office, the homely person on the bus, the kook in the neighborhood. In propaganda this definition of others is nearly the whole point: we are Germans of pure race, they are inferior; we are good Americans, they are beastly Germans, or fanatic Muslims. This is what makes it possible, as I said in the introduction, for us to kill children and their mothers and fathers and grandparents by bombing their homes, or to torture members of the enemy group when we have captured them, or to reduce a whole people to the status of chattel slaves or beasts of burden. One especially destructive form of this kind of speech, familiar to all of us, is racism, a discourse that assumes that all "blacks," to take the most flagrant case in our culture, are in some essential way the same, and different from "whites," and "inferior." The practice of racism does many terrible things, but among them is that it denies people in the race that is its primary subject their inherent right to grow and develop as unique and uniquely valuable human beings. In this way racism has kinship with the language and motives of war, the ultimate propaganda, which reduces whole nations, with all their people, of any age or condition, to objects of fear and hate.[3] It is upon this kind of denial of humanity that the empire of force, in its various manifestations, always depends.

Our dignity and value, as individuals and as communities, ultimately rest upon our desire and capacity to claim satisfactory meaning for our experience and that of others. This desire and capacity are distinctive to human life: one cannot imagine a fully human life without them, or

[3] For elaboration of the point that the language of race is the language of war, see James Boyd White, "What's Wrong with Our Talk about Race? On History, Particularity, and Affirmative Action," *Michigan Law Review* 100 (2002): 1927, 1951–53.

a nonhuman life with them.[4] To achieve or experience depth and reality in human speech—that which comes from the center—is of crucial value not only in the Quaker Meeting but everywhere. It makes us valuable; it confers dignity upon speaker and hearer alike; it respects the limitations of human language and the human mind; and it recognizes the value of every person as himself or herself a maker of meaning. It makes it possible for us to feel in our lives what it has been well said that Shakespeare's characters feel: that they live in heightened circumstances that call for heightened speech, speech in which they can make claims upon the world resting on the meaning of their own experience.[5] Living speech of this kind resists the empire of force as nothing else can do.

THE LAW

One of the ideas running through this book is that the law can be a place for what I have called living speech, and this in two ways. First, in thinking about the speech of others in the world, lawyers and judges can read the First Amendment as having living speech at the core of its concerns: speech that dignifies the speaker and hearer, that proceeds from central self to central self, and that has value not in an instrumental way, but value as speech itself. Where would such an experiment take us?

On such a view the central image of the speaking person would be that of a mind seeking and claiming meaning for experience, in relation both to others and to the language they share. The primary concern of the First Amendment would be with speech that was in this sense inherently

---

[4] Victor Frankl's book, *Man's Search for Meaning: An Introduction to Logotherapy*, trans. Ilse Lasch (Boston: Beacon Press, 1962), develops this point persuasively and at length. For a briefer instance, consider Barbara Myerhoff, *Number Our Days* (New York: E. P. Dutton, 1979), an anthropological study of life in a Jewish center for the elderly in Los Angeles: "Lacking hope for change, improvement, without a future, they had devised a counterworld, inventing their own version of what made 'the good life.' It was built on their veneration for their religious and cultural membership and it was full of meaning, intensity, and consciousness. This they had managed on their own, creating a nearly invisible, run-down, tiny world, containing a major lesson for any who would attend it. . . . It was especially their passion for meaning that appealed to me so deeply, this the Center folk valued above happiness or comfort" (20).

[5] See Patsy Rodenburg, *Speaking Shakespeare* (New York: Palgrave Macmillan, 2002), esp. 11–12.

alive and therefore valuable: not speech as taste, consumption, information, gratification, or use but speech as a way of achieving meaning—of which, as we know, silence is an important condition. For purposes of the amendment, that is, what would matter is not the fact that an expression uses words or that a gesture is in some sense communicative, but a judgment that this expression, this gesture, is offered as valuable for its own sake. Of course questions of definition would arise, and one should always display appropriate and honest modesty about making such judgments; likewise the Court should recognize that useless, damaging, stupid, gross, ugly speech may need to be protected in order to make the protection of the most valuable speech secure and meaningful. But in all this the Court's eye should be upon the nature and quality of speech, not just the fact of communication. It should always ask whether the utterance in question is offered as a claim of meaning or for the gratification of some other desire. If it decides that the amendment should protect dangerous, empty, trivializing, demeaning, or damaging speech, it should recognize that fact and what it means.

This view assumes that at its heart democracy works, or should work, by speech that is seriously meant, not by a calculation of preferences expressed in a series of interest votes, let alone by manipulative or dishonest speech. Democracy is a world of people talking to each other, on the street and in institutional places. The actions of public agents, including courts, derive their authority from this conversation, and from the way they themselves contribute to it. On the view I have been urging, the First Amendment would be committed to protecting and furthering this process and activity. It would see the world as a world of people talking, not making deals or transactions. Speech and what it can do are the center of its concerns.

Second, the law itself can be a place where people strive to engage in living speech. This is crucial for many reasons, not the least that the law will be able to protect living speech by others, in the world, only if its practitioners, both lawyers and judges, can understand and attain it themselves. Is that a real possibility? We have seen instances of failure—the cliché of the "marketplace of ideas," the emptiness of the formulas of *Free Speech Coalition* and *Virginia Pharmacy Board*—but also writings that have real elements of success: the opinions of Jackson and Frankfurter in *Barnette*, Jackson in *Thomas v. Collins*, Harlan in *Cohen*, and Brandeis in *Whitney*. These performances define possibilities we can both seek to attain ourselves and use in judging the work of others. In a sense we know this perfectly well, for when we evaluate an opinion or an argument, or the work of a judge or a lawyer, we normally do not speak merely in terms of analytic acuteness, skill in presentation, and intellectual coherence—though these are of course important qualities—but in much more general terms: openness to other ways of thinking; responsiveness to questions; honesty in facing difficulties; sensitivity to historical and social context; understanding of the situations and motives of others; awareness of the real costs and dangers of a particular decision; the capacity to make sense of the case as a whole, both standing alone and in connection with other cases. Beyond such things, we speak of even more general qualities: courage, for example, and wisdom, and a sense of justice, and good judgment. The legal intelligence in its ideal form would comprise nearly every intellectual, psychological, and moral virtue, and these qualities, when they are present, will manifest themselves in speech and writing.

Of course both the lawyer and judge are always tempted by empty formulations, by dead forms of speech and life—whether they take the form of legal clichés, as in *Free Speech Coalition*, or the importation of an authoritarian system of thought, as in *Virginia Pharmacy Board*. But these temptations can sometimes be resisted or overcome by a different kind of writing, offering a different sort of experience to the world.

Although we live in a mass culture it is nonetheless possible for our leaders—in the judiciary, in the legislature, and in the White House—to speak as responsible human beings, explaining themselves in a kind of expression that does not trivialize them and us but does honor to both. It is imaginable that in their expressions they could manifest minds that are honestly engaged in thought and expression of a deep and living kind, not the manipulation of formulas. We know this is true, for we have instances of it: think of Lincoln's letter to Hooker.

It is especially important for the Supreme Court to be able to do this, not only for us but for the institution itself, because the authority of the Court, especially its authority to review the actions of other governmental actors, depends entirely upon the justices' capacity to write in ways that compel respect. They have no power of a more tangible kind, over the police or the army or the budget. Their writing is the basis of their power. And this basis is fundamentally democratic, for the expression of reason is in the nature of things a submission, over time, to the audience to whom one speaks, who must approve or acquiesce if the power is to continue. It has been the point of this book to argue that what is called for in this writing is not merely good technical reasoning, but a kind of writing that shows that the author understands the empire of force to which she is tempted to submit, in the form of clichés and slogans and mechanistic modes of decision, and knows not to respect them. Then and only then can she offer us a judgment that is the product of her mind, in a text in which she is present as a person, responsible for what she says and does, and able, as Simone Weil puts it, to love and be just.

BELIEF: BEYOND LANGUAGE IS . . . ?

I now turn to a different aspect of my subject, not yet explicitly discussed but important for understanding the nature of living speech, for which my word will be "belief."

Think again of the way language works in the minds of Quakers at their Meeting. Language is here embedded in silence, where its shape can be seen, its adequacies and inadequacies made the object of attention; where it can be recast, both in the mind contemplating speech and in the mind listening as it is spoken. There is a constant sense of limit, both of mind and language, for whatever one says will come from a world of silence that is inherently inexpressible. This is so whether one thinks of what is going on as the leading of the Spirit or as something else entirely, say the confrontation of the conscious self with its buried voices. In this speech there is also a sense of the temporary, an inherent nonfinality. For everyone present in the room knows that whatever is said is said for this day, this moment only; as soon as it is over the present becomes the past and the silence out of which meaningful speech can emerge exists again, calling for something new. The kind of speech that takes place here is never conclusive; it always assumes and calls for further speech, and speech that emerges from silence. All this provides a context where simplicity can work with power—not as a cliché, but as truth.

This set of practices rests on belief. Not necessarily a "belief in God," as that phrase is usually meant: there is no need to imagine a creator, or a Christ or Messiah, or prophets or angels or devils, or sacred and inspired texts, or heaven and hell. None of the intellectual or imaginative apparatus of Jewish or Christian or other standard religious belief is required. The only constant is a belief in what the Quakers call "that of God in every person." Such a phrase can of course become a cliché or slogan, a sort of buzzword; but often it does not, whenever the community insists that it always be redefined as it is used in new contexts.[6] This means the phrase can be seen not as a conclusory gesture, a slogan or formula closing off conversation, but as a way of opening up continuing thought and reflection.

Ultimately the belief upon which these practices rests cannot be encapsulated in a phrase, or creed, or any other set of statements. It is not propositional in nature but experiential, a discovery or a commitment. This fits with the history of the word "belief," which does not etymologically mean what we often take it to mean, namely an assertion of propositions claiming to utter the truth of what cannot be known, but a form of love: it is cognate with the archaic "lief," as in "I would lief," and with our word "love" itself. The sort of belief I am speaking of is not an intellectual or conceptual position but something that lies beneath or beyond all such things: a kind of commitment of the self. The quotation from Simone Weil reflected in the title to this book suggests that there is an inherent connection between love and justice. This connection is I think true of the special kind of love we call belief, namely that it is essential to justice, and justice to it. Suppose you say: Whenever I hear the word "law," I will ask where justice is; and whenever I hear the word "justice," I will ask where belief is; and whenever I hear the word "belief," I will ask where love is?

Belief in this sense is an essential condition to the Quaker engagement in meaningful speech. It is the ground, outside of language, upon which the members of the Meeting rest, and from which they speak. It is what makes it possible for them to live with the knowledge that perfect speech and uncorrupted language, perfect knowledge and perfect virtue, are all impossible, and with the additional knowledge that one can never completely understand one's own culture and the way it has shaped one's mind. The constant return to the community of belief, both in imagination and in fact, is in this world the core of life, the place where the self emerges—the self that is necessary to meaningful speech. It is the center of the Quaker sense of human dignity and humanity. I think that some such belief as this is necessary to the kind of living speech I have been describing.

---

[6] For example, in the process of becoming a member of the Society of Friends each individual must explain, usually in writing, his own sense of what is drawing him to want to join this community and the practices that define it. In this statement each person must give content to whatever language he uses—including the phrase, if he chooses to use it, about "that of God."

As I say, it is not necessary that the belief be framed as a belief in "God" or some supernatural being or have any of the usual indices of religion. Indeed articulated beliefs of overtly religious kinds themselves often seem superficial or empty: not deep expressions of the mind and self confronting the puzzles and silences of the world, but phrases that make up a domain of cliché and slogan. The kind of belief I mean would include any way of imagining the world, and oneself and others within it, that would make possible living speech and coherent action.

This kind of belief has many forms. I think of one friend whose way of imagining human life is as a set of activities and experiences all in potential conflict, ranging from athletics to professional success to interest in the arts to intimate engagements in the family. His style of life is to realize these various potentialities, and the identities they entail, with as full recognition of the tensions and contradictions they generate as he can manage. It is a bit as though for him life were a quilt with many patches; the aim is to make sure that each is brightly and richly colored, in the hope, but not the certainty, that at the end it will make a significant pattern. Whether and how he succeeds or fails is the drama of his life. Another friend sees human life as grounded in the response to the beauty and coherence of the forms of nature, a response that at its best consists of acts of human creation, including his own—drawings, wood carvings, writings—which reflect and fulfill the process of natural creation itself. It is as though in all important human activity we are cocreators of the world, subject to the discipline of tuning ourselves and our achievements to the order of nature as we perceive it. Still another friend takes as the ground of life the use of language itself: one person speaking to another in language, never perfectly understood, never perfectly understanding— everything needing translation, and translation always imperfect. This becomes a model for all intellectual life, all ethical life, from the most personal to the most public. For another friend, the central question is overtly cosmological: how do we imagine the universe and ourselves within it? Is the universe, including people and their minds and imaginations, ultimately a physical system, working as a kind of enormous physical and biological machine? Or does our experience require us to imagine ourselves not simply as the product of a system, an emergent property, but as a person, a mind, a soul? I make these descriptions not in the hope that I can do justice to any of these ways of imagining the world but rather simply to suggest that all of them seem to me forms of belief upon which living speech can be based.

For my purposes in fact, statements of nonbelief, or failure of belief, can constitute a form of belief. Think of Ajax, first claiming then disclaiming a way of looking at the world. The important thing is that the side of the self that desires meaning of this kind, that wants to find coherence in world and significance in life, be present and continue its struggle. Not to do that, to refuse to commit—to keep one's options perpetually open—is to fail in the essential human endeavor. As Dante represents it, such a failure results in a fall into the anteroom of the Inferno, inhabited by souls that never chose either side in the conflict between good and evil. In this sense they never really lived at all, and they are accordingly regarded with contempt by people in every other condition in the Inferno, including the worst. The reason they are not sent into the lower regions, indeed, is that their presence there would give some sense of satisfaction, of superiority, to the wicked, and thus soften their punishment.[7] Of such as these, Virgil says, "Let us not speak of them, but look and pass by," *non ragioniam di lor, ma guarda e passa (Inferno III, 51).*

In the sense in which I am speaking of belief, it is ultimately the believing side of the self—the side that hopes to believe—that is expressed and recognized in living speech, and denied and trivialized by advertising and propaganda, both of which are ways of erasing the significance of meaningful speech or action, and in this sense of destroying belief.[8] The law by contrast requires belief. Think of what makes possible the life of the hardworking lawyer: a belief that what he is doing makes sense and has value in itself, as he himself works out the terms of a settlement, say, or a contract for the sale of urban real estate, and as he imagines his fellow

---

[7]   *Caccianli i ciel per non esser men belli,*
       né lo profondo inferno li riceve,
       ch'alcuna gloria i rei avrebber d'elli.   (Inferno III, 40–42)

"The heavens drive them out not to be rendered less beautiful, and the profound Inferno does not receive them lest the wicked there have some glory over them."

[8] For a line of argument congenial with my own, though cast in somewhat different terms, see Steven D. Smith, "Believing Persons, Personal Believings: The Neglected Center of the First Amendment," *University of Illinois Law Review* 2002 (2002): 1233. It is worth observing that the view I am articulating, and that Smith to some degree shares—that the kind of speech the First Amendment should be most concerned to protect, and enable, and foster, is what I have called living speech, grounded on belief—suggests that the connections between this part of the First Amendment and its other main provisions, protecting the free exercise of religion and prohibiting its establishment, may be much deeper than has generally been thought.

lawyers, across the country, doing much the same thing. If he lost that belief, and thought that all he was doing was working for money, or that what he himself said had no meaning beyond the instrumental or manipulative, that would make the life in a deep sense impossible. Without a belief in the real value of the conversation about justice that is the center of the lawyer's life he would be dead at the core. One can imagine a lawyer or a judge suffering a loss of faith almost as easily as one can imagine a priest doing so. In both cases the life led on such terms would become impossible, empty, dead, no longer full of the life and promise that were its essence. To recall the etymological roots of the word "belief," there would be nothing to love.

Law depends upon a belief in the reality of other people, in the possibility of meaningful speech in the heightened circumstances it provides, and in the kind of justice that consists of real attention, honest thought, and doubt. This belief is made express and manifest in writing that calls the reader into life. It ultimately takes the form of love, a love of other and a love of justice.

For our purposes, what this means is that the law, which is often represented as a closed and authoritarian system, is in fact grounded on wholly different principles of openness, and in two directions, of law and of fact. With respect to law, as we have repeatedly seen, what the good lawyer believes in is not the set of rules that she applies, but the process of thought and imagination and argument and speech by which the rules or other legal texts are given meaning in the world. This process or activity is the heart of the lawyer's life, and it is the heart of a legal education as well—we do not teach our students systems of rules, but how to engage in the process by which legal rules, and other texts, are given meaning.[9]

With respect to what we call the facts, the lawyer is constantly brought

---

[9] See Robert Burns, *A Theory of the Trial* (Princeton, N.J.: Princeton University Press, 1999). And compare Thomas D. Eisele on the teaching of law, "What We Share," *University of Cincinnati Law Review* 71 (2002): 493. Eisele quotes a fine passage by Brian Simpson denying that the common law consists of a set of rules. "[I]t is a feature of the common law system that there is no way of settling the correct text or formulation of the rules, so that it is inherently impossible to state so much as a single rule in what Pollock called 'any authentic [authoritative?] form of words.' How can it be said that the common law exists as a system of general rules when it is impossible to say what they are?" A. W. B. Simpson, "The Common Law and Legal Theory," in *Oxford Essays in Jurisprudence*, 2nd Series, ed. A. W. B. Simpson (Oxford: Clarendon Press, 1973), 89.

to face the world outside the language of the law: the world of physical and emotional experience, inherently inexpressible—the pain of a broken arm, or a broken marriage, or a broken career—and the world defined by other languages, from science to psychology to economics to geography, each of which has its own domain and way of functioning, different from the law's. The lawyer must find a way to talk about the world of human experience, and the worlds created by multiple human languages, in the places and language of legal speech. This always involves a process of translation that is inherently imperfect; a large part of his or her art is the recognition of that imperfection and the discovery of a way to proceed notwithstanding it. In all of this the law and the lawyer are resisting the claims of people, languages, and institutions alike that they have self-sufficient ways of describing the world and living within it that will work for all times and purposes—authoritarian systems of thought and life that cannot be questioned. The lawyer is a writer, one who believes in his own mind and its competence, and believes as well that those to and about whom he speaks are capable of understanding and responding to what he says.

This is not belief in the language of law as a system that can and will work to bring coherence and justice to the world. We could call that kind of belief legalistic. It would assume that the words of the legal rules, or of legal analysis, do by themselves all that needs to be done. All the lawyer or judge would need to do is memorize the rules, or master a mechanistic form of analysis. We have seen this attitude towards language in the work of Blackmun in *Virginia Pharmacy Board* and of Kennedy in *Free Speech Coalition*. The lawyer's belief is not in law as a mechanical system but in what can be done with it, sometimes at least, by an engaged and open mind, alone and with others. The lawyer knows that the language of the law will not work automatically in the world to realize the will or intention of the legislature or any other legal authority. Every case is new, and presents an opportunity to imagine it in new ways; to this end one calls upon other ways of talking, other languages, new perceptions and understandings, and one's own experience of life. Every case presents an opportunity for the judge or lawyer to call his reader into a fuller life of thought and imagination and feeling, all with the object of achieving justice—not for all time, but for this time, in the knowledge that in the next case it will have to be done again. The lawyer and judge live out of the belief that they can, that we can, create the world anew when we speak, making real for the moment the possibilities of love and justice of which Weil speaks.

For Weil justice and love are possibilities for the striving mind, not abstract entities or statically defined universals. They are not simply expressed by a single mind in its acts of language, even the most artistic acts of language, for the writer always depends upon the capacity of his audience to understand and respond. Good writing always needs good reading. In this sense, the belief of the lawyer is not in language, or language alone, but in what lies beyond language: in the unquenchable human desire for meaning and community, in others and in himself, upon which his every success ultimately depends. This is a vision of the world, and of the law, not as a mechanistic system that can be reproduced in language, reshaped, manipulated, and so forth, all to achieve something called the goals of the system, but as itself a source of life, infinitely renewable. In the end, the belief of the lawyer and judge in the possibility of justice, and love, is a belief in the possibility that they themselves can be called into life by the world—by another person, by a problem—and that they in turn can call others into life.

To resist the empire of force one needs to believe in the possibility of both love and justice, and believe it not merely as a general matter but in one's own writing. One needs to believe, that is, that one's own formulations can actually offer an experience of justice and love, in the way they define and talk about other people; and that they can also, correspondingly, commit what deserves to be called injustice, expressing not love for another person, or for what is most deeply characteristic of the human being, but the opposite—a kind of hatred, or erasure, or denial. At the same time we must recognize that because we have only our minds and languages and hearts to work with, our every effort at writing of a good kind will be incomplete and imperfect. We live with aspirations we can never fully realize. Our capacity for this kind of life is not a failure of mind or imagination, but a kind of success. It is what at our best we do.

DANTE

To return to an earlier theme, what I have said suggests a new way in which living speech depends upon silence, for it is silence that recognizes—gives a place to—the world beyond words, upon which we both draw and call in what we say.

Think once more of Dante the traveler. He begins as a frightened creature, almost without personality and character, lost, beset by beasts, in need of rescue. This is miraculously granted him in the form of Virgil, a protector sent by Mary and Beatrice, to guide him through the Inferno and most of Purgatory, when Beatrice herself will take over. In the Inferno Dante is introduced to a system of punishment and reward that looks at first like a logical system in which the type and degree of suffering are always proportional to the sinfulness in question. But this, as we saw in chapter 1, is not quite the case; Dante's questions open up inconsistency and difficulty in the system, especially in its claims to justice. Why, as I have asked, is it right that Virgil, the ideal figure of the classical world, should be consigned to the dark region of Limbo? He is not only Dante's own teacher and model, he was generally regarded at the time as the greatest figure of the classical world.

As Dante the traveler proceeds it becomes clearer and clearer that the reality to which he is exposed, including the questions of justice, cannot be reduced to explanations in the form of theory or principle. That kind of language cannot work, but dissolves under the pressure of what lies beyond language. We begin to see, especially in Paradise, that the expectations we form, based on our own habits of thought, will never suffice. The bright light and beautiful sounds of heaven erase everything else. It is the inhabitants of the Inferno who believe in language itself, and try to define themselves through formulas—like Francesca—or through mechanical or legalistic operations of the mind, like Guido. In the Inferno there is language, and nothing else; behind its claims is a vast emptiness, leaving the soul twisting on a surface of justifications and self-descriptions none of which can possibly work, for they consist of words alone. In Paradise, by contrast, language breaks down, over and over again, because of the force and reality of what lies behind it: the flooding light that represents simultaneously reason and love. Thus it is that the theoretical explanations given by Beatrice or Bernard, though they are authoritative speakers, do not quite work; in a way that will be familiar to the modern lawyer, every effort at explanation, or rule-making, raises new questions, requiring further explication, with the result that no direct statement can ever be wholly satisfactory. Beatrice's explanation why Piccarda should be ranked lower in heaven than others (distinguishing between the absolute and contingent will, *Paradiso* IV); Bernard's explanation of the presence of children in heaven, all by virtue of baptism—except for the pre-Christian Jews of course, who were not baptized, and except for some who are there by the prayer of family members instead (*Paradiso* XXXII); the Eagle's explanation of the elevation of Ripheus, discussed at the end of chapter 5; the placement of Virgil in Limbo (*Paradiso* XIX–XX)—in the end none of these quite works, despite the best efforts of scholars to see that they do. And they do not work for a good poetic and theological reason, which is that here we are beyond the reach of logic and analysis, in a world that has a reality that cannot be reduced to language. Every articulation of a truth is imperfect, and requires new articulation, which is imperfect, and so on indefinitely. The truth is beyond language. This is a point frequently repeated by Dante the poet, who tells us over and over again, especially in Paradise, that he cannot do justice in language to what he experienced, indeed that he cannot do it justice in his memory (*Paradiso* I, 1–12). After all, it is a vision of heaven including a vision of the Godhead, and who can remember or describe such a thing? In Paradise, we are told and shown, the heavenly creatures understand each other without language, mind to mind, unmediated. The real is beyond language.

Beatrice says something bearing on this point that may affect our understanding both of the Inferno and of the justice or injustice of what seem to be the punishments inflicted there. In Canto IV of the *Paradiso* she explains that Piccarda and the others who appear to Dante in the lower spheres of Paradise are actually not in lower spheres at all. They all inhabit the first circle, with all the other blessed ones, and make it beautiful; they "have sweet life in different ways, as they feel more and less the eternal breath," *e differentemente han dolce vita/per sentir più e men l'etterno spiro* (35–36). They appear to Dante in the ranked spheres as a way of communicating to him these differences, for the human being "grasps only through sense perception what it will make worthy of the mind" (40–42).[10] There are two points here. One is that the effort of Beatrice to talk nonquantitatively about the bliss experienced by different groups of souls quickly collapses, because our language ineluctably turns to notions of quantity to make distinctions. The idea is that all the souls are equally blissful in the sense that each is blissful to the extent of its nature—but of course, we say, that is not exactly equal bliss, if the natures are different; yet in another sense they are equally blissful, for each is as happy as it can possibly be. The language of quantity simply breaks down. Piccarda's own way of responding to this difficulty is to give up

---

[10] *Così parlar conviensi al vostro ingegno,*
però che solo da sensato apprende
ciò che fa poscia d'intelletto degno.

on this kind of comparative language entirely and simply say, "in his will is our peace," *'n la sua volontade è nostra pace* (III, 85). This is a small instance of a general phenomenon, the continual collapse of language in the *Paradiso*.[11]

The second point relates to our reading of the *Inferno*. If the spirits in Paradise are not what they seem, is the same perhaps not true in the Inferno? I have suggested that the characters there are all in various ways engaged in an activity of seduction, playing a series of confidence tricks on Dante the traveler, and on us as readers. It is our task to straighten them out: to see that Francesca is seeking to seduce us, as she was seduced; that Ulysses, the false counselor, in the famous speech to his men that stirs us so—"Don't live like brutes, but pursue knowledge and virtue!"—is in fact giving them, and us, false counsel. Beatrice tells Dante the traveler that what he perceives in Paradise is not really there, but a kind of theater, meant to make what is there intelligible. Perhaps the Inferno is a theater too, a series of challenges to the mind and soul of Dante the traveler, and of the reader, meant to recapitulate a moral education. On this view the souls are not to be imagined as real, not as alive, not as suffering; not as being thrust into boiling pitch, escaping for the moment, then being flayed by fiends and sent back into the pitch. They are all like Francesca, those who have given up life itself and become the phrases and languages of justification they employ—all of which are empty, false, dead.[12] They are in this sense all suicides.

Or think of Ugolino, in Canto XXXIII, telling the story in which his archenemy, Ruggieri, locks him in a castle room with his children, where they all starve to death, perhaps—the text is not clear—after he cannibalizes their corpses. This is the story of a man tortured to death with his children, and of course we sympathize. But Ugolino leaves out entirely the act of treason that brought him there, and like a stage magician he draws our attention away from the meaning of what he does tell us: that

[11] One thinks of contradictions, for example on the issue of original sin, which at one point is affirmed, another denied. Compare *Paradiso* VII, 25–31 (Beatrice) with *Purgatorio* XVI, 103–105 (Marco Lombardo).

[12] They become their language in another sense as well, for one desire of many of the souls in the Inferno is that Dante report to them on their reputation, or *fama*, in the world, or promise on his return to seek to restore or improve it. They live, that is, in the words in which people talk about them. No soul in Purgatory does this, though often one will ask to be prayed for. (This is because prayer increases the love in the universe, and this reduces their time in Purgatory.)

when his children spoke to him, asking what they should do, he was silent; and that his own "heroism" consisted in fact of his unforgiving hatred of his murderer, whose skull he gnaws throughout eternity, in a hunger that can never be satisfied. He could after all have forgiven his murderer, and taught his children to do so too—in which case, at least if he repented of his treason, he would not be in hell at all.[13]

Further light is shed on this story when we are told by another betrayer, Alberigo, that when a person commits treason his soul goes instantly to hell; his body is thereafter, for the rest of its physical life, inhabited by a demon (*Inferno* XXXIII, 130). He gives as an example one Branca Doria, a man who was still living in the world of Dante the writer; one of Dante's points is of course to suggest in this way that the real Branca Doria is actually a demon, and we are chilled by the thought. But we should realize that what Alberigo tells us is not true, or not always, for we know that Ugolino was not immediately dispatched to the Inferno upon the commission of his act of treason, or the whole story of his starvation would never have occurred.

We are being shown here by Dante that all of the appearances in the Inferno are theatrical, not real. In the imagined world of the poem they are a way in which Beatrice, or the Deity, is speaking to Dante the traveler, just as in the text itself they are ways in which Dante the poet is speaking to us. What is presented to us is not what the experience of the souls is like; they do not have choice, they cannot explain, they cannot lament; in reality they all share something like the fate of those in the last circle, who are frozen immobile in the ice. They are nonexistent, and

---

[13] I owe this observation to Alison Cornish and Anis Memon. To talk of possible forgiveness in these circumstances may sound far too easy and conclusory, but it actually is not. Suppose you found yourself dying with your young children in such hideous circumstances, and they asked you what they should do. Would you be silent? Or would you try to help them face the death that was coming, with all its pain? How would you do this? What the children need above all is a person in whom they can trust, who can offer them a way of making sense—or not making sense—of their experience, not someone who turns away from them in helpless and inconsequential rage. Forgiveness in such a case might have many roots, some of them pietistic no doubt, but some make good psychological sense: the one who forgives stands outside his suffering and asserts a kind of control over his situation, just when none seems possible. For the children, and indeed the father, to be able to do that might be the best thing they could do, not for Ruggieri, but for themselves. This is something we do not see when we read the Canto the first time because Ugolino so skillfully diverts our attention not only from what he did to betray his homeland but from what he failed to do as a father.

nonexistent by their own action and choice: by their refusal to repent, by their merger with one or another of the false languages they employ. In hell there is only language, nothing behind it; this infernal world has life only for the viewer, not for the soul that has perished. There are no punishments. There is only death.

Death is what it means to submit to the empire of force. Life lies in understanding—by experience and thought and imagination—the empire of force, and knowing the arts of mind and feeling by which one can succeed in not respecting it. Living speech does these things. Dante in his great poem gives us living speech, speech that still lives, as Shakespeare's sonnet and Frost's poem also do, indeed as the opinions of Jackson and Frankfurter and Harlan and Brandeis do too: living voices in living speech.

SIMONE WEIL

The very first words in this book, in the epigraph, are by Simone Weil, and it may be well that the last words be hers as well. In a sense everything I have written could be considered as a kind of preparation for the following, which is taken from her essay "Human Personality," written in the last year of her life, when she was thirty-four, and apparently intended as a kind of summation of her deepest views.

At the bottom of the heart of every human being, from earliest infancy until the tomb, there is something that goes on indomitably expecting, in the teeth of all experience of crimes committed, suffered, and witnessed, that good and not evil will be done to him. It is this above all that is sacred in every human being. . . .

This profound and childlike and unchanging expectation of good in the heart is not what is involved when we agitate for our rights. The motive which prompts a little boy to watch jealously to see if his brother has a slightly larger piece of cake arises from a much more superficial level of the soul. The word justice means two very different things according to whether it refers to the one or the other level. It is only the former one that matters.

Every time that there arises from the depths of a human heart the childish cry which Christ himself could not restrain, "Why am I being hurt?", then there is certainly injustice. For if, as often happens, it is only the result of a misunderstanding, then the injustice consists in the inadequacy of the explanation.

Those people who inflict the blows which provoke this cry are prompted by different motives according to temperament or occasion. There are some people who get a positive pleasure from the cry; and many others simply do not hear it. For it is a silent cry, which sounds only in the secret heart. . . .

In those who have suffered too many blows, in slaves for example, that place in the heart from which the infliction of evil evokes a cry of surprise may seem to be dead. But it is never quite dead; it is simply unable to cry out any more. It has sunk into a state of dumb and ceaseless lamentation.

And even in those who still have the power to cry out, the cry hardly ever expresses itself, either inwardly or outwardly, in coherent language. Usually, the words through which it seeks expression are quite irrelevant.

That is all the more inevitable because those who most often have occasion to feel that evil is being done to them are those who are least trained in the art of speech. Nothing, for example, is more frightful than to see some poor wretch in the police court stammering before a magistrate who keeps up an elegant flow of witticisms.

Apart from the intelligence, the only human faculty which has an interest in the public freedom of expression is that point in the heart which cries out against evil. But as it cannot express itself, freedom is of little use to it. What is first needed is a system of public education capable of providing it, so far as possible, with means of expression; and next, a régime in which the public freedom of expression is characterized not so much by freedom as by an attentive silence in which this faint and inept cry can make itself heard; and finally, institutions are needed of a sort which will, so far as possible, put power into the hands of men who are able and anxious to hear and understand it.

Clearly, a political party busily seeking, or maintaining itself in, power can discern nothing in these cries except a noise. Its reaction will be different according to whether the noise interferes with or contributes to that of its own propaganda. But it can never be capable of the tender and sensitive attention which is needed to understand its meaning.

The same is true to a lesser degree of organizations contaminated by party influences; in other words, when public life is dominated by a party system, it is true of all organizations, including, for example, trade unions and even churches.

Naturally, too, parties and similar organizations are equally insensitive to intellectual scruples.

So when freedom of expression means in fact no more than freedom of propaganda for organizations of this kind, there is in fact no free expression for the only parts of the human soul that deserve it. Or if there is any, it is infinitesimal; hardly more than in a totalitarian system.[14]

[14] Simone Weil, "Human Personality," in *The Simone Weil Reader*, ed. George A. Panichas (Mt. Kisco, N.Y.: Moyer Bell, 1977), 315–17.

Index

Shakespeare, William); world-imagining and claiming meaning in, 194–96

economic ideology/language/theory: and dehumanization in a consumer economy, 6; and democratic government, inapplicability to, 36–38; and human life in a consumer economy, image of, 27–28, 35–36; and regulation of price advertising, 77–83; value choices, ideology of the market and, 36; in the *Virginia Pharmacy Board* opinion, 79–85. *See also* marketplace of ideas

Eisele, Thomas D., 217n

Eliot, T. S., 60

empire of force: capacity for claiming meaning for experience, erasure of by, 168; Dante's *Divine Comedy* and (see *Divine Comedy* [Dante]); dead speech, maintenance of through, 89; death as the meaning of submitting to, 224; due process, argument for denial of as expression of, 65–66; free speech and, 29; giving content to the term, 8–9; language and the capacity not to respect, 1, 7–9, 12, 88–90; language and the capacity not to respect, Lincoln's letter to Hooker as example of, 48–49; law and, 9–10; the possibility of love and justice, necessity of belief in to resist, 219; in public speech, 26–40; resisting as the central question of life and politics, 204–6; speech that resists the, 189; submit to, desire to, 38–40; as system of thought and imagination, 4–7; teaching writing as means to come to terms with, 71–72; as war and dehumanization, 2–4

English language, 18–19

Eumenides (Aeschylus), 173

evil: meaningful speech and intentional, 76–77; of Polonius in *Hamlet,* 59; public freedom of expression and crying out against, 225; systems of meaning as potentially, 6; war's dehumanization as, 4

expectations, formal. *See* formal expectations

Ferber, New York v., 145–46, 149–50, 152, 155, 157

First Amendment: *Ashcroft v. Free Speech Coalition* (see *Ashcroft v. Free Speech Coalition*); Brandeis on, 165–66; *Cohen v. California* (see *Cohen v. California*); language of, 141; living speech and, 11, 210–11, 216n; questions regarding law made under, 10–11; *Thomas v. Collins,* 86–88, 141, 211; trivializing of by the Court, 158–59; valuable speech, reading as a call for, 42–43; *Virginia State Pharmacy Board v. Citizens Consumer Council* (see *Virginia State Pharmacy Board v. Citizens Consumer Council*); *West Virginia State Board of Education v. Barnette,* 45–47, 141, 211. *See also* free speech

flag salute case. See *West Virginia State Board of Education v. Barnette*

force, empire of. *See* empire of force

formal expectations: of judicial opinions, 112–13; the reader's desire for completion of, 97–99; Shakespeare's working with, 104, 108–9

formulaic/sentimental speech: by Ashcroft, 65–66; of Dante's Francesca, 61–64; in the *Free Speech Coalition* opinion, 151–56, 158–59, 211–12, 218; language not shaped by inner and outer silences as, 15–16; learning and avoiding tendencies toward, 51; living speech as the opposite of (see living speech); origins of in childhood writing, 51–58; presence and resistance of, 50–51; susceptibility to, 38–40; teaching writing, avoiding through, 66–72; in the *Virginia Pharmacy Board* opinion, 81–85, 89, 211–12, 218. *See also* advertising; clichés; ideology; propaganda

Fourteenth Amendment, 83

Francesca (the fictional character): language of courtly love, as captive of, 23–24, 61–64; reading, danger of her kind of, 116–18; seduce us, her efforts to, 222; sympathetic presentation of, 20–21